About the Author]

Born in Long Island, New York, Beatrice has always lived with and been interested in animals. Educated at Columbia International University, in South Carolina, she also completed two years Post-Graduate work in Science/Pre-Med at California State Polytechnic University in Pomona, California. She is currently a certified EMT-Intermediate who is also certified to teach CPR and First Aid.

In 1969, Beatrice discovered she had a unique ability to communicate mentally with animals. As a result, she has become the Pioneer in the field of animal-human communications. She has been tested extensively by many veterinarians, Doctors, and educators, which resulted in their endorsement

You can read about her amazing life story of how she won the battle with cancer through prayer and education with natural herb formulas and nutrition as God intended as well as her amazing Journey with her gift of being able to communicate with God's creatures in her book, SEASONS, MY JOURNEY THROUGH THE THREE DEMENSIONS OF NATURAL HEALING. Her DVD with YOU TOO CAN TALK TO THE ANIMALS and her COMMUNICATION SEMINARS teaches the viewer how to do what she does. Beatrice is a renowned animal psychologist, author and television personality and lecturer on holistic animal and human nutrition and use of herbs for healing. Her mental communication with autistic children, comatose people, and anyone unable to speak for other reasons, as well as with the animals, have opened a whole new approach to their understanding and treatment.

Beatrice presently resides in the Portland, Oregon area where she conducts her private counseling practice, and conducts her own herbal business, helping people and animals find health and healing. Her herbal and vitamin blends, books, DVDs/videos and Royal Rife Technology are marketed through mail order from her two centers, one in Oregon and the other in Kentucky. Her natural healing newsletters have been well received and can be viewed along with all her products on her website www.bealydecker.com

Beatrice Lydecker-Hayford

YOU TOO CAN TALK WITH THE ANIMALS
EXPLORE the FUN and MYSTERY of COMMUNICATING WITH your PETS

SPECIAL EDITION

PART I
A COMPLETELY UPDATED REVISION OF WHAT THE ANIMALS TELL ME

PART II
STORIES THE ANIMALS TELL ME

WITH

ANIMALS SAY AND DO THE DARNDEST THINGS

PART III
LEARNING THE ANIMALS LANGUAGE AND HOW TO USE IT

Living Free Publications
155443 S. Latourette Road
Oregon City, Oregon 97045
1-800-258-8589

Please don't let the dog out...

No Matter What It Tells You!
Thank you

YOU TOO CAN TALK WITH THE ANIMALS:
EXPLORE the FUN and MYSTERY of COMMUNICATING WITH your PETS
© 2008 BY Living Free Publications, a subsidiary of Bea Lydecker's Naturals, Inc. Author: Beatrice C. Lydecker-Hayford Editor: Bill and Mary Richardson   Jacket Design: Simply Art by Rose Mary Hayford   All rights reserved.
For information contact Living Free publications
Library of Congress Card Number:
ISBN 978-0-9622094-1-3

Warning
Prologue

PART I
A COMPLETELY UPDATED REVISION OF WHAT THE ANIMALS TELL ME

PART II
STORIES THE ANIMALS TELL ME
PLUS
PETS SAY AND DO THE DARNDEST THINGS

PART III

WARNING

Non-verbal communication is a form of Extra Sensory Perception or ESP.

Many people, having been once introduced to a new perspective of the world around them, decide to become involved in occult or metaphysical practices, such as talking with spirits, tarot cards, reading palms or leaves, astrology, reincarnation, transcendental meditation, and other related practices. The only part of ESP I feel is safe to practice is that which I have spelled out in this book. Please do not become involved in any of the above mentioned practices, because I believe you will place your safety and your soul in extreme danger. This is strictly my opinion based on years of experience in this field.

Non-verbal communication is an ability we all have at birth but tend to lose when we begin school and switch to a verbal and written mode of expression. To regain this ability is your birthright.

Beatrice Lydecker-Hayford

PROLOGUE

Over the years, I have known many animal owners who have lost a dearly loved pet. Their grief is just as real and deep as that of an individual who loses a human loved one. I experienced this myself when my first German Shepherd, Princess Royal, died.

One night, I was awakened by the sound of horrible kicking and thrashing. I flicked the light switch and stood in horror while Princess Royal writhed in confusion. The attack passed but was soon followed by another. I called my vet and within minutes he met me at the animal hospital to treat her for what we both thought was food poisoning. For four days I begged God to heal my precious dog, despite the vet's eventual diagnosis of a brain tumor. The case looked hopeless, he said, for no sooner did she come out of one convulsion, she went right into another in spite of the fact that she was heavily sedated. Eventually even the medication no longer stopped the convulsions, and yet, I couldn't bring myself to say the words that would have her put to sleep.

It was 4:45 p.m. on a rainy Thursday afternoon, October 1968, when I was driving to the hospital and asked God for specific help and guidance: *Please give me a sign so that I will know your will. If she is the same or worse, I'll say those words, but if she is slightly improved, I will know you are going to heal her.* At that moment, I finally released her into God's hands. I arrived at the hospital and the nurse told me that at 4:45 p.m., Princess Royal had suffered another attack and died. How good God was to spare me the agony of that terrible decision to put her down. He had taken her. It was His will. Yet I felt enormous guilt at not being with Princess Royal during her last agonizing moments. I felt overwhelming grief and loss. I sat on my bed, sobbing, my eyes closed in pain when God again showed His presence and purpose.

I had never had a vision in my life before this so I was unprepared for the feeling of being watched. I quickly opened my eyes and there sat Princess Royal, gazing up with the love she had always given me, one paw on my lap. I held her close in speechless joy. In a few minutes, without any sign of movement, she was out of my grasp. I called to her to stay, but she answered soundlessly, *I was allowed to come and tell you that I understand why you could not be with me in the hospital and that everything is all right. I came to say good-bye, but I'll see you again.* Suddenly she was gone and I sat alone but now with a sense of peace. I knew she was alive and with God. It was not until several months later that I learned that she could feel my love for her even though I was not in the hospital with her. Animals have taught me that we humans can hold onto them too tightly. At the moment I released Princess Royal with my prayer, she was free to go where God wanted her. Until then, I had been holding her here in her suffering body.

The pain of her loss stayed with me for some time, so much so, that I felt I needed a change of scenery, so I went to visit my parents in Florida. I was lying on the bed in their home where I first got her as a puppy, I felt the pain of missing her rush over me again and threaten to engulf me. Suddenly, the ceiling opened up and I saw her playing in the most beautiful forest, romping on a lush green carpet of grass, and then in a stream, diving under the water for rocks, just as she had on our hikes in the mountains near Azusa, California. Instantly, she was standing on the bank, as beautiful as I had ever seen her, her coat dry and fluffy. She trotted over to the edge of the vision, looked down at me and said; *we just wanted you to know that I'm all right and happy. I'm waiting for you and will see you when you get here.* Again she was gone.

After her death and these two comforting visions, I began to search the Bible for what God had to say about animals. I have found this a fascinating study through the years and it has resulted in my personal belief that animals live on after physical death, much the same as humans. Let me explain.

All mammals are biologically much the same as humans. They also have souls, in the sense that they experience emotions as people do and they possess a limited reasoning ability that I include in the "soul" part of the animal. The big difference between a human and an animal is in the area which is best described as the image of God. Humans possess an image of God that animals do not have. Humans have a conscience or a sense of sin, a complex sexuality that involves emotion, an ability to make

ii

intricate plans for the future and are able to think in the abstract. Animals have no sense of sin, their sexuality is only for reproduction, and they cannot plan changes in their environment. Since animals do not possess this image of God and cannot sin, I believe their souls live on. Job said, "For the soul of every living thing is in the hand of God and the breath of all mankind" (Job 12:10 LB) The Bible does not say whether or not these creatures live on, but I believe Princess Royal is spiritually alive and whole. The Bible helped assuage my grief with these words from Revelation 21:4 "He will wipe away all tears from their eyes and there shall be no more death, nor sorrow, nor crying, nor pain. All of that is gone forever." (LB)

Since my ESP ability has become generally accepted, I am often asked to speak to a dead pet or a departed loved one. My answer is an emphatic NO. I know the feeling of grief and the need to communicate and I have just described my personal visions of Princess Royal, but these were experiences I didn't try to conjure up, they just happened. I do not involve myself in the occult of any sort, or in metaphysical philosophies, or in anything that concerns trances or hypnosis. When I became aware of my ESP abilities, I was eager to learn everything I could. I attended meetings in which current cult philosophies were taught or demonstrated. In reading the works of J. Allen Boone, author of the book "Strongheart," listening to California psychic Fred Kimble lecture, and investigating the teachings of Edgar Cayce, I felt something was wrong. When a person is in a trance, or under hypnosis or anesthesia, he or she is open to many influences and is dangerously vulnerable. When I learned of my abilities, I prayed to God and told Him I would accept His work, but only if I could do it under complete control, wide awake and aware of my environment at all times. He has honored my request. The only Spirit I communicate with is the Holy Spirit and that is through private and conscious prayer.

I do believe in God and in His Son, Jesus Christ, and in the Holy Spirit of God. I also believe in the Bible as the Word of God. I do not believe in modern philosophies which teach that all humans have a bit of the God image in them, as Jesus did, and that

He was a human being just like the rest of us. I believe in His divinity and our non-divinity. I also believe that my prayers and God's guidance have helped me to use my gift for the good of animals and humankind or, in other words, to do His work.

God created the animals and then created man in His image to have dominion over the animals. Man sinned and when sin entered the world, man suffered; so did the animals. But I believe that when the second coming of Christ takes place, the animals will also be released from suffering. I take comfort from Romans 8: 19-23.

Yet what we suffer now is nothing compared to the glory He will give us later. For all creation is waiting patiently and hopefully for that future day when God will resurrect His children. For on that day thorn and thistles, sin, death and decay-the things that overcame the world against its will at God's command, will all disappear and the world around us will share in the glorious freedom from sin which God's children enjoy.
For we know that even the things of nature like animals and plants, suffer in sickness and death as they await this great event (LB)

I am also asked about reincarnation in animals because apparently the theory of reincarnation gives some logical answers to previously unanswered questions. "Before every man there lies a wide and pleasant road that seems right but ends in death." (Proverbs 14:12) In all my experiences with animals, I have never seen any evidence of reincarnation. I have asked many animals about this. One example should suffice. A dog owner, who believed in reincarnation and thought his dog was a former dog of his, made the living dog so confused he didn't know who he was and felt he didn't have the right to be himself. The dog communicated to me that all he knew was what was being mentally expected of him, namely the behavior of the dead dog, so he responded accordingly, in utter confusion. To return to the Bible, "We must be born again." (John 3:3) This is a *Spiritual* rebirth that takes place at the moment we accept Jesus Christ as our personal Savior this is not reincarnation.

In my studies, I saw animals all through the Bible playing a significant role in human life and in God's scheme of things.

Animals are described as instruments of God, either to minister to us, feed us, or bring judgment on the sins of men and women. (See I Kings 21:23 and II Kings 2:24)

Many people say they do not believe the Biblical account of creation, but I do. Reading Genesis, I am convinced that there was complete harmony between humans and animals until after the flood, and that all animals were herbivores. Adam and Eve communicated with the animals in the Garden of Eden. Why else would Eve talk to the serpent and respect its ideas as reasonable if it were not a usual experience to communicate with animals? I believe that all communication in the garden was nonverbal and harmonious; it is therefore not surprising that later the animals obeyed Noah's command to enter the ark and live there peacefully. After the waters receded from the flood, God told Noah that from that day on God was delivering every beast of the field and every fowl of the air to be food for humans and He placed the fear of man in the animals. I have discovered this natural fear in the wild animals with which I've communicated. They don't usually run away, but they let me know they do not trust me fully because I am a human being. I believe this true communication between humans and animals existed on its nonverbal level until the Tower of Babel. I also believe God made each creature reproduce after its own kind so that even today, when scientists attempt to cross breed animal species, the offspring is sterile.

In Numbers 22:21-35 we read about Balaam going along the trail on his donkey. Three times Balaam struck the donkey and then God allowed her to verbalize to Balaam what she was thinking. *Why do you hit me? Have I ever disobeyed you before?* Then God opened Balaam's eyes and Balaam saw the angel standing in the way. In my experiences of communicating with animals, I have found that they often see non-physical beings. The donkey had already seen the angel, and when it was given a verbal voice, was permitted reveal to Balaam the intelligent thought pattern that was already taking place in its' mind.

The ravens fed Elijah by the brook (I Kings 17:1-6), the perfect precedent to the story of Mrs. Ely Buffin's experience with the Eagle, found in Chapter I. In both incidences, the birds understood

EXPLORE

the dilemma of the humans involved and responded to their needs with intelligent actions.

Throughout the Old Testament lambs were used as sacrifices for the sins of men and women as a symbol of the ultimate sacrifice of the perfect Lamb of God, Jesus Christ, who died for the sins of all humankind. The unbroken donkey colt submitted to being ridden by Jesus when Jesus made His triumphal entrance into Jerusalem just before His crucifixion.

As you search the Scriptures, you will see the harmony God intended for human beings and the beasts in His creation. "No mere man has ever seen, heard or even imagined what wonderful things God has ready for those who love the Lord." (I Corinthians 2:9) Man's vision is narrow, but God's is limitless. "Are not two little sparrows sold for a penny? And yet not one of them shall fall to the ground without your Father's consent and notice. Mathew 10:29 Amplified Bible translated literally from the original Greek, "shall not fall on the ground without the Father being right there with it as it falls."

I believe God is trying to tell us that He made this earth and the creatures on it, that He cares what happens to His creations, and that He wants to help humankind toward a fuller and richer relationship with the animals of His earthly kingdom.

I also believe God sees the importance and the emotional necessity of animals in the lives of humans, especially when there is a void in those lives. A person, who tries to treat an animal as his or her lost child or lost loved one, puts a terrible emotional strain on the animal and may make it physically ill. It will certainly make both owner and animal neurotic. My animals are happy and well adjusted because they are loved as my substitute children and companions, but they are just substitutes and are still treated as animals.

As I began to understand God's concern for animals, I asked Him to show me what He would have me do with my abilities. This book is what I believe is His answer.

Beatrice Lydecker-Hayford

SECTION I

WHAT

THE ANIMALS

TELL ME

SPECIAL EDITION

COMPLETELY
REVISED AND UPDATED

CHAPTER 1

AWAKENING

I was living and working on an avocado ranch in Duarte, California, in charge of the irrigation necessary for food production in that often drought-ridden area. Perhaps it was that responsibility—and the extreme physical exhaustion I felt during my first few months there, that triggered a shift in my awareness, a shift so gradual that I can't pinpoint its beginnings.

For years an inner restlessness had plagued me. I was young, healthy, in charge of my life, or so I thought. I had worked in various interesting jobs, but I always became bored once I learned them. I had a loving family and the frequent company of caring friends, but I always felt restless and unsettled. I was always looking for something more, something different.

In Duarte, I worked among the trees, whose very lives depended on how well I did my job. I handled the soil, moved water lines, and later helped with harvesting the fruit. Sometimes, late at night, I would leave my bed and go outside to stand under the expansive branches of those mighty trees and listen to the breeze blowing through their leaves. These were precious times for me. I would sit and talk to God, and ask for answers to the emptiness I felt, knowing He was, and is, my source of strength and guidance. Little did I know the adventure He had planned, and the change of direction I was soon to experience that would fulfill that longing once and for all. I was tired of changing jobs only to become bored and restless again.

When I lived at the orchard, I had purchased a German Shepherd that I named Princess Royal. She had become my constant companion, until I moved to the city, where my job meant long hours of absence, and our time together became more the traditional dog/mistress relationship. I would take her to the park for a run on weekends, or to the beach in summer to play frisbee and run along the ocean's edge. I loved her, but it never occurred to me to see her as anything but a creature whose life revolved around my own, inferior to me in most respects. I'd watch her chase a butterfly or sniff the entrance to a gopher hole, and marvel at her ability to respond so completely to the hundreds of small happenings in her environment. Looking back, I think that because Princess Royal and I were unable to exchange our thoughts and feelings verbally, we began to share them on a more basic level. Nevertheless, this relationship was bringing about a change in my spirit. My feelings of restlessness were being gently soothed, replaced by a sense of awe at the oneness of life, at the absolute interrelatedness of all living things. When I wasn't working, we were inseparable.

Things were about to change, but never did I imagine it to be so drastic. She had a seizure, but after it passed the veterinarian assured me it was probably nothing since he couldn't find anything wrong with her and not to worry about it unless it happened again. Then two months later, it happened again, and again he could find no cause for it. Then the seizures began happening more and more frequently throughout the months, until one night I awoke to the sound of her thrashing about in the kitchen. Her seizure went on and on, not like the others that had ended within seconds. Somehow I managed to mobilize myself and telephone my vet, who agreed to see her immediately at his hospital. His final diagnosis was inoperable brain tumor! For four days I resisted his pressure to put her to sleep, insisting that her illness must be due to food poisoning. I was unable to bear the fact that my companion was leaving me.

In His mercy, God took her on the fifth day, releasing her from the torment her damaged nervous system caused her from the moment of first seizure. MY PRECIOUS PRINCESS ROYAL DIED AND MY WORLD WAS SHATTERED. I HAVE NEVER FELT SO ALONE IN MY LIFE BEFORE OR SINCE THAT HORRIBLE DAY.

I was so despondent that functioning efficiently was all but impossible. A close friend, concerned for my emotional state, urged me to join her prayer group. I went, but only half-heartedly. I felt too self-conscious about mourning an animal so deeply to talk much about her. My grief remained undiminished. Princess Royal was gone, and I was sure my recent feeling of peace had gone with her. As the weeks passed, I began to accept my loss and

I was able to get another Shepherd that I named Princessa VonRichtoffen.

One day, a member of the prayer group approached me. She was carrying a book, and as she handed it to me, she said, "I don't know why, but I feel moved to give you this. Please read it." The book was J. Allen Boone's *Kinship With All Life*. Shortly afterward, another member of the group approached me with a pamphlet about understanding how the subconscious mind works. I would later find out that the animal mind works much the same way, and that I would receive the impressions from them through my subconscious mind. Later, it would all begin to fit together. Yet at the time, my benefactors had no idea of what the other one had brought to me.

In his book, Boone wrote about his experiences of extrasensory perception (ESP) with animals, particularly the German Shepherd, Strongheart, a performing dog who had starred in a number of movies, and had for a short time lived with Boone. During their association, Boone came to realize that "behind every object which the senses can identify, whether the object be human, animal, tree, mountain, plant or anything else, and right where the object seems to be, is the mental and spiritual fact functioning in all its completeness and perfection. This spiritual fact cannot be recognized with ordinary human eyesight, but it is apparent to clarified inner vision."

Reading this, I realized that my work on the ranch and my closeness to Princess Royal were the beginnings of my own inner vision, which had not left me when she died.

Soon, I began to have some unusual experiences. I remember one day standing on a street corner waiting for a traffic light to change and hearing a voice call for help. I looked around to see where the voice was coming from and saw only a large Doberman Pinscher standing guard behind a warehouse fence.

According to the evidence offered by my five senses, a dog calling for help was impossible. The call was strangely soundless, yet I had heard it clearly. The cry for help grew in intensity until I could not ignore it. I had seen the dog before, growling at people passing by, occasionally even charging at the fence. But I could not resist going over to the animal which, to my astonishment, pranced over to me and nuzzled as far as he could through the fence, pressing his nose ever so gently against my outstretched hand.

After a few minutes, I left feeling confused about what had just happened. Why didn't the dog snarl at me as I had seen him do with other people who approached him? Why had I felt such overwhelming loneliness when I was near him? And where had that call come from?

That same day in January 1969 brought another vivid experience that left me baffled. It occurred while walking down a street in Monrovia, California, where I noticed a German Shepherd standing quietly behind the fence of a house. Almost as if he called to me, I went over and petted him through an opening in the gate. Suddenly a heavy sense of rejection and depression came over me. I was always around animals, but this was the first time I had experienced such a feeling, and it frightened me. Most dogs readily adapt to being alone in an outdoor yard, and there seemed no obvious reason for the emotional response I was picking up from him. It baffled me so much that I returned to the house later that day to talk to the owner. My questions surprised him at first, but then he explained. The owner had been injured in a car accident and had been confined to his home for several months. So he bought the dog Duke, for companionship for himself and his young son. That day, he had finally returned to work, and his son had just started nursery school. Duke was left alone for the first time. Learning this, I was no longer mystified by the feelings I had picked up from Duke.

I mulled these experiences over in my mind all day. The only conclusions that seemed to fit the facts were that both the sound and the feelings came from these two dogs, and that they had not menaced me because they knew I had heard them. They recognized what Boone called my "spiritual fact," and I, theirs.

These were my first encounters with animals on this level of communication, and they accounted for my beginning awareness that I had a strange, unusually perceptive ability. I was 31 years old and had worked as a supervisor of a women's prison, a bookkeeper, a bank employee, a waitress, and a cosmetic sales representative. But now, I knew I was heading into something new that would prove to be my life-long pursuit. My prayers were being answered.

The change was gradual and dreamlike, yet I remember the time clearly. Experiences began to happen that further solidified my understanding of the animal's ability to think and feel, and even calculate actions. I remember an experience with Blacky, my Pomeranian, who was then 8 years old and living on the ranch with me. One afternoon I had planned a shopping trip to Pasadena, but I dreaded the prospect of driving several hours through smog and traffic, parking in the terrible heat, and traipsing from store to store. I dawdled in my room while dressing and delayed leaving as long as I could.

The familiar sound of the screen door opening and closing told me that Blacky had already headed for the car. He always knew when it was time to go for a ride and could be found patiently sitting at the car with a whatever-took-you-so-long expression on his face. As I was getting ready to leave, I said to myself, "Okay, friend, I know you've planted yourself by the car expecting to go with me, but this time you're in for a surprise because you're staying home. It's too hot for you to sit in the car and wait while I shop."

But when I reached the car, he was nowhere in sight. I looked in all his favorite hiding places until I was tired of searching. This surprising disappearing act added to my growing impatience. I was already late getting started, and I wanted to put him inside before I left so the coyotes wouldn't get him. I called, yelled, and whistled, but still no Blacky. I finally gave up and drove off.

A quarter mile later, I found that little black puff sitting in the middle of the road waiting to be picked up. I was stunned! Imagine being outwitted by a dog! Needless to say, he got his ride. There was no way he could have known that I would not drive all the way back to the house again. How could he know I was running late? I looked straight into his eyes, and he stared right back at me—*through* me, it seemed. This didn't exactly calm me. I pondered the possibility of mental telepathy, even X-ray vision, and drove on unsure of the answer. How else could he have known what I had in mind and how to manipulate me?

Shortly after that experience, a friend of mine who bred Alaskan Malamutes shared an astounding experience he had with his male Malamute. My friend had been watching television while his dog lay beside his chair. Then my friend decided to eat some cookies, but before he could leave his chair, the dog bounded into the kitchen where he planted himself in front of the cabinet where the cookies were kept. My friend explained that earlier that same evening, he had gone to the kitchen several times for food that he normally did not share with the dog, and each time his pet had remained by the chair. How the animal had known to respond at the precise moment his master headed for the cookie jar—and a treat he regularly shared with his four-legged friend—was another experience that brought me to search for a better understanding of this new world of communication opening up for me.

I began to suspect that mental telepathy was possible in animals, yet I speculated that overt signals by people might exist and serve as clues for pets. I finally surrendered all doubt when another incident revealed that this telepathic communication was not due to mere coincidence or signals.

I had been sick with the flu and resting in bed for several days. During my second day in bed, I was awakened by five ranch roosters crowing directly under my bedroom window. My head throbbed with each ear-splitting call. I tried shooing them away, but failed. Growing enraged, I finally threw a bucket of water at them through the window screen. The roosters scurried a short distance away but, to my chagrin, shortly returned. Princessa sat watching the scene.

Their noise became torture. I took hold of whatever I could throw. Shoes and slippers went flying at the roosters from the doorway. I finally dragged my weary body back to bed. Princessa still watched. I was barely under the covers when the roosters were at it again. I felt totally defeated and fighting back tears, buried my head underneath my pillow. In a little while, Princessa started to paw at my bedcovers. As she continued to tug, I suddenly became aware of the silence. Silence! Curiosity finally overcame me, and I followed my Shepherd's lead out of the house. As we rounded the corner, I was shocked!

Princessa had silenced the roosters permanently. They lay on the ground in a dead heap. I was sick at the sight and baffled. Princessa had been trained not to harm the livestock. I was shaken by the experience. How did she understand? Why did she risk a reprimand? How could she know how ill I was and that it was only those five roosters that were causing my pain? We had sixty hens and roosters milling about, but they were not disturbing me as those five had been. (I had raised them, so I was able to recognize each individual chicken.)

Meanwhile Princessa was prancing about, wagging her tail, kicking up dirt. She was so proud of what she had done! I looked at her and told myself that dogs did not experience feelings like joy and pride at doing something to alleviate a human being's pain or irritation. Or do they? The violence of the act shattered me, yet there was an even deeper lesson to be learned here. I began to accept the fact that animals can react to the mental wavelengths of human beings. It was a turning point for me.

Inner vision, that was it! That's what I was getting in touch with during my stay at the ranch, and what was still developing in me. I now realized how much more there was to existence when seen through clarity of vision.

"Ask the dumbest beast, he knows that it is so; ask the birds, they will tell you; or let the earth teach you, or the fish of the sea. For the soul of every living thing is in the hand of God, and the breath of all mankind" (Job 12:7-10).

In June 1972, I was invited to lecture on thought communication with animals at the German Shepherd Club of Fresno, California. Afterward I received a letter from Mrs. Ely Buffin, a member of the club. It was one more confirmation of what was becoming a deep belief and way of life for me. She wrote, "Last weekend, some friends, my husband, and I took a backpacking trip into the mountains. On our return, I was hiking alone and took a wrong turn at a junction. I had hiked for about two miles when I was confronted by a huge, beautiful gray eagle. He squawked and scolded me so that I stopped to talk to him. He would not even let me speak with his intense scolding, but swooped closer and closer.

"Finally, his apparent concern made me ask, 'Am I going the wrong way?' He became totally silent and flew closer, holding himself still and quiet. I felt a need for hurrying; so I ran back down the trail and found my way to the proper path. I had gone two miles out of my way. Had I been just two minutes later, a search party would have gone out after me, and it would have meant many hours gathering up everyone. Your 'gift' has given me the knowledge of how knowing, thinking, and feeling animals are, and I wish to thank you for giving me the sense to listen to the warnings of my new found friend, the gray eagle."

Mrs. Buffin had the sense to *listen* to the gray eagle and interpret it correctly, thus avoiding a dangerous crisis. She was given a glimpse of another world and knew it. We all possess sensitivity and inner awareness, but she was directly open to it.

After receiving her letter, I felt my confidence in my own abilities grow, and my first tentative theories deepen to belief. My aim now in writing this book is to help everyone become aware of his or her potential: the knowledge that each of us has the ability to tune into the sensitive world within, to become one with nature and then hear, just as the animals hear, the voice of the animals and nature around us.

CHAPTER 2

EARLY ENCOUNTERS

After this first awakening, I deliberately sought situations that would offer possibilities for communicating with animals. When my animals were sick and had to go to the veterinarian for treatment, I would arrive early and spend time in the waiting room, mentally communicating with the dogs and cats there. I would mentally ask each animal what was wrong, and then I'd speak to the owner and discover that the animal's pain or trouble was exactly what the animal had communicated to me.

During visits to the veterinarian hospital, I grew to understand animals' physical reactions as well as emotional feelings. One day, when I looked into the eyes of an old, sickly gray-and-white cat, a sudden wave of nausea came over me and I felt a stabbing pain in my kidney area. I knew there could be nothing wrong with my kidneys because I felt fine, but I allowed the feeling to grow to see what would happen. I felt sure I was vicariously experiencing the cat's physical pain in its kidney, as well as its strong feeling of being old and tired. I had the sensation of wanting to die, and as I thought of death, I felt sleepy and peaceful.

It began to dawn on me that the cat was telling me it was in great pain and looked forward to dying. There was no fear of death, just a sense of peace. I asked the owner what was wrong with his cat, to which he replied, "His kidneys are very bad, and we've brought him in to be put to sleep."

The communication itself is like experiencing a dream; I see, hear, taste and feel, but it is all going on inside my head, but I am wide awake and aware of everything around me. Someone took a movie of me once while I was working with an animal, and the only change they observed was while I was *looking inward* to the pictures in my head, my eyes went out of focus.

I must admit, though, that I was terribly confused when I first began receiving mental impressions from animals. These strange sensations shook my sense of logic and reality, and made me feel isolated from other human beings. In the early days, when I told my friends about my mental communication with animals, most tended to be kind or tolerant, yet some were patronizing. As my strange talent became more widely known, I experienced the gamut of reactions from open-mouthed wonder to ridicule, from laughter to suspicion, and from embarrassment to open hostility and unconcealed doubt about my sanity.

Fortunately, I learned that Fred Kimble, a psychic who lived in California, also communicated with animals via ESP. I attended one of his lectures, and it was soon clear that he believed the source of his understanding sprang from occult inspiration and was supernatural. I believed mine was natural. I did not attend his classes, but I was greatly relieved to know that I was not alone in this ability.

After a period of about six months, I began to understand more clearly how the communication worked. And as the accuracy of my nonverbal reception from animals increased, I lost my fear of criticism and began to share what I knew with my friends, most of whom were animal lovers and owners. They were fascinated with what I told them about their own animals and shared it with their friends, who also quickly spread the news.

In time, feature reporters from newspapers like the San Gabriel Valley Tribune, Los Angeles Times, and Los Angeles Herald Examiner began to write about my work. Invitations to speak at dog clubs began pouring in, and eventually I was appearing on radio and television programs. Then appearances on the Mike Douglas television show, along with other network programs, gave my work national exposure, and newspapers and magazines began requesting more interviews. My credibility was being accepted, and my level of accuracy in consultation with animals had anchored itself on solid ground.

Meanwhile, more and more people called for appointments with their sick or misbehaving pets. Most of the animals had been taken to veterinarians but were not helped, which may have been because many of their problems were emotional rather than physical. Each case was a challenge, and as I refined my technique, my private practice grew.

One memorable case was Poi, an Australian Shepherd dog. He urinated in the house, ate tissues, chewed furniture, and was covered with a rash. He also suffered from edema, or some form of body swelling. All medical treatment had failed.

When his owner, Mrs. Griffin, brought him to me, I asked Poi what was wrong. He told me he didn't use his dog door because a bird attacked him and pecked at him whenever he went out into the yard. He also said his owner was sad and cried a lot. So to comfort her, he ate her tissues to convey to her that he wanted to help. He was sad and lonely too, he said, and wanted a companion to play with during the day.

After our conversation, I spoke to Mrs. Griffin, who verified everything Poi had told me. There was an attacking mockingbird in the area. Mrs. Griffin had recently lost her husband, so Poi had been left alone a lot. Poi had shown both his own needs and his empathy with his owner. He had literally grieved with her by eating tissues. The frustration of loneliness, the desire to help his owner, and the undischarged energy were all causing his physical symptoms of excessive itching and swelling. The owner got rid of the bird by moving its nest, and got a companion for Poi. In almost no time, the rash disappeared and Poi was going outside to urinate, and began living a normal, healthy life.

Another memorable case became a personal breakthrough. Because I vicariously experience what the animal experiences, if a dog has a headache, I have a headache. I realized for my own health and sanity I needed to close myself off, to a degree, from some of the animals' physical and emotional problems. I had to learn to communicate with the animals, yet separate myself from their pain or close off pain identification. This posed a real problem until Casey, a Boston terrier, dramatized it for me and forced me to discover what I now call my technique of pain separation, or closure.

When Casey was brought to me for help, his owner, Rachel Hill of Santa Ana, California, was receptive to the idea of using ESP. Her only concern was to discover why her normally affectionate dog had suddenly become an unpredictable, uncontrollable animal, barking and biting anyone without warning, even biting off his owner's fingertip during the frenzy.

I mentally asked Casey why he was behaving this way. He explained that hearing noise of any kind, even the doorbell, was so painful that he lost all control of his behavior. He was terribly ashamed and sorry for biting his owner. I received the image of a brain problem, which caused an unbearable pressure that intensified whenever sound reached it. I took this to be the source of Casey's pain.

When Mrs. Hill took Casey to his vet, the doctor rejected my diagnosis because he could find no pupil dilation or loss of coordination, the normal clinical signs of brain damage. Casey's doctor was unable to X-ray the dog's skull because he did not have the proper equipment. An electro-encephalogram could have been taken, or Casey's vet could have recommended another doctor with the appropriate X-ray machine. Unfortunately neither of these happened, and subsequently Casey died of the brain problem indicated.

When Casey left my home after that first consultation, I developed a headache of such intensity that I had to take an aspirin and lie down. When the headache still did not diminish, I began to question its source, since I had been feeling fine before he arrived. I soon realized my headache was the same as Casey's symptomatic pain, and since Casey's headache was experienced by my subconscious mind, not my physical body, aspirin could not make it go away. I learned then how to close off the empathy pain by telling my subconscious that the pain belonged to the animal and not to me. I then ignored the symptoms, acting as though they did not exist, and they immediately disappeared.

Soon after this important insight I received a letter from Rachel Hill that gave me much comfort and encouragement. Apparently she had taken Casey to the veterinarian again for further treatment. She reported, "Our vet confirmed your diagnosis of a brain tumor. Casey began having trouble with his coordination (which I think you noticed), but which we didn't pay too much attention to as [Casey] has always been kind of floppy and awkward. But last evening it seemed more pronounced, so I took him to the vet this morning. The vet is keeping him for a couple of days, but these are just stop-gap measures, we know, so tonight our hearts are very heavy, and my tears have made my eyes red and sore. But all the tears and all the heartaches are unimportant compared to the pleasure he's given us in the years past. He was a funny little clown with a slapdash sense of humor and, above all, was so devoted to us and so happy for some petting and attention. It was because I knew he loved me that I could never bring myself to do anything about his biting me. I always knew he didn't mean to hurt me, and I'm surer of it now than ever before. Thank you for your help and using your great gift to help all animal lovers."

Despite such successes and a growing reputation, I am often asked what qualifies me to be an animal analyst. My response is that I cultivate the gift of a free, open spirit that allows animals to speak to and through me. My answer may garner only indulgent smiles or quizzical looks, but I could not be more sincere. Contrary to popular belief, ESP is not limited to a gifted few, but is an innate human quality. I believe everyone possesses the ability to communicate with other forms of life, and with other people, using ESP. The time has come for this to be freely and responsibly acknowledged.

I am also a firm believer that for one to be a responsible animal analyst it is not enough to be able to ask animals questions and get answers. One must be educated in breed characteristics and animal behavior before being qualified to give advice. Simply put, just because I can speak Spanish doesn't make me a qualified psychologist in Mexico. Too many people have come out of the woodwork, so to speak, since I took my stand years ago and are giving, in most cases, inaccurate advice because they don't have the knowledge to back up their counsel.

This was brought to my attention recently when a famous animal communicator told one of my clients that her dog was attacking other dogs because "in its past life, it had been attacked and killed by a pack of dogs and there was nothing she could do about it." Had this communicator had a proper knowledge of animal behavior, and of the influence toxic substances have on temperament, she would have known that this particular breed is naturally dog-aggressive. She would have also known that since this dog had been exposed to Lysol, a coal tar derivative that makes some of these dogs aggressive, she could have corrected the problem.

But once the owner came to me, I located the problem, cleaned up her dog's environment, and sent the owner to a knowledgeable trainer who helped her learn how to control his aggression. Then the dog improved immensely.

Another case with this same uninformed animal communicator involved a friend of mine who had purchased a beautiful thoroughbred horse from the killer pen in Canada. One day the horse would act just fine; the next day he would race off with her on his back, running through fences, stumbling, falling and other such behavior. The following day he would be fine again. This particular communicator told the horse owner that he was acting that way because he had been abused in a past life and was now afraid of people and that it was the owner's *karma* to keep this horse until he died.

When I learned of this, we traced the horse's bloodlines and discovered he was from a famous horse that sired offspring that were great runners but often crazy killers. This horse had an inherited genetic mental deficiency—which could, I reasoned, someday cause him to kill his owner.

Now had that communicator known her horses, she would not have put my friend in jeopardy or tried to use her horse to teach the concept of reincarnation. I was so thankful my friend came to me before she got hurt. Her poor horse was crying out for help because he didn't want to behave this way, but just couldn't help himself. He was put to sleep mercifully before he had a chance to hurt someone else or himself.

Another time I was called in to chat with a sick cat in Oakland, California, that had been suffering from cystitis. I determined that it was caused by an improper diet and exposure to toxic substances in the home. I worked with the owner to clean up its environment and change its diet. With proper nutrition, the cat got well.

The whole experience had been so positive for the cat's owner that two years later, she called in the same communicator who had talked to my horse friend, for a "follow-up" chat with her kitty. That communicator told her that she had no business making her cat well, but should have let it "pass on so it could have come back in a younger, healthier body." This communicator brought such negativity into their home that from the day she left, the cat started getting sick and eventually died. Had I learned about her visit *before* the cat died, I'm confident that I could have prevented it.

A lack of knowledge isn't helpful to anyone, including animals. So be sure you know the qualifications of the communicator and be certain that they don't overstep their bounds and use your animal to propagate their personal philosophies.

The basic difficulty in discovering one's ESP ability lies in reawakening an ability that has become dormant. There are no economical, social, or educational barriers to its renewal. My formal education had little to do with awakening my ESP abilities, I hold a bachelor's degree in biblical education from Columbia International University in Columbia, South Carolina. It is only since my involvement with animal healing that I have seriously undertaken a study of sciences, which includes two years of chemistry, physics, zoology, genetics and other related courses at Citrus College in Covina, California, and California State Polytechnic University in Pomona, California.

The more I worked with the animals, the more I realized that more education was vital because, simply pointing with my index finger to an animal's body part or telling the vet the animal hurts "here" or "there" was hardly a sound or professional approach. My education has given me, among other things, the knowledge of animal anatomy that I needed to relate animals' physical symptoms of pain to veterinarians.

Two particular courses, anatomy and organic chemistry, and two particular dogs, both German Shepherds, one being my own Princessa, showed me how formal study really complemented my ESP abilities.

A German shepherd was brought to me with one of the more unpleasant and puzzling problems of dogs: eating sticks, stools, and gravel (an inclination Princessa also demonstrated). The dog's owner said she had taken the dog to the vet, but nothing was found that shed light on this disturbing behavior. As I mentally visualized the animal's stomach, an image materialized of some sort of tiny ducts that entered the stomach and were nearly empty and dry. It was so clear that I felt like a camera observing a scene, and was even able to zoom in on particular areas. I had no idea what to do with the image, and I admitted as much to the owner, unable to offer any advice.

Later, while I was in my organic chemistry class, the solution surfaced quite unexpectedly. As the professor lectured on the digestive process of the human body, he explained that hydrochloric acid (HCL) is secreted by the body and passed through tiny ducts into the stomach. This secretion breaks down proteins in order to make these particles small enough to be assimilated by the body as they reach the small intestines.

I was seized with excitement! Those were the same ducts I had seen when working with the Shepherd. The stomachs of both dogs—both of the Shepherd and my Princessa—were not producing sufficient amounts of HCL to effectively break down the ingested proteins that later fermented in the intestinal tract and produced uncomfortable amounts of gas.

Because the stomach was unable to do its job, the dogs were eating gravel and stools as an attempt to get relief. When I discussed this with our vets, Dr. Darrow and Dr. Christiansen of Arcadia, California, they explained that the dogs were looking for the HCL used in the digestive process of healthy animals, which is present in their excretions. They also said that was an inherited problem in many breeds such as Dalmatians, Shepherds, Aussies, and Bostons.

To correct the problem, the vet suggested using salt, which contains chloride, but that did not work. He then recommended an enzyme supplement, which also proved fruitless because a stool sample analysis had already shown that Princessa's pancreas was producing enzyme amounts sufficient to dissolve carbohydrates. I decided that if HCL was lacking, then why not give her precisely what she needed? I purchased some HCL tablets from the health-food store and gave Princessa one about ten minutes before her meals. I also found that when HCL is given along with a dry food mixed with water, the already-deficient amount of HCL is diluted in the stomach, and the problem is intensified. But when the food was fed dry, with water not given until after the feeding, I was able to reduce the amount of HCL supplement needed. It was this situation that later, when I started the herbal business, prompted me to develop a formula I call Digestion that will stimulate the body's natural production of HCL, and will even more effectively correct the problem.

Soon, I was working with veterinarians as I do today. We are a sort of team, complementing each other's knowledge. I tell them where the animal hurts and how their pain is conveyed to me. They determine the diagnosis and decide on treatment. Many times a vet knows an animal is in pain, but he does not know where it originates. I think of myself as an interpreter for the animals and an aid to the doctor.

I once treated a Boston terrier named Mickey who had a unique problem. Vivian Wolf of Anaheim, California, brought the dog to my office to see if I could determine why the animal was acting as if he had pain in his nose, for which his vet could find no cause. Mentally, I asked Mickey what had happened, and through a movie-like sequence of mental images, the Terrier explained. He had been sniffing around during a walk in the desert, when he suddenly felt a sharp stab in his nose. This set off a series of sneezes that lasted for about forty-five minutes. When the sneezes finally stopped, his nose hurt quite badly.

Vicariously, I experienced Mickey's pain and identified it as an insect sting, and realized that the insect had been expelled during his sneezing fit. By the time Mickey had been brought to the veterinarian, there was nothing visible in his nose to pinpoint the problem, but my interpretation unlocked the mystery. Sometime later, I met Mickey's vet, Dr. Richard Dahlum of Orange, California, who told me that my information had enabled him to successfully diagnose a similar case.

Mickey also had a chronic ear irritation that was being treated with liquid medication. When I mentally looked into his ear, I saw a form of bacteria burrowing into the moisture. Mickey had allergies that produced excess moisture in the ear canal, making it a perfect breeding ground for bacteria. Because liquid medication could not penetrate the moisture barrier I suggested an antihistamine also be given to dry out the ear canal so the medication could reach the bacteria. Dr. Dahlum agreed, and Mickey's ear problem was solved.

Sometimes a physical problem may be the source of an emotional problem. Such was the case with Bala, a cross between an Australian Shepherd and a Dingo, a wild dog of Australia (a cross that, in the breeder's opinion, created a better herding dog). Because Bala did not respond to his owners' training, they thought he was unusually stubborn. But when Bala and I communicated, he explained that he wanted to learn but could not hear their commands. I mentally looked into his ears and saw large wax plugs had built up in the ear canals. I also saw that the dog had no ear drums.

Bala's vet suggested surgically removing the dog's ear wax at the Veterinary Teaching Hospital in Davis, California. When the wax plugs were removed, they discovered that the dog had no ear drums and no scar tissue to indicate that he ever had any.

My teachers have also been the animals themselves. It is they who have helped me become increasingly receptive to their messages in this exciting, exacting work. Only through accurate communication can I assist an animal, particularly in cases that require a probe that spans several years or one that dates back to the traumas of birth itself.

Such was true in a case that I consider to be a breakthrough in my work. I began working with a poodle who demonstrated very erratic behavior. One moment the dog would be lying down calmly and then, if anyone touched him, he would leap up and viciously attack them. At other times, unprovoked, he would suddenly attack the straw of his igloo-shaped basket. No medical reason could be determined to cause the dog's hostility, and his owners were in despair.

When I communicated with the dog, he revealed an experience that had occurred at birth. I received an image of a newborn puppy with his mother lying underneath a bed where she had gone to give birth to her litter. I saw the mother trying, but failing, to release that poodle puppy from her embryonic sac. I experienced what he had felt as he gasped helplessly for breath; the life-sustaining oxygen still denied him in the sac. Then I felt hands pulling him out.

The poodle's vet was Dr. Howard Kurtz. I suggested that his owners relate my image to him, along with the explanation or *diagnosis*: possible brain damage due to lack of oxygen resulting from the puppy staying too long in his mother's embryonic sac. I had seen a similar case while working at a women's prison, with an inmate who had a form of epilepsy called *rage syndrome*. The illness produces seizures that cause a person or animal to attack anyone or anything around them with no apparent reason and with nothing specifically triggering the episode. Those afflicted with the illness never know what they are doing or how they can control their behavior. Based on my findings, Dr. Kurtz successfully treated the poodle for a possible condition of epilepsy, a frequent result of this type of brain damage.

As a follow up, the owners called the dog's breeder and received undisputed confirmation. They were told that two puppies had been born: one that died before the owners were able to retrieve it and the other puppy had to be removed by hand, from his mother's embryonic sac. It had taken so much time to extract him and his mother from under the bed, that by the time they removed the sac, he had already suffered brain damage from oxygen deprivation.

Dr. Marvin J. Cain, a veterinarian from Cincinnati, Ohio, who had heard about me, asked if I would come to his horse farm in Kentucky and consent to various animal-communication tests. He raised a few race horses there for himself, but mostly they were injured horses that were there to be treated with acupuncture or to recuperate from injuries. Dr. Cain had previously X-rayed and diagnosed those injuries so he knew what was wrong with each of his animal patients and he wanted to know if I could pick up by ESP what he had already discovered. Unaware of his findings, I was to describe their problems through what they "told me". As a result of this successful and fun experience, we have become great friends, often to this day, calling on each other for help with difficult cases. Here I will cite just two examples of what happened.

The first involved a horse trained as a jumper that had been forced to end his career because he came up lame after a series of jumps. The horse told me he enjoyed jumping, but the pain afterward was so great that he was forced to limp. When I mentally looked into his front legs, I saw affected splint bones, and I felt him landing very heavily on his front legs. He was a large horse that did not shift his weight quickly enough from front to hind legs, so his front legs took the shock and weight of the landing. I determined that his splint bones were far too delicate to handle the sudden pressure, resulting in a crack that extended up the full length of the bone. Dr. Cain told me he had reached the same conclusion through a leg X-ray.

I then worked with Dr. Cain on a dog case in which X-rays did not reveal any specific information. The dog continually chewed at its foot and nothing appeared to be lodged there. When I mentally entered the dog's foot, I saw a tiny glasslike substance embedded between its toes. Dr. Cain investigated surgically and found an area of scar tissue that could have held such a tiny particle. After Dr. Cain removed the scar tissue, the dog stopped its chewing.

The animals have helped me to help them, and the experience is rewarding to all. They have also enriched my life in a much deeper way. My lessons here began like so many others—with one of my own animals. One of my greatest teachers was Princessa VonRichtoffen, the one who killed the noisy roosters to give me silence.

CHAPTER 3

ANIMALS ARE ANIMALS

It was one of those rare autumn mornings when light and color are perfectly blended. As I sat on a hillside in the California sunshine studying for a final chemistry exam, Princessa lay near me, content to share this almost lyrical moment. My eyes rested on the back of her head as I thought *how bored you must be! I get to do so much, but you have to stay home alone, day after day.* Slowly Princessa turned her head around, looked me straight in the eye and communicated a direct answer, *but my life is wonderful! I have time to see the things you are too busy to see!*

What do you mean, Princessa? I asked her.

Hear that bird? Listen to that dog! There goes that car again, coming our way. Just smell this earth! Hey, look at that rabbit! There goes another bird.

These sights and sounds were out of my physical range, but once I took Princessa's advice and began mentally "listening" through her ears and "seeing" through her eyes, the countryside became an enchanted ground, filled with exciting life. Princessa could not possibly be bored! As we sat there on the hill, she told me about her day, which was literally filled with activity: play, sights, sounds, sensations and excitement. Sometimes she ran about retrieving sticks the ranch hands threw for her. The men tired quickly, but she flew over the ground, stretching her muscles with the sheer joy of racing and running. When the game was over, she returned to the comfort of her own world, savoring an old bone, smelling the earth, experiencing the subtlest puff of wind. Since that first lesson, I have learned to look at the world through animal eyes, far beyond the range of human sight and hearing. The secret was to stop long enough to absorb what was going on around me, even in the desert which often seems so barren.

I was in Las Vegas once, playing bingo and asked a lady from the East Coast if she had visited Death Valley yet. She looked at me with horror and disgust. "Death Valley! It's nothing but sand!

How boring and dull! Las Vegas is where I belong." It takes all kinds and this lady and I were sure opposites. Little did she know what she was really missing! I find Las Vegas a dull, unchanging place, though plenty of money changes hands, it leaves the soul empty as well as the pocketbook. But, when you travel through the desert, Death Valley in particular, and take the time to really observe what is there, you'll find it is always changing. The beauty is endless and the quietness and serenity uplifts the soul. I spent a week there recently, sitting for a couple of hours every day, just listening and looking through my animal-trained "eyes and ears". The desert is teeming with life if you look beyond the heat and sand. This was brought home to me in an even greater sense as I walked across the desert, remembering all those pioneers who, in their rush to get to the gold fields of California, walked across some of the richest gold mines right under their feet. Yet, until Princessa's lesson, I was just as rushed as the next person, so intent on tomorrow that I missed the experiences of today. Now life is exciting and the most everyday experiences have a dimension that was totally lacking before. Now living "only for the moment" is a cliché for me because I have been given the grace to experience what it means to live "within the moment".

In real life and in literature, most people are quick to interpret animal behavior in human terms. Princessa taught me not to do this. Animals have different motives. We should let them be animals, not anthropomorphize their actions, giving them human motives. They are much more exciting as animals than as actors in Aesop's fables or the Cat in the Hat. One needs to be careful about trying to make our pets into people, especially that special person who is missing from your life. I often see this in older people whose children have grown and "left the nest". The animal is a wonderful substitute and one I highly recommend as long as you remember it is still an animal, and not a child. Too many times empty-nesters will indulge the animal the way they always wanted to do with their children, but it doesn't work with the animals either. They will often exhibit behavior problems like excessive barking, chewing, defecating and other obnoxious behaviors when they are left. An animal, like a child, wants to know its limits because it gives them a sense of security to know what they can do to please us. Discipline bad behavior, but ALWAYS reinforce good behavior

The biggest mistake I made before learning to communicate with animals, believed that being human was a far superior state of existence. This idea is shared by many animal lovers who say, and really believe, "My dog thinks he's people." It's not the dog who thinks he's people, its people who give humanlike qualities to the dog. When I asked animals if they wanted to be like people, they were emphatic in telling me they were perfectly content to be themselves. Their behavior resembles that of humans at times because it is their way of making their wants and needs known and their attitudes understood.

Although I now know how stupid it is to consider an animal in human terms, I have been just as guilty as the next person. After all I had learned from Princessa, I reverted to this error. I was trying to teach Princessa to speak by training her to bark for something she wanted. I was enthusiastically saying: "Come on, Princessa, speak! Say woof, woof!" I kept repeating this so-called training instruction until I was hoarse, but all she did was sit there with a puzzled expression, her head cocked to one side, refusing to utter a sound. Finally in exasperation I mentally asked her; *Princess, what's the matter with you? Why don't you speak?*

She mentally answered: *You already know what I want. Why do I have to bark?* Her answer was so sound and so sensible; I was ashamed that I had tried to reduce her to human "doggie" talk.

It is vital to accept the differences and similarities between animals and people in order to pave the way for communication. Accepting the animal as animal and valuing it for that alone, is the first avenue to receptive listening and response. While some information in this chapter may appear elemental, it may come as a surprise to discover how many intelligent and well-meaning pet owners disregard the obvious.

My anatomy studies taught me what similarities there are in bodily functions between animal mammals and humans. Both species require sound basic nutrition and both reproduce life in the same miraculous way. That is why animals fall prey to many human diseases and research experiments on them are often responsible for discovering cures that benefit humans. I am 100% against useless, repetitive experimentation on animals, especially for the development of cosmetics or products that are not vital to our lives or when those same experiments can be conducted without animal involvement. I am aware that there is a legitimate basis for some limited experimentation on animals, but only when testing is done on laboratory raised animals where the genetic background is known. Let me explain.

Take for example the average "Fifi" who has only known love and sleeping on the living room couch. She somehow gets lost and ends up in the pound or with some animal broker. She is then sold to a lab where she gets very little human contact, and now has to sleep on a cold cage floor, grieving for its' owner. The lab knows nothing of the genetic makeup of that animal, and treating it like it is a piece of lab equipment, does not take into account the animal's emotional state and its effect on the outcome of the testing. How do they know whether Fifi's diarrhea, or the skin problems, or chewing on herself, is coming from the chemicals she was given, or from something in her unknown gene pool, or possibly from a past exposure to something in her previous environment, or could it be from grief and stress? They don't know, so their results are not legitimate proof of what their product or chemical does. Only when we know the gene pool, and have raised the animals in the same environment all their lives where they have never known anything else, can we call the results legitimate. They usually will not be stressed if the environment is comfortable, like a nice kennel with companions and good care. This leads me to the next thing I have learned from the animals.

Animals have told me they are capable of feeling love, hate, resentment, frustration, jealousy, depression, and joy, but one attribute that sharply differentiates us is in the area of conscience. Humans wrestle with the question of morality. It is different for animals. While a pet may feel upset after he has done something wrong, his guilt does not stem from a sense of morality (right or wrong) but from the reprimand they know is coming their way because of their actions. There is a part of man I call the Spirit, or the more complicated thinking process, which includes an ability to make intricate plans for the future. Animals do not possess this ability. Ah, I hear you saying now "But they do plan for the future. Look how animals store food for the winter." That is instinct and involves no reasoning or special mental process in most cases. I even question how much of an animal's behavior is actually instinct and how much is taught by the mother. Behavioral psychologists are just beginning to discover that some animal behavior, once branded as instinctive, is actually taught by the parent. This subject is covered at length in Chapter 8. Animals are capable of sensing a situation and acting accordingly, but they cannot, as humans can, decide where they want to go on a vacation and execute all the necessary preparations, such as reservations, how much they have to save each month to prepare, and so on. An animal is not capable of such complicated thinking or action.

Another important area of difference is environment. Environment shapes human lives to a large degree, but our growth does not solely depend on it. When we realize we have a problem resulting from environment, we can decide to do something about it and by various actions and counseling, bring about the change. Animals are under the control of their environment. Even though they sense something is wrong or unhealthy or dangerous in their environment, most domesticated animals usually cannot make necessary changes without the help of their human. An animal can make deductions such as "when Uncle John comes over, he always leaves the door ajar, so the next time Uncle John comes, I will dart for the door and escape," or they will chew and dig to get away from a situation they don't like, but their capabilities are limited.

Experiencing time is another difference between people and animals. Animals are not aware of time in the way humans are. During our communications, animals will tell me about an event that occurred one year ago, and then jump to something that happened yesterday. They do not experience time sequentially.

However, if I ask specific questions about the particular event, an animal can give me the information in chronological sequence.

Awareness of time duration is also a difference between humans and animals. An owner can be gone for ten minutes or an hour and still receive the same greeting from a pet upon returning. It "feels" the same to them. I am speaking of the emotional aspect, not the physical. Confinement over a long period of time will create a build-up of energy in an animal that may produce physical symptoms of frustration, but this reaction is not related to the animal's concept of time. Absence from an owner for an *extended* period of time of several weeks however, will produce a homesick longing in a pet. This is because it is aware of missing someone loved, not because it is aware of dates, or days of the week.

Horse breeders or pet owners, who show their animals, frequently want me to ask their animal about a show on a specific date. This is impossible. The animal has no idea what the "fifteenth of the month" means. But if the owner gives me a specific experience that identifies a particular show, I can ask the animal about an event. For example, a question such as why the horse refused to jump at the third fence can bring a specific answer.

A common misconception among animal owners is that an animal possesses a sense of time because it does the same thing every day at the same time—such as waiting at a window at 3 p.m. for the children to return from school, or going to the train station daily to wait for an owner who arrives at 6:00 p.m. There are two explanations: one, emotional, two physical. Emotionally, the dog is "tuned into" the children and knows they are on their way home. In the case of the dog waiting at the station, there exists a biological "feel" about that time of the day. This same physical or biological principle holds true for cows at milking time. The cow feels its udder fill with milk and "knows" that it is time to be emptied and get dinner.

A great difference between humans and animals concerns the question of sex and sexuality and, of course, propagation. There is considerable controversy and confusion over the question of spaying and neutering animals, along with the pros and cons of allowing one's pet to breed because it is believed to make a better-adjusted animal when it has had one litter and then is spayed. This is an old wives' tale. I deal with these subjects in detail in Chapter 10. Here I want to report briefly on the biological and psychological differences between animal and human sexuality and reproduction because, according to my animal friends, we humans know very little about what *they* feel about sex and propagation.

From what the animals tell me, males and females alike, sex is a tremendous *physical* pressure and there is absolutely no emotional content to the experience. Male animals, for instance, do not seek females for mating unless the female is in heat. Sex then becomes a strong, uncontrollable physical drive, like hunger for food, and not an act of love as it should be in humans. Too many times sexuality in humans becomes like the animals, a drive to satisfy one's own pleasures instead of an act of love; but, for the animals, it is not an act of love, it is strictly a natural drive. Many humans tend to identify their sexuality with that of the animals and feel that because sex is important and enjoyable for them, it must be important to their pets. This could not be further from the truth. Spaying and neutering automatically removes that pressure, thus freeing them to be more loving pets and more involved in other activities that they enjoy far more.

The same applies to propagation. My communications with dogs and cats reveal that 99 percent of them do not want litters. This is no exaggeration. Physical drive is not something animals can control, nor do they connect it with the end result of puppies and kittens.

One animal mounting another is another commonly misunderstood behavior. When two dogs meet, and one animal mounts the other, it is an expression of dominance. There is no sexual connotation to it at all. So if two males do it, there are no "homosexual" overtones. When one dog rides another and the second one permits it, then the "rider" becomes dominant in their relationship. I have often seen this when my spayed bitch and her neutered son play together. If the son has a toy she wants, she will ride him as a way of telling him to surrender the toy. This also happens when I am busy and one of my dogs wants attention. If I continue to ignore him, he will try to "ride" me, forcing his way of "domination" on me. Whenever I have observed this "mounting" behavior and asked the animals about it, they have revealed its nature clearly. It is a matter of domination, nothing else.

There are exceptions, of course, and these should be checked. The male dog, who habitually "rides" a person, may have an overactive hormone stemming from an enlarged prostate gland. He cannot control his behavior and should be examined by a veterinarian. According to veterinarians with whom I have discussed this problem, the only solution is to have the dog neutered as soon as possible. The younger the dog is neutered, the better for the animal. In older dogs, surgery can be fatal. Prostate problems and prostate cancer are common killers of older, unaltered male dogs.

Sniffing at people, particularly in the genital area, has no sexual connotation. An animal identifies a person the same way they identify each other, by our unique body chemistry makeup. They love to "read the doggie newspaper" on their walks to find out who has been out and leave their mark to let others know they have been there too.

One last point. Sex is as pleasurable to the animals as it is to humans. If it wasn't, or if it was painful, they would try to avoid it. You will occasionally see the animal that literally masturbates with a stuffed toy. This is not emotional, but again, strictly a physical pleasure. I don't know if it is good for them or not, but I do know, it is strictly a physical enjoyment like you eating something you like.

Sex for the animal usually means reproduction or a drive they cannot control, and this is one more good reason to understand that our pets are animals with their own needs, distinct from that of humans.

CHAPTER 4

THE NON-VERBAL LANGUAGE

Non-verbal communication is natural to everyone. Most people tend to get "hung up" on words as they begin to learn vocabulary and literally lose communication. This can even happen between people within our own country. For example, when I first moved from New York where I was raised, to South Carolina where I attended college, I was baffled by the clerks' response as I left the store. "Ya'll come back, ya hear?" I went back to ask what I had forgotten only to have her look at me with the most quizzical look on her face. After a few minutes, we both had a good laugh as we realized it was her way of saying, "come back again, I enjoyed serving you". Had this happened in New York, it would have meant that I had forgotten something and I needed to go back and get it.

As I explained earlier, ESP, or nonverbal communication, is a natural ability we all have as children. It's something we're born with, but obscured later in life as we learn words and focus on the use of verbal communication only. A visit to a special education school in Northern California in July 1974 provided an excellent example of this natural ability. One student was a twelve-year old boy who had cerebral palsy and had never been able to verbalize anything beyond grunting noises. We met, and as I mentally received his thoughts, he ran away as fast as he could.

"I can't understand that," one staff member said. "He always greets strangers with affection. Sometimes he's so demonstrative he makes a pest of himself." The staff member tried to coax the boy out of the corner of the room, but he refused to budge. I stayed where I was, but across the distance I mentally asked the boy, *why did you run away from me?*

I was not surprised when he replied in the same, silent communication. *I can read their minds,* he answered, referring to the staff. *That's how I get my way. They want me to work, but I like just sitting still. Now somehow you know my secret. I was afraid you were going to tell on me. Then I wouldn't be able to do it any more.*

I talked with the staff members and gradually the youngster relaxed and left his corner to join us. Wanting to test the validity of this communication, the staff members agreed to an experiment. They all mentally told the boy to mop the floor. The boy had already admitted to me that he was lazy and didn't want to work. But he read their thoughts and his eyes widened and he grunted, "Uh!Uh!' He shook his head no and ran away again.

You may think this child a special case, but your experience will show you many examples of normal children communicating nonverbally among themselves, with animals, and with adults. Haven't you seen a small child look at an adult and immediately love or dislike that person for no apparent reason? Some adults who love children elicit an immediate happy response from children without doing anything special to entertain or win them. The child is using his or her natural ESP to look into the adult and discover what the adult's *true* feelings are. You may also see children from two different countries (parents speaking different languages) play together for hours with no communication barrier. They are basically conversing with their minds. This is also true between twins who eventually develop their own language. Unfortunately, once children begin to verbalize feelings, this marvelous ability ceases to be used, becomes dormant, and by adolescence may be lost entirely.

Young children who still use this nonverbal language can also communicate with animals. Two families, both friends of mine, had this experience. Mo and Till Moen of Lompoc, California, and their young son, Trajen, are very good friends of Mr. and Mrs. Stan Appelt of Bradbury, California, the owners of Burgie, a black German Shepherd. Trajen and Burgie had a beautiful ESP friendship for the first four years of Trajen's life. The little boy often came into the house to tell his mother, "Mommy, Burgie says he's thirsty, " or "Burgie hurt his leg, right here," pointing to the area on his own leg which Burgie had conveyed to him was painful in *his* leg.

This sounds like childhood fantasy, but when it was checked out, we knew it was genuine communication: Burgie was indeed thirsty or hurt in some specific way. Then the friendship was interrupted when Trajen and his family moved to Florida for a year. During that year, Trajen entered school and developed a much larger vocabulary, depending more and more on words instead of mental communication. Trajen and Burgie were reunited when Trajen returned to California and visited with the Appelts, but something had happened to their ability to communicate. After twenty minutes with the dog, Trajen ran into the house in tears. "Mommy, why doesn't Burgie talk to me any more?" When I visited with the boy's parents at the Appelts' home, I sensed Trajen's hurt and disappointment and Burgie's deep sorrow. I explained to the parents and the dog that Trajen had lost his ability to communicate nonverbally. As the little boy outgrew his nonverbal language, a special friendship ended. Once children begin to verbalize feelings, this marvelous ability becomes dormant and by adolescence may be lost entirely. The only children who never lose this "ability" are ones encouraged by their parents, teachers or others in their environment, to maintain it.

Unfortunately, at that time, I did not know how to help Trajen recapture his ability. Today, in 2008, I would have instructed the parents from the time he was very little and still had a good open communication between dog and boy, that whenever he told them what an animal said, to respond by saying, "thank you sweetheart for telling me". The parent then must check out what the child says, in front of the child so that the child knows the parent believes him, and he will rarely lose the ability to talk to the animals and "hear their voices back". Children need to understand that this ability is normal and something to cherish as you respect it in them. They need to have that communication believed and nurtured by the adults in their lives in order to keep the channels open. This is a great gift you can give your child. Being able to communicate with animals enriches our lives, and I couldn't imagine not being able to do it. It doesn't just help maintain a better and greater relationship with animals, but will help in their relationships with people throughout their lives.

Animals also communicate with one another. I learned more about this one day when riding a friend's pinto mare, Dawn. Dawn asked me if she could visit her good friend Kelly, a gelding with whom she had shared a stall when she was injured.

Dawn's owner, Buz Olmstead, of Stallion Springs, Tehachapi, California, commented that Dawn had indeed been injured and had spent quite a bit of time with Kelley during recovery, but Kelley had been returned to her owner and they didn't see each other any more. We decided to find out what the horses had to say to each other, so we allowed Dawn to go where she wanted to. As we approached Kelly's driveway, Dawn quickened her pace and trotted quickly up to Kelly's corral. As we approached, I experienced a sense of *greeting* pass between them. Kelly asked Dawn where she had been. Dawn responded by showing Kelly the exact places... trails, hills, forest and river. Kelly received these pictures as he stood staring into Dawn's eyes. It was like watching a silent movie—incredible!

Kelly told Dawn how lonely he felt and how he wished he could have been with her by showing her pictures of himself standing alone in the pasture and projecting the feeling of loneliness. I experienced two horses exchanging feelings of parting, after which Dawn willingly turned for home.

Intelligence is another factor in the nonverbal language. There are several theories about the relative intelligence of various species of animals. Personally, I do not find any one species any more or less intelligent than any other, although many people, including members of the scientific community, base the species' intelligence or IQ on its relationship and similarity to humankind. For example, monkeys are considered more intelligent than other animals because their anatomy is similar to humans and they can mimic us in many ways. But mimicry is not intelligence. In my opinion, if dogs and horses had the same anatomy as humans instead of four paws, horses had arms and legs instead of hooves; they could perform just as well as monkeys and often, better. Another way some people measure intelligence is based on the animal's degree of dependence or independence. Cats and horses are more independent and usually relate better to one another than they do to people. Dogs, however, are more dependent on humans both emotionally and physically. People, therefore, tend to think dogs are smarter than cats and horses. This is both illogical and unfair. Each species should be considered and accepted as equal, and each individual within that species should be judged solely by comparison to its own kind.

There are many different levels of intelligence within each species which can be measured. My personal criteria of an animal's intelligence is by its ability to clearly communicate; how much depth perception it has of the world around it; and its ability to distinguish and communicate the events of its life in the actual sequence in which those events occurred. An animal of average or above-average intelligence can relate details in sequence. A retarded animal can only relate fragments of events, not necessarily in the order they happened, neither can they retain what they are being taught.

For example, a Labrador was brought to me because he refused to obey commands, even nipping at his owner at times. The Lab communicated that he really was trying to learn, but he became confused because he could not remember the meaning of the command for very long. When punished, he snapped out in sheer frustration because he did not know what else to do. He responded as many learning disabled children do under pressure. Once the owner understood this, she treated the dog differently, demanding less from him and rewarding him in a more positive manner for good responses. Their relationship improved dramatically and the dog stopped biting.

Retardation is a basic cause of many animals' inability to develop love for, and loyalty toward, its owner. Some retarded animals may outwardly express its joy of loving, but what it is really expressing is its joy in receiving love while not being capable of returning love. Only time and working with that animal will help you understand them better.

Normal animals, in general, operate on love, but they also respond to fear, anger, and distrust. The mail carrier who genuinely loves animals and is not afraid of them, sees them in terms of friendship and pleasure, and most of the animals the mail carrier meets, will be friendly or simply leave him alone. The mail carrier, who is afraid of dogs, will be in danger of being attacked because the animal will feel that fear, vicariously, and act accordingly.

45

We saw this when I lived in North Hollywood, California. We always knew when our regular mailman was on duty because the dogs never stirred when he came around, or just lifted their heads, looked at the door, and quietly went back to sleep. We always knew when the substitute who hated animals was on duty, a man who was so paranoid about dogs, he often didn't leave people's mail claiming they had vicious dogs when in reality they didn't even have one. We could tell exactly where he was on the street because every dog went crazy as he approached, including ours.

My animals tell me a human emits no scent when he or she is frightened. The animals pick up the person's mental picture of expecting to be bitten. The animal may then bite, but it is reacting to the fear in the individual and the mental picture they are holding, not any scent.

One day, my friend Jean Salmon of Covina, California, was taking her German Shepherd to a dog show. Her children and the dog got into the car first. Jean followed, but not without some emotion. She was angry at one of the children and intended punishment. As she approached the car, the Shepherd who had had his back to her, wheeled around and clamped his teeth onto her arm. Just as suddenly, the dog realized who she was, released her arm, and hung his head in shame. Later, when I talked to the dog, he explained his action. He had jumped into the car after the children with his back toward Jean. He was unaware of who was coming, but acutely aware of the anger directed toward one of the children. He turned and bit Jean, trying to protect the child from the anger coming toward the child he was protecting. Animals react strongly to human feelings.

Another friend of mine was trail riding on her motorcycle. Her boyfriend was with her, riding his own bike. As he rode down the wooded path, a German Shepherd darted out, growling and snarling at him. He feared the animal, which caused the dog to react strongly with aggression. A few seconds later, my friend rode by that same spot and once again the dog started attacking. She continued riding, thinking friendly thoughts and telling the animal she thought he was a beautiful shepherd. The dog stopped running after her and sat at the side of the path with his head cocked to one side. No one could convince my friend that the situation was coincidence. She knew the dog picked up her positive, loving feelings.

My work with animals has shown me that you just can't fool them. One day, Princessa sat in the back of the station wagon as we drove past a school yard. She begged me to let her go play with the children. I stopped (remember this was a long time ago, back in 1974, before the modern day dangers children are presently facing from strangers) to allow a ten year old girl to come up to the car to meet Princessa. She asked if she could pet the dog. For the first and only time in her life, she growled at a child. I asked the girl, "Are you afraid of the dog?" She answered, "Yes." I explained that Princessa loved young children and she need not be afraid of her. As she realized that Princessa was no danger, her attitude changed toward the dog who immediately licked her hand. It was beautiful watching the change in both of them as they began to play together.

My first experience in testing this non-verbal language was with my Pomeranian, Blacky. I wanted to experiment with mental commands to see if Blacky would respond. I knew he loved liver-flavored dog biscuits, so while he was lying under the bed one day, I visualized in my mind Blacky coming out and getting a dog biscuit I held out for him. He came. Then I visualized him asking me for another one by first going to the box, sniffing it, and then returning to me, sitting patiently until I handed him another one. He did just that. Then I actually gave him the whole box of dog biscuits. An astonished Blacky picked it up and scurried under the bed, dragging his treasure. After I listened to him munch happily for a few minutes, I mentally pictured him pushing the box out from under the bed with his nose, myself looking at the box, then Blacky taking it back under the bed to eat the whole thing. He would not budge, but went on hurriedly munching. Mentally I said, *if you keep the box, I'm going to reach under the bed and take it.* I pictured the action in my mind, slowly, step by step. In a couple of seconds, Blacky pushed the box out from underneath the bed with his nose. I must admit, I was somewhat overwhelmed that he had responded so obediently to my mental pictures. He was actually reading my mind. I kept my part of the bargain and gave him the whole box. He was like a kid let loose in a candy store!   After this successful experiment, I started using mental pictures as a regular part of my work.   In the second part of this book, I will explain the exact techniques of how this language works, and how you too can learn to use it in Part III of this book.

People who show dogs often have difficulties in the ring because they are not aware that their thoughts are being picked up by their animals.   For example, when a dog is taken to show for obedience trials, the animal is told verbally, "Down, stay," but while standing back, the handler is thinking, " *Oh boy, last time we were here he got up and ran out of the ring. I hope he doesn't run out again this time.* The dog picks up the handler's mental picture of running out of the ring and it does exactly that.   The handler then usually punishes the dog for disobedience.   The dog cannot understand this because it did what it was told mentally: *Get up and run out again this time.*

So far, I have been talking about short-distance communication in which the person and the animal are in sight of each other.   However, I have also learned that ESP is not limited to space or distance and can be nearly as effective over thousands of miles.   The next chapter explains this phenomenon and how it has enabled me to locate lost animals and help pet owners with all kinds of animal problems, emotional and physical.   Now most of my work with animal communication is done over the phone, one day a week.

CHAPTER 5

LONG DISTANCE COMMUNICATION

Mental or non-verbal communication is not limited to time or space. An animal may be in another room or thousands of miles away from its owner, but ESP communication is not affected.

J. Allen Boone, author of *Kinship with All Life,* got an inkling of this phenomenon when he realized that his dog Strongheart always seemed to anticipate his arrivals. His book tells how a friend took care of Strongheart while Boone was away, the friend reported that Strongheart always walked to the window and sat there waiting, just minutes before Boone's arrival to pick him up. Even though no outward warning was given to the dog and Boone's returns from his trips were irregular, Strongheart was always constant in his vigils and accurate on the timing.

A client of mine who "dog sat" a Poodle during the owner's out-of-town trips recognized this same sort of behavior in the dog just before the owner's return home. The Poodle would gather up his toys, put them in his box, and then sit by the window and wait. A check with the owner's time of departure after an absence of several days, confirmed the fact that the dog's behavior coincided with the exact moment the owner had boarded a plane for home.

When I saw my own dogs acting the same way, it removed all doubts about the existence of ESP over distances. I decided to test this when I visited with my sister Florence in Bradenton, Florida. I had to be out for the day, so Florence agreed to watch the dogs and record their actions with the times. I recorded the times along with my actions so that we could see how they correlated. When I returned that evening, she laughed and said, "I know exactly when you started for home, changed your mind and went somewhere else."

"How on earth did you know?" I asked.

She said that at 8 P.M. my four dogs got up from the kitchen floor and ran to the front door to meet me. About twenty minutes later, they returned to the kitchen. Just ten minutes after that, Flo said, they went to the front door again. "And then you came home!"

I had indeed started for the house at 8 P.M., but about twenty minutes later I felt hungry and decided to take a side trip to a hamburger stand. Ten minutes later, when my order was ready, I got into the van and headed back to Bradenton. My dogs had been mentally watching me and knew when to expect me back. .

Blacky, my Pomeranian, is another good example of this phenomenon. I would leave Blacky with my friend Evelyn Appelt, and though my trips were of varying duration, Evelyn soon learned my travel plans from Blacky. His actions clued her in as to when I would return so she made sure she was at home when I came to get him. She said, "While you're gone, Blacky sleeps behind the couch and hides. He only comes out to eat, but when you are on the way home, he comes out and begins to play." A quick check showed that Blacky did indeed change his behavior the very hour I started for home.

Then something occurred that made me realize there was more to this phenomenon: My animals were receiving my thoughts the *whole time I was away.*

I went to San Francisco on business and asked Jerry DeMent, an old friend who knew my dogs well, to stay at my house and take care of them. Throughout the three-day trip I felt alone, lost and inexplicably frightened. I missed my animals terribly. I wished they could have been with me. The last day in San Francisco, I had to walk along Market Street at 6 a.m. It was raining, and I felt miserable and nervous as I waited for the bus to take me to the airport, not relaxing until I was actually on the plane safely headed home. When I arrived, Jerry said he figured I was headed back because the dogs radically changed their behavior. During my absence they had been restless and refused to eat. This was unusual because they had always had fun with Jerry in the past and had always eaten heartily. At seven that morning, the very time I entered the plane, they suddenly relaxed and started eating again. They had actually experienced my tension and relaxed only when I did.

LONG DISTANCE COMMUNICATION

I learned that animals can mentally "see" and "hear" what is going on around their owners while the owners are away. I questioned a number of animals who all told me that communication across a distance is exactly the same as when they are in the same room with their owners. It is just as clear to the animals. To test this, I visited a number of boarding kennels in order to ask the animals what they perceived about their owners while they were gone and how they felt about being left. From what the animals told me, I have concluded that cats can accept the absence of their owners more readily than dogs because cats seem to be more independent. Dogs tell me they have a difficult time being away from family because they are so bonded with them, not only mentally, but an actual physical need to be with them as well.

While working in Florida in January 1975, I was asked to communicate with two Boxers. The owners had gone to England for a month, and on their return were shocked to find that each dog had lost about fifteen pounds. The owners blamed the kennel staff for not feeding the animals, but when I asked the Boxers about it, I got a different story. They told me the food was there, but they sensed their owners' concern over them not eating. This made them feel something was wrong with it, so they refused to eat it. The owners then admitted that during their entire trip, they had worried that their dogs would not eat. The dogs had "picked up" this worry and acted accordingly.

There is a lesson to be learned from these Boxers. First, if you have to leave your pet, be sure it is in a good, safe place, and then if you still tend to worry, send the pet thoughts of love and reassurance of your return. Send them happy thoughts, tell them mentally that you will be back; knowing that the best thing you can do for them in your absence is to have a good time yourself. This will help them relax and have as good a time as possible in their circumstances. Another thing you can do is be sure they are used to being away from you. You can do this by taking them to doggie day care and maybe one or two nights in a boarding facility before you make the major trip. This lets them know that you will always come back to get them.

Most animals can get along well during a limited separation from their people. If they know you are coming back, they can handle the break. Only if the animals are confined for several weeks or they are experiencing stress from you, may there be trouble like diarrhea, nervous scratching, or chewing.

While you are away, animals can also "see" through your eyes; they can "see" your surroundings and what you are doing. A client brought his friend's dog to me to see if the dog realized where his owners were and how he felt about staying with the friend in the owner's absence. The dog gave me mental pictures of a service station and a restaurant in a forest of huge redwood trees. We made a note of the day and time of these communications. When the owners returned from the redwood forests of Northern California, they checked their itinerary. They had indeed been walking into the restaurant for dinner that not only fit the description the dog had conveyed, but also the time of day.

In the cases described so far, my communications with the animal had occurred when I was actually with the animal. Now, I wondered if I, too, could communicate with an animal over a distance, so I decided to try it. I was giving a lecture at the Madonna Inn in San Luis Obispo, California, when Dr. Werbel, a physician who was in the audience, asked if I could " pick up" or "tune into " his son's Samoyed dog, some distance away. I visualized the dog and mentally called him by name. Suddenly, I realized I was "seeing" the dog's surroundings. I recognized the area as being near Lake Tahoe, some four hundred miles from where we were. The doctor confirmed the fact that his son lived eleven miles south of Lake Tahoe. The dog "showed" me himself playing with a little blond-haired boy. Next, I saw a man lying in bed, obviously in pain, eating ice. From the mental pictures the dog conveyed to me, I concluded the man was Dr. Werbel's son and that he had the flu. Dr. Werbel shook his head. There could be no "little blond-haired boy" in his son's life since he was a bachelor, and his son couldn't have the flu or he would have called his dad. Later that evening, the doctor's curiosity got the better of him. He called Lake Tahoe. His son admitted to having the flu and had been eating ice to try to settle his stomach. He also said that his dog often played with the landlord's son, a blond-haired little boy who lived downstairs.

Another instance really brought this home in an even stronger way. I was in Holland speaking to the University's veterinary and agricultural students, many of whom were there from other countries. One man, who was the head of agriculture in Australia, asked me to "talk" to his dog back home. He had been in Holland for several months, so he didn't know how things were going except those things that his wife had told him. The dog first told me how much he was enjoying the man with the beard. They were having a lot of fun playing because the man would throw sticks for him to fetch, and took him around the farm with him. The student was shocked! He said there is no man there, especially one with a beard. He thought I was wrong, but curiosity finally got the best of him, so he left the room. About 15 minutes later he returned, obviously in shock. As he sat down, he told the group that I had been right. He had called home and learned from his wife that the dog was right. His wife had planned to surprise him by adding a front porch to the house. The builder was a man who loved the dog, did indeed play with him, and sported a beard. She was mad that the dog had "squealed" on her and now the surprise was spoiled. It sure changed the atmosphere in that room and definitely influenced those students to respect their patients more than they had ever realized possible. This put a new dimension to their future practice as veterinarians.

After this, and several other successful communications, I found that distance was no barrier. I began consulting long distance with animals while relaying their problems and solutions to the owners on the phone. I don't need pictures to do this as pictures only show me what the animal was feeling when the picture was taken, not what they are feeling at the time communicate with them long distance. The process is the same as if I was with the animal physically, but one condition is necessary, I need to know where the animal is located or where it was last seen. If I cannot visualize the animal in its proper geographical location, I often get a blank mental response or will "tune in" to another animal that has the same name. When I'm directed to the right area, the mental picture comes in clear and strong. When I do not know where the animal or person is, I will try sending my mind in a mental circle, similar to the circling of a physical radar beam. When I feel a strong tugging sensation, I know I have located the correct direction. I then move in that direction until I locate them. This ability comes in handy when I attend large functions and get separated from my fellow attendees.

This ESP "radar" can also draw pets to their owners over great distances. One such example can be found in Alexander Key's book *The Strange White Dove*. The author tells about a family who had lived in Florida and moved to Temple City, California, a suburb of Los Angeles. They had left their cat with a neighbor in Florida, but two years later, their cat turned up on their doorstep in Temple City. In another situation, a cat belonging to a friend of mine had been left behind with an acquaintance when he moved. It disappeared, only to find its way from Beverly Hills to Ventura, California, a distance of about one hundred miles - again, a place where it had never been before, but had missed its original owner so much, it "tracked" him to his new home.

Not long after reading *The Strange White Dove*, I met a cat who had found its way cross country. It had lived all of its life in one apartment in North Hollywood, California. The owner had a job transfer and had to move back East, so she loaded her belongings and her cat into the car and took off. When she arrived in St. Louis, Missouri, the cat escaped. The owner was frantic and searched for days, to no avail. Three months later, the cat showed up at her old apartment in North Hollywood, thin but OK. It seems that many cats get very attached to a place and find it hard to leave no matter how much they love their people.

A client once brought a Yorkshire Terrier to me to find out how the dog, which had gotten out of the car in Colorado during his move to San Diego, made it all the way to San Diego, California, even though the dog had never been there before. The dog's story went like this. *"When I couldn't find my owner, I could feel the direction he was headed. I stayed around the truck stops and restaurants until I felt someone headed in the same direction. People thought I was cute so a lot of them fed me. I would jump into their car or truck and ride with them until I felt them turn away from the direction of my owner. I waited until someone else came along and hopped a ride again and that is how I got here. I could feel where my family was the whole time and just kept walking until I got here."* Wow, and who says dogs are dumb; pretty clever guy in my book.

Now that I knew I could work with animals over a long distance, I started doing consultations over the phone. One of my first cases was with a Hackney Pony, Midnight Ace, a champion owned by D. L. Arkenau in Kentucky. The pony was having trouble with its tail. Three veterinarians had examined the pony, but could not determine a successful diagnosis or treatment. Arkenau then decided to dock the pony's tail to relieve his suffering, an action which would also have ended the pony's show career. Pat Wood, a horsewoman in Hamilton, Ohio, who had recently read about me in a magazine, decided to contact D. L. to suggest that my ESP diagnosis procedure is a possible alternative to docking. Pat contacted me in San Francisco. I "tuned in" to the sick pony, who communicated what had happened. While he was scratching his rump on the stall door, he felt a sudden prick, like a sliver of wood entering his tail. A pus pocket had formed against the spinal column in the tail, and it was deeply embedded, invisible to the naked eye. Mrs. Wood and Arkenau decided to risk lancing the supposed abscess area. When Midnight's tail was lanced, the infection came out and with it, the splinter.

A year later, Mrs. Wood contacted me again, this time about an American Saddlebred she owned which had become partially paralyzed in her back legs. So far, her veterinarian had found no physical cause. While Mrs. Wood and I were on the telephone, I mentally went over the animal's body. A scar and an injury at the high point of the rump became "visible." The horse transmitted to me the picture of a heavy board falling on her back, hitting the spinal column between the vertebrae. Nerve damage seemed possible. Mrs. Wood took the horse to Dr. M. J. Cain, the Kentucky veterinarian who uses acupuncture. Dr. Cain found the scar and the spinal problem causing the paralysis, and used acupuncture to treat her. She gradually regained feeling in her legs, though a little paralysis remained that Dr. Cain felt was due to her unwillingness to roll over on her back, an action needed to make vertebral adjustments on the spinal column. For a horse, rolling is a vertebral adjustment as good as any chiropractor can do for a human. American Saddlebreds are not allowed to roll because it could break the tail set, a surgical procedure in which muscles in the tail are cut: the tail is wrapped into a ball and tied in a way that makes the tail stay in a vertical position. This is done so that when they are shown, the tail will be carried high. Since her horse needed to roll to affect a cure, I went to Ohio to meet Mrs. Wood, with the hope that the two of us, using visualization techniques, would help the horse break her mental training block. We took her into an arena where there was plenty of sawdust. For an hour or more, we visualized her rolling in the sawdust, but to no avail. Although it is natural for her to want to roll, the training block was so strong that every time she seemed about to roll, she hesitated and got back on her feet. After the visualization session, we turned her loose in the pasture. To our amazement, she promptly started rolling on her own. We could actually hear the vertebrae popping into adjustment as she rolled for the first time in her adult life. She made a rapid and complete recovery after that.

Not long after, I began communicating with animals by long distance, I started receiving letters from people asking, "If you can talk to animals at a distance, can you use that to find lost animals?"

Ten percent of the time I can and it works. The rate of success is low because I see only through the animal's eyes. This "view" is often so general that it is extremely difficult to distinguish one terrain from another unless I have personally been there and know what that area looks like. Sometimes an animal conveys where it has been, but not where it actually is now. I don't know why this happens, but it does.

One dramatic success at finding a lost animal occurred in 1974, while I was working in Cincinnati, Ohio. On December 1, Herman Koopman, a horse trainer who lives in Portola Valley, near San Francisco, California, telephoned me about his lost Arabian mare. She had been trained for dressage, a fancy form of riding that takes horses years to learn, like the Lipizzaner horses of Austria. I had once visited Koopman's ranch, so I recognized the area she was showing me with the mental pictures she was transmitting to me. When I was finally able to "tune into" his mare and hear what had happened, she told me she had strayed from the rest of the herd while they were heading up the winding road to the pasture at the top of the hill. She saw that the other horses were above her so she tried to take a shortcut-straight up the hillside. In the process, she slipped and fell back down the hill, seriously injuring her left shoulder. Here she remained because her pain was too great to attempt climbing the hill. An hour after we had hung up, Mr. Koopman called back to tell me he had found the horse at the foot of the hill. Her shoulder was cut and bruised, and her left front leg was sprained. However, the mare eventually recovered, and Koopman was able to continue exhibiting her in dressage.

A call came from Julie and John Crawshaw of Pasadena, California. They owned a jet black cat called Jasper who suddenly disappeared. I "tuned in" to Jasper who showed me where he was lying under the house next door. I knew it was next door because I had been to the Crawshaw's house before and recognized it through Jasper's eyes. I asked Jasper why he didn't go home. He said he knew he was dying so crawled off to die alone. I do not know why many animals do that, but they do. The owners found Jasper lying under the house as he had "said" and rushed him to the veterinarian. Unfortunately, it was too late and he could not be saved.

One of the most gratifying cases I've had locating a lost animal, was a Poodle named Gigi in San Felipe, Mexico. This is terrain I did not know. The Poodle's owner, Ann Fischer of Los Angeles, California thought that Gigi had been stolen while she and her daughter were out boating. On their return to the camp site, the dog was gone and so was the family camping next to them. I contacted Gigi mentally. Apparently, she had started out for the desert and then decided to return to the campsite. On her way back, she was captured by a Mexican family. Gigi's mental images showed her tied up outside an adobe hut with chickens nearby. Ann Fischer returned to the San Felipe area, posted a reward for Gigi's return, and the Mexican family responded the next day.

Another successful case, was finding a Labrador that had disappeared with another dog. When I "tuned in" to them, they showed me a housing pen. They told me they had pushed open a gate and run across a well-cared for field with short grass, and then into a farm. They were sniffing around the calves in a pasture when the farmer saw them and penned them up. The owner soon recognized the area. Next to the housing development, where he lived with the dogs, was a golf course. On the other side of the golf course was a farm. The dog's owner called the farmer who said he had confined the dogs because he was afraid they might harm his livestock. This took place near Ashville, North Carolina, another area that had been unfamiliar to me at that time.

One of the most interesting cases I remember was a champion Bichon Frise, one of the top dogs in the nation that had been stolen from her crate at a big dog show in Chicago, Illinois. The owner was frantic to find her very valuable and beloved dog. When I asked the dog where she was, she gave me a description of the man who had taken her. She said that he had taken her home where he had clipped her down to look like his poodles. She heard him say it would hide her identity until they could sell her and ship her to Japan with falsified papers. The Bichon's owner recognized the man as an acquaintance from the dog shows. She called the police, went to his house, and sure enough, there was her dog.

The last case I will describe is about a Standard Poodle that had been traveling with her family, when they decided to stop at a rest area to walk her. While they were walking in the pet area, a large truck hit its airbrakes very close to them. The dog became alarmed and bolted from the owner. She disappeared into the woods. They searched frantically for her for hours, but to no avail. They finally left the area in despair, but the next day a friend gave them my phone number. They called me. Once I had located the area, the dog "showed" me that when running, she had spotted a culvert that went under the highway. She fled into it and just hid in fear. Even though she heard her owners call, she was too frightened to come out. I told them to go back there, take a flashlight and crawl in if they had to, but she was still there. They returned immediately to the rest area, found the culvert, and sure enough, there was the poodle. It was a very happy reunion.

I rarely take lost animal cases any more because of the deluge of calls I started to receive, as many as twenty a day. It just became too overwhelming and since the animals can't tell me addresses or distances they travel, it is very difficult to find them. The cases I have related above are ones that really stand out to me and, of course, were successful. I wish they could all be that way, but they aren't. I can only locate about 10% of them. Unless animal's can show me specific things they see that makes their area stand out, it is very difficult to tell where the animal is. It becomes very frustrating. I have an assistant, Linda Thomas, who is happy to do this. If you contact us, we will be happy to get you in touch with her.

Finally, this skill has been very effective in helping people, too. I remember a time when I lived in Los Angeles, California. I received a call from a lady in Apple Valley, about 150 miles away, concerning her teenage daughter who had run away with an older man and her car. She was concerned about where her daughter was and how she could help her. I "tuned" in to the girl to find out what she was doing. I could feel her riding in the car, looking out the window. She was really scared, feeling she had gotten into more than she realized and wanted out, but didn't know how. She was thinking about calling her mom for help, but scared she was going to be in worse trouble for what she had done, so was weighing her situation against her mother's anger. I could see from her eyes the sign that said, "Entering El Paso, Texas." I relayed this information to her mother who was relieved to find out she was alright and going to call home. I advised her to let the girl talk without showing any anger, only concern that she was alright. I then told her to let the girl know what she did was wrong, but that they could work it out if she would come home. Just show her love, concern and a desire to help her get through this without retaliation. I knew that if the mother got angry and yelled, she would never see her daughter again. Together, they could go to counseling and get the help they both needed so that her daughter would not feel she needed to run away again. The next day the girl called from El Paso, Texas, pleading with her mother to help her because she knew she had made a terrible mistake. Her mother took my advice, flew to El Paso and drove her daughter back to California.

Another incident took place in Florida. I was called by the police in Bradenton, Florida, concerning a woman with Alzheimer's who had disappeared and could I locate her mentally. This was the second time I had helped them track a missing woman. The first time was when an elderly lady had disappeared a few years prior to this incident. At that time, I could "see" the woman sitting up against a tree in a semi-wooded area, next to a large road under construction. There was one area like that next to highway 75. They went there and found the lady propped up against a tree; unfortunately she had died of exposure. I don't know how I did it, but I simply visualize the person, and it comes to me. All I know is that I am not getting it from the person who is deceased. When they called this time about an Alzheimer's patient, named Myrtle, I could see her in a swampy area in either dry brown grass or under something the color of dried grass, no houses or people close, but I could hear a clunking sound like cars going over a bridge. They couldn't find bridges anywhere near the trailer park where she had lived and wandered away from, so they asked if I would come and help them. I went to different areas around there, but could not feel her anyplace we went. Finally, I went to her trailer and mentally tracked where she had gone. I ended up at a small church just outside the park that had a small swampy area next to it. I could feel her very strongly nearby, so they sent in a search – and - rescue team to comb the area. As I stood there, I could hear the clunking of a manhole that had an opening under the road leading from the swamp which sounded like the cars were going over a bridge. I knew I was in the right place. Each member of the team was given a walkie talkie, making it possible for me to communicate with each one, to help guide them to her. Finally, looking through her eyes, I saw a pair of boots very close by. I described those boots to the rescuers. One man said, "I am wearing those boots, but I don't see her. All I see is a cream colored bedspread" (the color of dried grass). I told him to look under it and sure enough, there she was, dehydrated, but still alive. Because she knew her mind was going, she wanted to die, so had gone into the swamp to lie there until she died of starvation or exposure. She never dreamed anyone could find her.

Another case took place in Tampa, Florida, not long after that incident. There was a little girl named Martinez, who had started home from school, but never arrived. She was about 9 years old. When I asked her where she was, she showed me a picture of a man on a bicycle that had abducted her and taken her into the woods near the school. She said, "When I told him I didn't want to play with him, he hurt me and then buried me and I am gone". Once I picked up that the Martinez girl I was reaching was dead, I stopped the communication since communicating with the dead is forbidden in the Bible. I got together with a police artist who drew a sketch from my description. The next day I received a call saying they had found the man in the picture, had searched his room and found hidden in his drawer, every newspaper article about the missing girl that had ever been written. He had also been identified by neighbors as the man on the bicycle near the school the day the child had disappeared. Since he was now in a mental facility, they could not prosecute him, but were able to get him out long enough to visit the woods. He admitted to being with the girl that day, playing with her in the woods. He took us to the site where we found her shoes and some other articles of clothes, but no child. He said he had buried her, showed us where, but said she was alive when he put her in the ground with a straw to breath from. The grave was there, the straw was there, but no child. He said he came back a few days later to dig her up and play again, but he said he found only a dead dog dressed in children's clothing so he took the dead body and dumped it down a sewer. He took us to the manhole which had definitely been opened. It was a very sad ending as all the evidence was there, but since there was no way they would ever find a body in the sewer, he was never prosecuted and the poor family never really had closure. So you see, some cases end well, and others don't. This is a challenging area I love to work in, but do on a very limited basis. Again, not

EXPLORE

every search is successful because I am dealing with the human mind that doesn't always "see" things literally like the animals do, and some don't want to be found, so they can send the wrong pictures.

CHAPTER 6

IDENTIFYING EMOTIONAL PROBLEMS

Like humans, animals have emotions which run the gamut from joy to grief. They also have emotional needs which, if deprived, may produce emotional problems. The way an animal expresses these problems, however, is very different from the way a person would. The healing process, on the other hand, is not so different. Understanding and communication are the two essentials.

Medical science today tells us that nearly 85 percent of all physical illnesses have emotional roots. This is an alarming percentage, but true. Dr. Arnold A. Hutschnecker, author of *Will to Live*, is emphatic in his belief that the human mind can actually cause death. This psychotherapist contends that the "will" to live can end or cease, and when the subconscious knows and accepts this fact, the body reacts and physical death becomes a reality. I personally know of two incidences where this has happened. The first was my mom, Louise. She and dad were very close. When my dad died, she really didn't recover very well. After several years of living alone, she finally moved into a nursing home. She liked it there and was fine until we had to sell the house and disperse all her belongings. This broke her heart because she had always held onto the idea of "going home." At Thanksgiving she seemed in good spirits, had a great day visiting all her children and grandchildren and that night, quietly slipped away. She felt there was nothing to look forward to anymore; she wanted to go home to be with the Lord and her loved ones.

Another lady I knew, who lived on St. Armands Key in Sarasota, Florida, also wanted to die, but she was not physically ill. She threw a party, had all of her friends over, had a great time and after everyone left, laid down on the couch and died. An autopsy proved there was nothing wrong, she just died. I explored this concept in depth in my book, *Seasons, My Journey through the Three Dimensions of Natural Healing*.

Animals are also influenced by the "will" to live. From long experience and close observation, I know that the emotional quality of an animal's life and its physical well-being are directly related. The animal can receive excellent physical care, but if the outward physical symptoms are rooted in an emotional disturbance, healing will not occur and in some instances, may result in death.

There is one major difference between humans and animals, and the reader needs to be aware of it. In a human, the physical disorder which originates in, or is aggravated by, the psychic or emotional process, is considered psychosomatic. A human being, faced with a difficult life situation or crisis, may develop a physical illness—headache, nausea, chronic fatigue, and the like—which will reflect the tension or enable them to "legitimately" avoid the situation. Animals do not have psychosomatically induced physical problems, but they do use physical symptoms as signs or signals to express emotional distress. This is what I hope you will understand better after you read this chapter.

Each pet's life is different. Only you, the owner, are capable of evaluating your pet's environment, noting day-to-day behavior changes, eating patterns, and any physical abnormalities which may or may not be signs of emotional problems. The first step, if you notice any unhealthy change, is to take your pet to the veterinarian for a physical examination. Do this before concluding that your pet has an emotional problem. After a clean bill of health, then look into the possible emotional root of the change. Animals brought to me for consultation are those that exhibit unusual behavior changes or suffer from physical symptoms of distress or serious illness with no apparent reason and no verifiable medical cause.

Near-death and recovery was experienced by a race horse, Eagle's Dynasty, owned by Mr. and Mrs. Darrell Clingman of Arcadia, California. Eagle suffered a leg injury when he got cast – he rolled over too close to the wall, thrashed to get up, and caused damage to his legs. This ended his racing career. Several veterinarians were called in on the case, but their prognosis was dim. All agreed that Eagle would never run again, much less race. Some even doubted he would ever walk again. Mrs. Clingman, accepting this no recovery diagnosis, traded Eagle for a jumper. The new owner decided the horse could be used for breeding, but kept Eagle at the Clingman's farm to be cared for during his convalescence. Eagle's condition worsened. Two months later, the new owner decided it would be best to put the animal to sleep. At this point Mrs. Clingman, who still cared for the horse, called me and asked me to come over. She hoped that Eagles life could be spared. I talked to Eagle for an hour, asking him what was wrong and what was happening to make his physical condition so much worse. Finally Eagle lay down, placed his head in my lap and mentally transmitted his message. *"I want my former owner (the Clingmans) back. They are the only ones who ever loved me and I want to stay with them. I know that if I get well, I will have to leave. I would rather die than go to a new home!"*

I conveyed the horse's feelings to Mrs. Clingman. As I did, Eagle raised his upper lip, quickly shook his head up and down, and whinnied in approval. The next day, Mrs. Clingman retraded the jumper back for Eagle. The horse's condition immediately started to improve; he began to eat properly and his leg injury began to heal. Since the Clingmans and I are now friends, I've seen Eagle's progress. He not only walks, but he runs in the pasture alongside the beautiful foals he has sired since his recovery. Eagle cannot race again, but the Clingmans still use him for breeding.

When a mysterious physical symptom surfaces or healing just won't happen, never overlook the emotional quality of the animal's life. Eagle's Dynasty is a prime example because before we knew of his fear, he had had the best possible veterinarian care.

Animals have also told me that they are affected by their owners' lives and their emotional states. An argument between two people may upset an animal because he feels the anger and cannot discern its direction. Pets will automatically blame themselves as the cause of the anger and react to this frustration by scratching, chewing, or running to hide. Few humans understand what's going on during a heated discussion. Logic and reason are lost when tempers are flaring, so how is the poor animal to understand what we don't? They tell me they just need to know that they're not the object of that anger. You can reassure them by telling them "you are fine. Everything is ok. Just go lie down and relax". They can understand that concept and even if they don't respond immediately, it will help calm their fears.

A consultation with Liebchen, a Dachshund belonging to a friend of mine, Wanda Selling of Covina, California, revealed just how damaging human conflict can be to a pet. When I first saw Liebchen, her body was covered with a skin rash and she was constantly chewing her feet. A veterinarian diagnosed it as a grass allergy and advised confinement to the house as well as medication. After one week, the animal's skin condition worsened.

I asked her what was happening. She mentally said," *my owners argue about problems in the house as well as the veterinarian cost for my skin treatments. It's all my fault. I don't know how to help them and since I can't chew on anything or I will get in trouble, and now I can't even run around to help release stress, I just scratch and chew myself all the more.*" The confinement heaped yet another frustration on her for she missed running in the yard and the company of the dog next door. This longing and lack of exercise intensified her compulsion to scratch and chew. Based on what the pet told me, I advised the Sellings to increase her exercise and reassure her that the family quarrels were not her problem. Within two weeks, Wanda notified me that the skin condition was greatly improved. It did not clear up entirely, but I am reasonably sure that this is because of the dog's sensitivity to domestic turmoil.

When we humans face frustration, we can go for a walk, eat, do something to divert ourselves from the problems and release tension. Animals do not have these options. They cannot escape their environment or give vent to frustration by tearing at whatever is around them because this behavior means punishment. The alternative then is to direct the frustration inward, to *tear at themselves, by scratching and chewing.* Domesticated animals need plenty of exercise, often a wonder cure for the ailing, urbanized pet. Owners sometimes believe two or three short daily walks on a leash are enough for a dog, but most dogs require far more. Apartment living is tolerable for pets, even large ones, provided the exercise requirement is fully met. One of the classic symptoms that your dog will exhibit if it isn't getting enough exercise is licking the feet. Run them more and it will usually stop.

The most common physical symptoms of an emotional problem are hot spots and rashes - skin irritations that cover the entire body. A hot spot is one point on the body where an animal chews until the area becomes raw and inflamed. Hot spots are often blamed on something in the environment like grass or fleas, but I believe the real reason is more often emotional frustration the animal cannot solve. There is one incident where the hot spot is caused by an internal organ malfunction. If they chew ONLY on the loin (on the side just in front of the stifle, or what is commonly called the knee in the back leg), it is an acupuncture point connected to a problem in the liver. They are trying to stimulate healing to a damaged or congested liver. A blood test can show liver malfunction, but will not show that the animal has a congested liver (one that is either toxic or not able to do its job to full capacity). Both acupuncture and our Liver formula can stimulate the liver to clean out and work to full capacity again.

Princessa helped me understand this emotional behavior more fully. She was accustomed to running free on the ranch in Duarte. Whenever she was in season, I confined her to the house. Within a few days of confinement, she started scratching herself until a hot spot appeared on her rump that remained until she had her freedom again. This was before I recognized and understood about animals' emotional needs and the symptoms of emotional problems.

Another example of the connection between confinement and skin rash is illustrated by a German shepherd named Thor, belonging to Mr. and Mrs. Beckett of Sacramento, California. I was speaking at a club there when the Becketts contacted me. Thor had been plagued by skin rash most of his life and at one point had been taken to the Davis Veterinary Teaching Hospital in Sacramento. The doctors there located some staph infection but not enough to have caused an irritation as extensive as this one. The staph infection was cleared up, but he still suffered with skin problems. During the consultation, Thor conveyed to me a whole chain of emotional problems dating back to early puppy hood.

Now confinement was adding a physical frustration to the emotional ones. After some work with Thor, during which I helped him resolve his emotional conflicts, I advised his owners to lift the confinement and let him loose in his fenced yard. After this, whenever Thor started to scratch, a member of the family took him out running alongside a bicycle as a way to relieve the energy build-up. The Beckets contacted me two weeks later to report that Thor's skin problem had finally vanished and upon further checking a year later, it had not returned.

Increasing the amount of exercise is one way to eliminate skin disorders, but there may also be a physical reason, such as too much bathing, using the wrong soaps, the food, legitimate allergies, and over vaccinating. I will deal with this later in detail in chapter 11, Consumer Awareness.

One of the most common and unpleasant expressions of emotional problems is urinating or defecating, marking territory, or expressing dislike for something or someone. Animals can experience personality clashes just like humans can. I learned this from a Poodle who told me that every time her owner's daughter came home from college, he became upset and marked all the tires on her car, as well as soaking her suitcases and shoes. He told me that he just could not tolerate the young woman and wanted her "eliminated" from the home. In another case, a Keeshond was brought to me for consultation because each morning he defecated on the wife's side of the bed, but never on the husband's side of the bed. He told me "*I hate the dog shows, but she makes me go. He doesn't go to the shows and tells her I should stay home too, but she won't listen. I want to eliminate her taking me to the shows*". Incredible? You bet, but true.

Sometimes this urinary behavior crops up when two animals are feuding. It may be outwardly fighting so you can tell, or it maybe subtle fights that you can't see. Two cats, Nupkins and Puffins, had a real battle going on between them. Their owner Marjorie Sutton called me because the cats were not getting along, and one of them was urinating on the drapes. She wanted to know which one and why. Nupkins readily admitted she was the one doing it because her owner had "*changed our litter brand recently from clay to one with the green stuff in it. When I use the box, it smells awful and the litter sticks to my paws. I finally can't hold it anymore so I head for the box. Puffins is a grouch and gets in my way and won't let me in. I have to go so badly that I can't hold it to fight her for the pan, so I spray what I can reach, which is the drapes. They never punished me, so I thought it was ok."* The next day, Mrs. Sutton purchased a second litter pan which she put in a different room, and went back to the old form of clay the cats were used to. I asked Puffins why she was so grouchy. Her reply was *"I don't like to eat a big meal, but like to snack throughout the day on my favorite dry food. She took that away and now I have to eat only when she puts it down.."* "Well," Mrs. Sutton said, "that can be easily remedied." She purchased another food dish, which was also put in a separate room, filled it with the dry food so she could eat whenever she wanted to snack without the other cat barging in. From that day on the fighting and urinating stopped - the two cats, at least for now, tolerated each other.

Jealousy will also cause bad behavior. A Scottie, Rowdy, had this problem. Mr. and Mrs. Edward L. Coughlin of San Gabriel, California, called me because when their new dog, Rowdy, first arrived at their home, he immediately started urinating on their older dog's toys that were lying all around the house. This behavior intensified every time he returned from the groomer's kennel, where Rowdy had been raised. When asked why, he said, *"I loved the kennels. I have my own run and nobody shows any one dog any favoritism. I want to go back there and live because they love me and make a big fuss over me when I am there. These people love their old dog more that me because they pay more attention to him and won't let me enter in with them."* The family told me they really loved Rowdy and didn't mean to show partiality, but realized they had been, so they gave each dog equal attention. I suggested that the groomer ignore Rowdy when he went to be groomed. Even though this was hard for them as they were his breeder and loved him, they complied with the family wishes. On his next visit, they groomed him with no fuss, placed him in a crate and kept him there for the day. After two visits, Rowdy was content to go back to his new home where he was lavished with attention and the urinating stopped.

Behavior changes can also be brought about through mental projection coupled with the laying on of hands. Let me explain what I am talking about.

The idea first came during a consultation with an unmanageable, nervous horse. Whenever he was touched on the rump or back legs, he balked and kicked. This made showing him almost impossible as he had to be bathed and handled over every part of his body. I gently, but firmly, placed my two hands together, palms down, on the horse's neck and stood still. At the same time, I made my own body go almost limp in the most relaxed state I could get into while standing. After a minute, I slid my hands about 6 inches down the neck toward the body and repeated the relaxed state, with my hands pressing just hard enough to show a slight dent in the skin. After another minute, I slid my hands another 6 inches down the neck, repeating the relaxing feelings in myself (which is what I wanted the horse to experience, too). Again and again, I worked my way down the horse's body and finally down the rump and legs, encircling them, gently pressing inward, all the time picturing the horse relaxing and enjoying it. It took quite awhile, but eventually the horse allowed me to touch him all over without resistance, even lowering his head, closing his eyes, and actually seeming to enjoy it. I instructed the owner to repeat this process every day until the horse felt safe enough and trusted her enough to allow her to go immediately to anyplace on his body without fighting. After four of these treatments, anyone could handle the horse. He had been reconditioned by thought and touch. When using this method, always slide the hands; never pat or lift the hands to change position as that will disrupt and stimulate rather than calm them.

One of the most dramatic examples of this treatment occurred when I was working in a veterinarian's office. A man and woman entered carrying an injured cat whose cries sounded like a baby screaming in pain. The distraught owners told me they thought the cat's front legs were broken. We had to wait for the doctor so I approached the animal, laid my hands on it and mentally projected the positive sensation of pain leaving its body and being replaced by quietness and peace. Slowly, like the horse, the cat laid his head down and closed its eyes. I explained to the owners that their own emotional state was greatly contributing to the cat's fears and her screaming was a reaction to their own fears and feelings of guilt about the injury (she had gotten caught in the closure of an electric garage door). I showed them how to lay hands on their pet, relax and send their love and reassurance to their cat, and gradually, they all relaxed. The cat no longer screamed, he just rested quietly under the umbrella of their thoughts. This method is a reassuring way to transmit much needed understanding. I have found the procedure extremely helpful, an important and innovative aspect of ESP healing.

One of the most successful trainers in history was Barbara Woodhouse from Great Britain. I had the privilege of meeting that wonderful woman; she confirmed my belief that she projected her ideas to the animals. When she held obedience classes, she instructed owners in her famous "Walkies," which in our terms meant healing. When the inexperienced owners tried to make the dogs obey, the animals acted terribly, pulling, jumping, and being just plain obstinate. She knew the owners felt out of control and didn't know what they were doing, so the dog took advantage of them. She would take the leash, and instantly the dog would stop the bad behavior and act like an angel. When I observed that sudden change, I could see that the dog was thinking, *Oh Oh, she is on to me. I better behave and do what she is mentally telling me!* She knew she was in control and so did the animal. I have never seen anyone like her. She could get any animal to do anything; she even trained cows to be ridden, and to jump over jumps with a rider on them. Her books are a delight to read and certainly an eye opener.

Animals who know when someone is receiving their thoughts will often exhibit some interesting reactions. For example, during consultations, animals rarely exemplify the bad behavior for which I was contacted. Instead, they appear relaxed, almost as if they were falling asleep. Animals that normally run from people, or even bite people, will usually lie quietly at my feet while I am communicating with them. An exception is the cat that hid behind a flower pot to stare at me from a safe vantage point, while it tried to figure out why its own thoughts (mental images) were in my mind. As a general rule, animals just relax, and fully project their feelings to me.

Another common reaction among animals is their emotional response to grief. I was working in Bradenton, Florida, in January 1975, when a woman called about her cats and the radical change in their behavior that she noticed shortly after the death of her husband. Before his death, they had been extremely affectionate; now they were aloof to everyone, including her.

When I asked the cats why they had changed, they said, *"We are sad and really miss our owner. We feel alone, as if nobody understands our grief. They don't understand that we loved him very much. That is why we never left him until they took him away and now we are very lonely."* I explained this to the widow who immediately gave them sympathy and love, sharing her grief with them. You could see the change taking place as they finally realized she understood that they had suffered a terrible loss too, and missed him as she did. The next day, she called to tell me the cats had returned to their normal, affectionate behavior. I attribute this change to the fact that they finally were able to express their feelings. It may sound trite, but is nonetheless true, these cats needed someone to talk to. They needed to be relieved of their sorrow and anxiety. Once this happened, there was no longer a need for abnormal behavior.

Two important symptoms of an emotional problem are shyness and over - aggression. These are both learned behaviors that are most often not genetically linked. I will explain this further in chapters 8 and 9.

Summing up, the symptoms of emotional disturbances are:
1. Chewing the feet or excessive licking of the feet. The animals are trying to tell you they are not getting enough exercise. Cure: more exercise.
2. Wetting or messing. They are trying to tell you they want to eliminate someone or something from their lives. Try to connect the defecating or wetting with a person or situation that is upsetting them and resolve the problem if possible. If not possible, discipline the animal. I'll explain how later in the book.

3. Rashes and hotspots. The main cause is frustration. Find out what is causing the frustration and resolve it, if possible. Also check the animal's diet, frequency of bathing and the products used in their bathing, and their bedding.

4. Shyness and over aggression.

CHAPTER 7

SELECTING YOUR PET

Selecting a psychologically sound animal is not a matter of luck. If you look at a litter of puppies or kittens, or walk along a line of cages of animals up for adoption, you can tell next to nothing about the animal and how it will fit into your home, or how well it will adjust to its duty if it is to be a working animal. It is wise, then, to take some time to get to know the animal better before you make that final decision. This can help you avoid a lot of heartache in the future. The following criteria are some of the things you need to look at:

1. What are your needs?
2. Where should you purchase the animal, and from whom.
3. When available, get an evaluation of the psychological and physical condition of the animals' mother and father.
4. The animal's early environment. While there may be a vast difference between a home environment and a kennel environment, they may both be excellent places to purchase an animal. It all depends upon the physical health of the animal, the cleanliness of its environment, its early exposure to stimuli, and how much the animal has been socialized and handled.

PETS FOR THE FAMILY

Bringing a pet into your home means you are seeking a relationship that may span a good many years. You will be living with breathing, feeling creature that will endure emotional trauma at the change of ownership and environment, so be prepared to make the purchase at a time when you are able to plan on a long-term relationship and can give them some quality time when they first arrive to help them through the adjustment.

First, decide on your needs, what fits with your lifestyle and what you want from that new relationship, then study the breed's best suited to those needs. There are many wonderful books available that will describe the various breeds, their characteristics, temperaments and what they are best suited for, such as the

American Kennel Club standards book, Dog and Cat Fancy Magazines and many more in your local pet shops as well as on line if you have access to a computer. Dog and Cat shows are wonderful places to meet breeders, see the quality of animals they produce and find excellent breed books. Shows give you a comprehensive view of all available breeds and the best animals of those breeds. Newspapers list the times and places of these shows near the section where pets are advertised for sale. A "Specialty" listing refers to one breed or one class of breed only. A "Sporting Dog Specialty" refers to dogs that are used for hunting, "Toys" are the small breeds; and, "Working" are those used for guarding, pulling and police work.

When you attend shows, walk around the rings to the breed you are considering and ask the breeders questions. They are usually happy to share their knowledge and you will get to know the points to look for. Talking to several breeders will give you differences of opinion, which will also be useful. The reputable breeder will be willing to show you his or her stock when you visit them and the mother of the pet you wish to purchase. He or she can also show you records of wins and the places or people who have purchased from him or her in the past. This will enable you to follow up on the reliability and health of the animals. If a breeder won't let you visit their kennel and insists on meeting you or bringing the pet to you, then there is probably something wrong that they don't want you to see. I have the people visit us, meet the animals and then I usually deliver the animal to be sure they are going to be a good placement, but I always have them visit us first.

The breeder should also be willing to give you a guarantee against Hip Dysplasia, a bone problem most commonly found in large dogs, which should surface by the time the animal is one year old. The cause of Dysplasia is disputed, but the effect is undisputed - the hip ball and socket do not fit properly and the animal either becomes crippled or develops painful arthritis. It is hard to detect in the pup, but is only found by X-ray in the grown dog and then only by a veterinarian who knows how to properly position the dog for the AKC requirements. Not all veterinarians know the requirements laid out by the Orthopedic Foundation for Animals so they could give you a misreading. If you have a written guarantee, the breeder should specify whether they will refund your money or a part of it, or replace the animal.

A responsible breeder will also be willing to take responsibility to care for the animals they produce. In my case, if you can't keep the pet you obtained from me, then I will very happily take it back. An example is the Samoyed breeders in San Francisco and Sacramento where their club will rescue unclaimed Samoyeds from the pounds and place them in good home if the original owner can't be found. Another breeder, Wilna Coulter of San Carlos, California, once took back an eight - year - old female that the owners could no longer keep. She was past the normal show dog age, but was nearly perfect so Wilna decided to show her. She became a champion and was nearly unbeatable until she was over ten years of age. Star was quite the show girl. She fully understood what it meant to win. She loved winning so much that if the judge passed her without looking, she would keep barking until he turned back to acknowledge her presence. For many animals, the conformation does not develop for a year or so, so when you sell or buy a puppy, you may have unknowingly sold your best dog or bought a champion.

If it is to be a family pet, give the children an opportunity to learn the proper care of the animal and understand what is involved in that care. A reputable breeder will give your family that opportunity. Be prepared to take over that job if the children fail. Children must be taught the proper way to handle the animal and to respect the animal's need for love.

If you want a family pet that will provide companionship for young children, I would not recommend Chihuahuas, Min Pins, Yorkies, or any other very small dogs like those, as they are too delicate. I rarely sell one of my Chihuahuas to families with small children at home. They don't mean to hurt these little ones, but they can accidentally drop these wiggly bundles and, since their heads are the heaviest part of them, they will usually land there and the fall will either kill them or cause seizures or break a leg (that often happens with them jumping off a bed or couch too), which can run you into the hundreds or even thousands of dollars to fix, say nothing of the pain it causes. I raise and show Chihuahuas and as careful as we are, these things have happened to us too and it is no fun. Children can get rough with little dogs which can also lead to snapping and aggressive behavior in animals that have no other way of defending themselves. A large dog can handle the roughhousing of children much better. Find one that has been born and raised in a family atmosphere, preferably around children. The pet's early conditioning is important and because children's feelings are changeable - one minute they are very happy, the next sad and the next very angry, only an animal that is familiar with children can cope with such volatile changes.

For the family environment, consider the calmer temperament commonly found in the larger breeds such as the Great Dane, Standard Poodle, Samoyed, Collie, Labrador, Newfoundland and German Shepherd to mention a few. Be sure it is well socialized, especially with children about the age of your own children.

I am pretty partial to German Shepherds because of my teacher, Princessa who was not raised with children, but instinctively loved them. We went to the beach one day with a friend and her two - year - old boy. I watched her as she and the boy played in the water. It was really quite funny as the boy became frustrated because Princessa stayed between him and the deeper water and wouldn't allow him to go in above his ankles. She never left his side the whole time we were there. No one had taught her about the dangers of deep water and children; she just knew it and protected him. I had another friend tell me she was in her kitchen one day when she heard her baby screaming. She looked out to an incredible site. Her crawling infant, who had gotten out of the yard, was in the road and here came her German Shepherd, carrying her by the diaper, the only thing she was wearing. She was screaming bloody murder because she wanted to stay in the road. Neither of these dogs had been trained to protect children, they just knew what to do and where the danger was, and instinctively took care of the problem.

Princessa, who came from a kennel and had never been exposed to children even in my home, was an incredible dog as well as a wonderful companion and protection for me, but had such a great love for children. We lived near a large apartment complex that housed a lot of families with small children. The children would come knocking at our door every day and ask, "Can Princessa come out and play?" The parents never worried about the children as long as the dog was with them as she wouldn't let anyone harm them. I had a toy tied to the back screen door which she used to pull the door open and come in when the children went in. I tell you this only to encourage you to check out all sources for your pet and not be afraid to get one from a kennel if they are from good stock.

When you live in a small area, larger breeds are fine as long as they are able to get enough exercise. I have been very surprised when talking to dogs that live in New York City, in apartments, to learn how they love their lives. They tell me life is very exciting because their owners have to walk them several times a day, giving them a companionship with their owners that dogs who live in a large yard, rarely get to experience. They love the constant new smells and seeing so many new things as they walk. This surprised me at first, but made a lot of sense. When the owner is home, they are always with the animal, not stuck in a backyard by themselves.

If you live in an apartment where sufficient exercise may be difficult or you are unable to walk them frequently, consider getting a small dog that can be trained to use newspapers or piddle pads, They get a lot of exercise running back and forth if you play with them or have a companion for them to play with. You may also consider getting a cat. Cats make excellent apartment dwellers and they are good companions even to children; they also take relatively little care, are naturally clean if provided with a litter pan and do not require walking for exercise. I have spoken to many animals that have been raised indoors or in captivity, such as in a good zoo and they have told me they are perfectly content. They do not know any other way of life and since their surroundings are clean, comfortable and their food is provided, they are happy. The only time I have found discontent in a caged animal or one confined to the indoors, is when it is not cared for properly or has previously been free to roam in the open or the wild. After this, confinement indoors will often produce emotional frustrations that result in either skin rashes or hot spots, or destructive behavior such as wetting, digging or tearing furniture or paper. I'm not talking about baby animals that will get into destructive behavior motivated out of boredom and mischievousness, and just look for something to do the same as any little child would get in to when left alone: this is different. This is going from the wild and freedom to captivity.

Birds, hamsters and other small animals also make excellent apartment pets for shut - ins, and can easily adapt to children.

Be prepared to protect your new pet with good solid fencing and proper locks on the gates. The theft of small dogs even from fenced yards is all too common. They are easy to resell and do not put up a fuss or bite savagely enough to defend themselves from the thief. Every day, purebred animals are stolen from cars and yards and often resold under falsified papers as guard dogs or as animals used to train fighting dogs. Dog fighting, as a sport, is against the law, but it is still a common illegal practice. Any barking dog is a deterrent to a house thief, but a small dog cannot stop a dog thief from stealing it when left out in a poorly protected yard. Even worse is the time you come home and find your dog who had escaped from a weak fence, lying in the road, dead.

Under no circumstance should any animal be allowed to run free. No matter how well behaved your pet may be, there is always that one time when it will see something across the street and will dash in front of an oncoming car. You also risk animal control picking up your pet or people thinking it is a stray and taking it in. In coyote country, coyotes will lure a loose female dog into their pack by mentally calling her to join them. They tease her into following them. They integrate the large female dogs into their pack, but will kill and eat all small dogs, female or male, and cats. They also use their female coyotes in heat to lure male dogs out to a spot where the pack can kill the male for food.

Lastly, if you have to keep a dog tied up all the time, don't get a dog, get an alarm system. I have conversed with many that were tied up and they tell me it drives them crazy, often making them aggressive. It is one of the most frustrating existences for an animal that you can put them in. That wonderful little puppy is so happy to have a home and thinks it is going to be loved, only to find itself on a chain, isolated from everyone, and lonely. That is no existence for anything to have to endure. If you could feel their emotions, you would understand why I call that animal cruelty. They don't know why they are rejected. I can't emphasize enough how cruel that is. If you only have them out there for a couple of hours to exercise and potty, that is different. They can tolerate that, but not a life on a chain. That is no existence for anything. They can handle a small confined area better than a chain.

WORKING GUARD DOGS & ANIMALS FOR PROTECTION

If you are looking for a guard animal, consider the more aggressive breeds or ones that people think are aggressive, such as Dobermans, Giant Schnauzers, Rottweilers, Boxers. It should be raised in a kennel or outdoor situation so that it doesn't become too dependent on humans for companionship. This will prevent the animal from being lonely during the long hours of guarding the yard, garage, store, or whatever area needs protection. The guard dog must be taught not to eat anything in its area unless you, the owner, say it is all right. This will prevent it from eating poisoned food someone may throw to it. The dog must also be spayed or neutered to prevent its being led off guard by a dog of the opposite sex. Spaying or neutering does not in any way deter the aggressive guard from it protective duty, just keeps its mind on the job.

It is also best to have at least two dogs at the same time. They become very lonely when by themselves, besides, they work better as a team because they can back up each other in case someone tries to break in. Animals do get terribly lonely; especially guard dogs that have very little human companionship.

I cannot tell you how important it is with our present day problems to have one or two good companion dogs at home for protection. I'll give you some examples of why I feel so strongly about that.

I was a single woman who traveled by myself in a camper all over the United States, lecturing and counseling with pets and groups. I took three German Shepherds with me all the time because I felt that anybody or any gang trying to harm me would probably be able to subdue one dog or even two, but they would have an awful time trying to overcome three sets of powerful Shepherd teeth. An experience I had once really backed that up. I was in my motor home, parked on the beach at the end of a long line of other motor homes parked there overnight. About two in the morning, I was suddenly awakened with an eerie feeling that something was wrong. When I peeked out from behind the curtain, I was shocked to see my motor home surrounded with trucks, jeeps, and a large number of young people. They were very quiet and so were my dogs until they tried to open one of the compartments with a screwdriver. All of a sudden, my three German Shepherds stuck their heads out the windows, with teeth bared and almost got the head of one of the guys. All they could see where German Shepherds hanging out of several windows. I heard them say, "#*#*+***# there's nothing but Shepherds in there. Let's get out of here." I was sure grateful my guys were with me that night. Another time, I was traveling through Kansas when I saw a family stranded on the side of the road. There was a woman and some children huddled under blankets in the back seat and a man standing by a raised hood. It was cold, dark and remote, so I stopped to see what I could do to help. The man approached me on the driver side while, unbeknown to me there was a man hiding in the bushes on the passenger side. They didn't see my three German Shepherds lying beside me and in the back, so while the man was talking to me through the window, the other man quietly opened the passenger door. At that, he was suddenly met by three sets of teeth and one loud growl. I never saw a door shut so fast in all my life. I sure learned fast that it was a setup, but they learned even faster not to mess with a van full of dogs.

Another case was in San Bernardino, California. I was called in by a family to ask the Malamute dog for a description of what happened to the woman of the house and the two little girls. The husband had come home from work, found the front door open, the toddler in the crib, crying and wet, the body of his wife tied to a chair in the living room and the two older girls missing. The dog had been in the back yard, but could see what happened through the kitchen door. He was totally distraught for he told me he had tried to get in to protect the family, but couldn't. He described the intruder, said the man had rolled the children in a rug and carried them out the front door which was later confirmed by neighbors who saw him leaving with the carpet but thought he was a carpet layer who was just taking the old rug out. They couldn't see what was in the carpet, never realizing he had the girls rolled up in it.

When I asked the husband why the dog was locked out in the back, I was informed that they didn't want the dog hair in the house. Believe me; I would rather have the hair and my family than a clean house and a dead wife and missing children. They never did get the girls back even though they knew who the person was from the dog's description. Giving your dog access to the house may save your life.

WHERE NOT TO GET OR BUY YOUR PET

Many people complain about having to pay for a dog when there are so many free ones available. This is true, but the free pets may not have had the proper care and nutrition. The average person cannot afford to give proper care to a pet he or she intends giving away. Free pets often develop problems that eventually cost a great deal more in veterinary bills than the purchase price of a guaranteed pet.

Never buy a pet from a swap meet or a flea market. These are favorite places for thieves to unload stolen animals. You have no way of checking out the papers on these animals or the conditions under which they have been raised. Be sure you have some way to verify their address and get a written guarantee that if the animal is not healthy or the papers cannot be verified, you will be able to recuperate your investment.

Be extremely cautious when buying from an ad in the newspapers. Be sure you have the privilege of going to the home or kennel and checking the animals breeding conditions. Be sure the animal really belongs to the person selling the pet because this is another common way of unloading stolen animals. One family had their Irish Setter stolen from their yard. Two months later they saw a "For Sale" ad in the local newspaper for an Irish Setter. When they went to the address, they discovered their dog with falsified papers. Another time, when I was rescuing Shepherds from the pound in Los Angeles, I overheard two men standing near a lovely Doberman Pincher that was up for adoption. "I have papers for a bitch about that age. I can use them to sell her and no one will know." In talking to the kennel people, I learned that these two men were in there often doing the same thing we heard and saw that day. Unfortunately, there is no way you can prevent this from happening. How sad for the people buying that dog from these men for they had no idea what they were getting. They could have gone to the pound and purchased the same dog for about $25.00 instead of hundreds they would pay those crooks. An honest person will give you the opportunity to contact the owners of the sire and dam listed on the papers to be sure the animal is what it is represented to be.

Last, I do not recommend purchasing a dog from a pet shop. In my work with breeders all over the country, I have not found one that will sell their stock through a pet shop. Responsible breeders want to keep track of their dogs to be sure they are in good homes. When I place my pups, I try to go to the home and see if it is suitable for the pups' mental and physical well being. I make sure the dog will not be used for indiscriminate breeding or for creating another "puppy factory"- an inhumane practice where people breed bitches every time they come in heat, raise the pups as cheaply as possible, and sell them to pet shops or wherever they can make a dollar. The kennels are usually too small for the animals; conditions are generally unclean; there is no room for exercise; the ventilation is bad; and no or little care is given to the animals. The mother suffers greatly, crammed into a small cage with a litter constantly hanging on to her. Such a condition existed in El Monte, California, for several years before it was discovered and put out of business. On the evening news, our local television station showed eighty Poodles and litters crammed into small cages in a dark garage. This is all too often the conditions under which these dogs and cats are raised for sale through pet shops. When you feel sorry for that cute little animal in the pet shop and pay those exorbitant prices, remember, by buying that one, you are encouraging the industry to continue and more than that one animal you are saving will be harmed.

Another good reason to stay away from buying dogs from pet shops is that they never have the mother and you have no way of seeing her or the conditions under which the puppies or kittens were raised. Unless the pet shop has been in business a long time, your guarantee, if you can get one, may not be worth the paper it is written on. If the pet shop is reputable, you will be given the breeders name and address so you can check on all the information you receive. Don't be fooled when they tell you they will get you the papers. Usually they will only give you a bill of sale, but no AKC papers. A few years ago, there was a pet shop called the Swill Chalet in Pasadena, California. It specialized in Saint Bernards. It seemed reputable, had been in business for some time and many people purchased dogs from it at about $300 (would be much higher now) a dog. One potential customer asked for a dog from a certain sire. The store owner said he would produce a puppy from that sire within a couple of months. The pup was produced and the papers signed. Later the shop owner was found guilty of falsifying the puppy's papers. That particular famous sire had been dead for quite some time. Needless to say, this owner too was put out of business. Pet shops are notorious for being dumping places for puppy mills and for people who have bred dogs or cats they can't sell or give away.

FINAL WARNINGS

Do not be fooled by the claim that your pet has champions in its pedigree and therefore, is more valuable. Almost every purebred animal on the market has pedigreed champions in its lineage, a fact that means very little. It is the present breeding, recent health and show records that count, and most of all, the structure of the animal itself.

Beware of the claims of a new registry. There is no such thing. The most recognized registry is the American Kennel Club, AKC, second is the United Kennel Club, UKC. Another registry is Federacion Canofilo International, FCI, which is the official world registry for most other countries (except Canada, England, Australia, which have their own official registry) and it, requires that the parents be registered with them or the offspring cannot be registered. Many breeders or sellers are claiming registration with Continental Kennel Club. I have not been able to confirm or authenticate CKC as a national registry. To show in both AKC and UKC shows, the dog must be registered in each club registry, but dogs registered with CKC only, cannot be registered or shown in AKC or UKC shows. If you can't get your dogs registered by AKC or UKC, then you can usually get it into the CKC, which does not require the parents to be registered. They just have to look like the breed it is claimed to be. I had an experience in a small town in Mississippi in January 1976 on my way from Florida to California. I drive my camper on my travels so that I can take my animals. On this day, we needed some pet supplies so I stopped at a pet shop in a mall. As I usually do, I began looking at the animals there. The sign on one cage read $89.00. The dog looked like a Poodle, but didn't look purebred. When I asked the owner of the shop if it was purebred, he proudly told me it was a rare new breed called a Cockapoo. This is supposed to be a cross between a Cocker Spaniel and a poodle, but in reality nearly any breed that is crossed with a Poodle is called a Cockapoo. I asked him how he could charge that amount of money for a mongrel. A Cockapoo, Peekapoo, Schnauzapoo, or whatever "poo" it is, is a mixed breed and will never be registerable by any dog registry. We are presently seeing the same thing happening where people are now calling mixed breeds, "designer dog", but again, are really nothing but mutts. This shop owner told me that the breed was recognized by a special registry and he had papers to prove it. He also claimed that this dog was a real bargain. Breeders in other states were selling these dogs for one hundred fifty dollars. The poor locals who didn't know better were going to be taken for this was just an outright lie. You cannot mix breeds and get a pure bred any more than you can mix soda and liquor and get a pure liquor drink. They are called mixed drinks and dogs that are mixed are called mutts.

Run from the shop owner or breeder who crosses or mixes his stock and check out all claims of this nature, either with the AKC or with your local breed clubs. They can be found by looking in the papers for dog shows listed in the dog section. Purchasing these animals at inflated prices only fosters continued breeding abuses. In my counseling, I find that the worst traits of the two breeds often combine to produce psychological problems.

Now that you have decided upon your need, and examined all the possibilities to meet that need, you are ready for the final step. Get to know the mother of your desired pet and its early conditioning. An overwhelming majority of problems come directly from the mother and her early conditioning. Many breeders have told me they have bred their male in order to get an animal with the same personality, they want one just like their boy, but in reality, all they got was fifty percent of the genetics. This will help determine the physical appearance and mental ability, but the not necessarily the personality because it is formed more by the mother and the environment. If the breeder desires an animal like their male, get an approximately nine week old baby that was whelped by an emotionally solid mother, bring it home and let the male finish raising it. Once you as the buyer, determines that the puppy has been raised in a good environment by a psychologically and physically sound mother, and the papers are what you are looking for, then you are ready to take your new pet home.

I prefer the purebred animals over mixed breeds because I pretty much know what I can expect in its characteristics; however, I do not want to put down the mongrel or mix breed, because, as a general rule, they make loving pets. If you don't care whether the animal is a mixed breed, then the best thing to look for is a healthy mother and the happy environment of her young. No matter what the breed, pure or mixed, you want a psychologically sound pet.

CHAPTER 8

THE PSYCHOLOGICALLY SOUND ANIMAL

For centuries humankind has believed that animals live strictly by instinct, but I believe, from my own experience and from recent studies on imprinting, that little of what constitutes animal behavior is instinct. Animals learn from their mothers. This process starts prenatal and continues beyond weaning to the time they become independent and or are removed from their mother's presence.

THE MOTHER

The pet's mother is all important; her health, both physical and mental, her environment, her prenatal attitude toward her litters and last, the training she provides her young. To have sound offspring, it must start with the mother.

Physically she needs good nutrition to prevent health problems. I believe most of the dysplasia problems stem from the lack of certain nutrients. I believe this because I bred dysplastic dogs to dysplastic dogs, fed them high minerals, collagen, vitamin C and Calcium along with vitamin A & D to help them absorb Calcium and came out with the best hips I'd had in any litter. I developed my Love Your Pets Puppy vitamins based on what I learned from my years of testing that theory and watching what the mothers ate when they were pregnant. For instance, three weeks before the puppies were due to be born, I noticed my females eating oranges and buds off the roses (high in Vitamin C). In researching it, I found that the unborn puppy skeleton turns from cartilage to bone during that period making the need for Vitamin C greater because it helps hold the calcium in the bones. I kept increasing the amount of Vitamin C I fed the female until she stopped eating the roses buds and oranges. The level of vitamin C that I was substituting was at about 750 mg. per day so I determined that is the level I needed to put in the puppy vitamins I feed to not only the puppy during growth, but the mother during pregnancy. I also observed her eating dirt so I increased her minerals and the dirt eating stopped. Because the ligaments are made of a collagen type protein, I increased her collagen intake to strengthen the baby's ligaments. I truly believe that by observing the plants she ate, supplementing the nutrients found in those plants is what produced good results.

Another interesting phenomenon I have discovered is the relationship between parasites and the immune system. After I developed my Living Free Immune formula, I decided to give it to my dogs to strengthen their immune system. I feel this is very important if I want healthy, strong puppies so I made sure all pregnant bitches get it throughout their pregnancy. Ever since I started this practice, I no longer find any worms in the puppies. I don't see any fleas on the dogs anymore either, so I have made it a practice to feed the immune formula to all of the dogs in my kennel for about a month, twice a year and in addition to my pet vitamins. The little extra money it cost me has saved me hundreds in flea products and wormers.

Of course, one of the most important aspects of breeding is to be sure to breed the best quality possible; guarding against breeding genetic defects, each female should be bred only once a year to give them time to recuperate from their last litter. They may be able to produce two litters a year or every time they come into season, but at what cost?

Vaccination schedules are very important, too. We have been running titter tests on our dogs for several years and found that the vaccines hold for a minimum of 7 years. In the horses, it appears to be 5 years, but we don't know for sure, since we didn't test the horses the way we did the dogs. When we asked the vaccine companies how long their vaccines hold, they told our vet they didn't know, they had never tested them, but they did admit that they knew the Tetanus shots in horses held for a minimum of 5 years. I'm sure that is true because they don't want us to know the truth. They would lose too much money and unfortunately, I somehow don't believe they are in the business of making vaccines because they love our animals so much. The bottom line is profit.

If the mother's immunity is up and the babies nurse on her within the first 12 hours, they will also receive the colostrum that contains the titters and will maintain immunity for the first 9 weeks. If you give the vaccines to the babies sooner than 8 weeks, you will compromise the immunity they received from mom and leave them susceptible to diseases. I start the DHLP shots at 8 weeks and the Parvo at 9 weeks because they hold the Parvo titter longer from mom. I don't like to give all the shots at once as I feel that is too much on their tiny systems. For the Chihuahuas, I only give a half vaccine and only two of those the first year. In giving more than that, I have seen health problems like seizures, and general malaise. I only give one booster shot at one year of age and none for several years after that. When I gave the vaccines every year I found that all the dogs in my kennel came down with cancer in their lifetime, but not after I stopped that annual regimen. The Parvo vaccine destroys the thymus gland which, in the adult animal or human, produces T Cells that eat cancer. The original Panleukapenia did not, but since they now combine it with other cat vaccines, we can't get it separately any more. Since Parvo was originally a cat virus prevented with Panleukapenia vaccines, it was used on dogs to stop the epidemic when it first spread from cats to dogs. It prevented Parvo in dogs but didn't harm the Thymus gland like the canine version now does. It's no wonder dogs come down with cancer when we vaccinate them year after year, destroying their immune systems. Vaccines work on the principle of injecting a small amount of the disease so the body can gradually build up antibodies to that particular disease. In case your animal comes in contact with the disease, it will have the antibodies to fight it off. The blood titter tests will show you the level of antibodies your dog has to any particular disease. The more one is exposed to the disease, the stronger the body becomes in building antibodies; the more your pet gets out, the less chance they have of losing titters. We don't lose antibodies, so why keep loading their systems up year after year? Veterinarians are now becoming more aware that over vaccinating our animals is detrimental to their health. If you have any doubts, run a blood titter test.

One final word about the Parvo vaccine: do not give it within 30 days of breeding as it can cause sterility for that length of time.

An ingredient that can cause birth defects is Ethoxyquin. There was a lot written about it several years ago and many of the pet food companies removed it from their products. It is a cheap antioxidant, developed by Monsanto, as a stabilizer for rubber tires. It is so toxic that the plant workers have to wear full body suits when around it, yet they use it in pet foods as a preservative. It should be listed on the package, but many times it is hidden in products that are added, such as in fish and chicken meal. Menhaden makes the only fish meal on the market that we know of that does not contain it, so check with the manufacturer if you have any questions. If they can't tell you for sure it is Menhaden, then it is probably best if you avoid that food. I went through several years and about $25,000 in dead and deformed puppies before I found it in the fish meal used by a major pet food company that sells their products under private labels. After having several litters of pups born dead or deformed, from mothers who had had good litters before switching to the dog food made by that food company under the name brand of a major warehouse chain.

I had found that the healthy pups from those litters were able to have perfectly healthy litters themselves as the pups' owners were using a dog food that did not contain the Ethoxyquin. When checking further, I found that the food I had been using did contain ethoxyquin in the fish meal. When I called the warehouse headquarters and spoke to the head of product quality control, they told me that the dog food company assured them there was just a trace of it in the fish they were buying and shouldn't harm my animals. Unfortunately, a trace was all it took with my Chihuahuas and Chinese Cresteds for when I switched to an Ethoxyquin free food, the puppies no longer had birth defects nor were there dead or fading puppies. A friend of mine fed a dog food containing Ethoxyquin and in every litter, had either fading puppies that died, or pups born with one eye. She finally switched her Pomeranians to an Ethoxyquin free food and no longer has problems. I may be a little paranoid now after losing about $25,000 in vet bills and dead dogs, but I will no longer buy anything containing fish or poultry meal unless I can verify that they use Menhaden fish meal.

BIRTH and GROWTH

Psychologically, I have found that the mother will pass on her temperament to her offspring, so be cautious about breeding females with "hang - ups." Animals develop feelings and attitudes, good and bad, based on genetics and what they learned from the mother through mental communication, much the way humans do. Breeding the best animals with the best pedigree doesn't always mean champions; a champion is made up of more than physical appearance. It has to have a champion attitude, too.

From the time puppies are born, socialization with their litter mates and with humans is essential for good mental and emotional growth. From the age of four weeks until they go to a new home, it is important to expose them to new situations. Since many of our dogs will be entered in AKC shows when they are old enough, it will require a lot of traveling, thus they must be accustomed to a lot of new circumstances. When I was breeding German Shepherds, we visited the beach, the forest, parks, watched fireworks, road construction, city traffic and every situation I thought they might have to face later in life. They got very excited and tense with each new experience, but quickly learned to relax and enjoy themselves as they watched their mother enjoying herself. When my pups went to their new homes, they were ready for most conditions they might live under. Obviously, I did not allow my pups to go to a home where they would be placed in a back yard and left to themselves. You can purchase kennel raised animals that can handle isolation better than our heavily socialized pups.

When animals go to new homes, their emotions are still delicate, and they must continue to be exposed to new situations or the early training will be lost. Pups and kittens should never leave their mother and littermates until they are about 9 weeks old. When taken before that age, they often become shy and insecure or overly aggressive. Up until 9 weeks, the mother is training them and teaching them how to think and react to life as an animal must. You cannot give them that because they learn by thought transmission and you don't think like a dog or a cat.

It really grieves me the way most horse people take the foal away from the mother at 4 months of age. That is so cruel. Sure the baby can eat on its' own, but there is a lot more training that needs to be done, emotionally and mentally. A four - month - old being taken away from mother is like a child at two years old was being taken away and sent to boarding school. If you could feel what I feel, you wouldn't do it. Most mothers know when the baby needs to get on their own and will let them know in her own way.

Puppies should be leash trained and know some basic obedience by the time they are 4 to 6 months of age, but because their attention spans are so short, the training should be limited to only a few minutes at a time. One owner I observed pushed her four month old puppy for ten minutes or longer at a session. The pup became so nervous it stopped eating and started throwing up, she scratched excessively and tried to hide when the owner came near. When the training time was cut to just a minute or two at a time and treated as a fun time instead of serious as she had been doing, the pup responded in a more positive way. For their own safety, they must be trained to *sit, stay* and *come* on command. If they ever got loose, it could save their life. Basic obedience can continue with increased periods of training, but serious obedience, attack training, or retriever training, should not be attempted until the dog is at least two or three years old because they do not fully mature emotionally or mentally until then. This is why a female dog should not be bred until she is physically and psychologically mature enough to settle down and train her puppies to be well-adjusted dogs. This could take a few years, depending upon the breed.

Many owners complain that the mother animal will not allow anyone to come near her young, but tries to "protect" them. I don't accept this. If the mother animal loves and trusts you, the owner, what is there to protect her babies from? I have found from talking with mother animals that they are really jealous, not protective. Until the birth of their litter, they have received a lot of attention, especially during pregnancy. Suddenly, everyone is making a fuss over the little ones and ignoring "momma." When Princessa had her litter, everyone who came to see the puppies was instructed to first make a big fuss over her. They were to praise her and tell her what a wonderful thing she had done. After about two or three visitors treating her like that, Princessa met people at the door and even led them to her puppies so that she could get a great deal of

92

praise and petting. She never once showed any concern over the pups, joyfully allowing people to handle and cuddle them. The only time she showed any concern was when a stranger started to carry one of the pups out of the room, and then she trotted along after the stranger, without showing any aggression, just to see what was happening to her baby. She knew I would protect her pups; there was no need for her protection or jealousy.

It has been a beautiful experience watching her daughter, Philea, with her first litter. She did not trust strangers, so I made sure that plenty of people, particularly children, were present during the birth and immediately afterward. Philea tried to show aggression, but it was curbed until she accepted visitors and their praise. I also engaged children to help stress-train the pups, which proved to be a growing experience for both animals and children. Princessa was present during the births of Philca's pups and even helped clean them up. Philea's brother, Loverboy, enjoyed sniffing them and trying to figure out what was going on. The cats also investigated them, as well as my sixteen year old Pomeranian, Blacky. It was a beautiful sight to see the mother, Philea, sharing her family with the rest of my animal household.

STRESS TRAINING

Stress training is quite important from birth to maturity. It is a way of conditioning the newborn animal's nervous system so that when it gets older and must face stress situations; it will be able to withstand the pressure. The Air Force stress-trains its military dogs because the stress-trained pup develops into a dog that can work better for longer periods of time. According to an article in the Los Angeles Times, May 3, 1970, "To Do in the Army".

Super dogs are also taught alertness, obedience, and the ability to relate to their handlers. Among the tests are a pup's reaction to a rag waved at him; ability to escape from a maze; reaction to noises, lights and mirrors; alertness to hidden decoys; and the ability to read hand signals. Training begins at birth and continues until the age of eleven months when the animals that pass these rigorous tests are shipped out for active duty.

What does this have to do with you and your pet? Everything!

EXPLORE

A new home is a stress situation. So also are traffic, strange visitors, fireworks, horns honking, another pet of a different species, being put in a kennel while you are away, and children, not to mention a children's birthday party. You may wonder whether a centrifuge is necessary. It isn't. Handling does essentially the same thing. Here's what I do with my newborn pups. On the first day of their life, I pick it up and stroke it. The second day I repeat the stroking and then slowly turn it around in a circle. The third day I repeat the first two days procedure and then hold the pup upright on end, head up and rear down. The fourth day I reverse this position to head down, rear up. In this routine, I also increase the amount of handling time. By the time they are three weeks old, each puppy is handled for a minimum of ten to fifteen minutes per day, turning them on their backs, tickling their tummies, and so on.

LEARNING INDEPENDENCE

From birth until the puppy leaves, the mother animal teaches her young how to survive. When adopted too soon, the young learn to think like the surrogate mother, who is often its human. Later in life, they have difficulty relating to their own species, often not wanting to breed or be around them. This was brought home to me by a Unicorn I once met. Yes, you read it right. It was a unicorn, a white angora goat with one horn sticking out of the forehead. A white angora goat with a mane was the original Unicorn, not a horse. Mythology dressed it up and changed it to something more dramatic and appealing, like a horse. When the owners first called, asking me to visit with the goat, they were trying to find out why the goat wouldn't breed. They wanted to produce more unicorns, but the goat refused to cooperate. At first we thought it was a joke, but they kept calling back until we agreed to see him. When the goat arrived, he was spotless, did not smell like a goat, and rode in a van like a dog. He was an incredible animal that had been hand raised by people. When I asked him why he refused to breed, he told me he didn't want anything to do with the other goats. He thought like a human and as far as he was concerned, the goats stunk. He was so imprinted on people, he

94

could not correctly relate to his own species. You may have seen him at a Renaissance Fair or with the Ringling Brothers Circus. He loved people and loved performing. The only way they would get babies from him was through artificial insemination.

The advantages of leaving puppies with their mother for nine weeks or more, depending on the breed, some need more, is beautifully illustrated by Princessa. This shepherd weaned her pups as individuals. Some she weaned at about 5 weeks and others that needed special attention, she let nurse longer (I called it Southern Comfort at that stage), but all of them nursed until she knew they were ready. Every day she would take off to the woods with them trailing behind, their tiny, round bodies bouncing up and down, feet scrambling furiously to keep up. Whether she kept them out for a few minutes or half an hour, the pups returned in the same gleeful spirits as they had left. One day she and the litter disappeared for more than two hours. I frantically searched for them, terrified that something dreadful had happened to them. Later, I sighted her trotting down the road, her head held high, a look of triumph on her face. Dragging behind her, strung out in a row, were seven soaking wet little puppies, so tired they could hardly walk. When I asked Princessa why she had taken them away, she told me, *"I was teaching them how to hunt. I was protecting them. I know what I am doing and they are fine."* I would never have let them roam like that if they could have gotten off the property or were in any chance of danger. I have learned so much from Princessa and feel such gratitude for her forthright communication with me. There is absolutely no substitute for the education a mother provides her young during those early weeks. I exposed Princessa's puppies to every new experience I could find and still the best lessons are those they learned from their mother.

Another important lesson I observed was with Princessa's son, Loverboy. For his first year and a half, he had little to do with children. This lack of exposure makes most dogs timid and untrustworthy around children, but Princessa made up for Loverboy's disadvantage. Princessa loved children. I had had trouble with children throwing things over the fence at the dogs, so I taught her to get whatever they threw over and take it back to them. You wouldn't believe how that changed the kid's attitude toward dogs. Whenever they came around, she loved to fetch sticks and other things for them. Loverboy watched, perplexed that those jumpy, unpredictable little creatures could be such fun for his mother when they were so changeable. Soon I saw Loverboy could stand it no long. He approached the children slowly, until he discovered that these children loved to play as much as he did. He became what I can only call "kid crazy". After that, whenever he saw a child outside, he begged to be let out to play. When Loverboy ran with a child, it was as if his spirit was being freed. I could feel his joy and his capacity for loving a child, especially a disturbed or handicapped child. Without question, Princessa had done a good job.

Through my work and Princessa's teaching, I have discovered that puppies of most breeds that are still living at home should be taken away from the mother for periods of time, from 9 weeks to one year. This will prevent the mother from dominating the pup and controlling its actions and thoughts, which, in turn, could result in an insecure submissive adult. Puppies must also be exposed to situations without the mother so that they learn to think and act on their own. This is not as important with a strong-minded male because he has a natural aggressiveness which will enable him to assert himself; however, watch for any signs of shyness or submission in him toward his mother. Investigate the mother of the animal you intend to buy, and guard against buying a pet with an overly protective mother. You may have some severe shy or insecure problems to overcome. She can be easily identified by her effort to keep people from getting near her offspring.

For example, a thoroughbred yearling colt in San Diego suffered tremendously from his experience with his mother. I was called by the colt's owner to find out why the yearling backed people into a corner of his stall to kick them, and why he refused to allow anyone to put a halter on him. He also turned his head away when someone passed by him, and he frequently walked with his head down, making strange motions with his mouth. The owners could not understand his behavior because they had never abused the animal.

I asked the colt what was wrong. He communicated to me, visualizing it graphically, "*My mother hated racing and she told me people would take me away from her and force me to race. She told me to reject all people. That is why I turn my head away or try to back people into a corner of the stall and kick them."* When I related this to the owner, she recalled that every time she had gone into the pasture, the mother had stepped between her and the colt. The colt also told me of a terrible experience he had had at about three months of age: *"My mother and I were sent away to a terrible place. They took her away from me and I got scared. They put this thing on my head; they called it a halter, and tied me to the wall. I was frantic! I reared up but got my legs tangled in the rope. My face was pushed against the wall and I fell down. I hung with my legs in the air and my rump on the ground. After struggling for a long time to get up and breathe, they finally came back. When I was free, my nose and my rear really hurt for a long time."* The owner told me that this was the time the colt had been transported to the farm where his mother had been bred. The owner said she often wondered where the colt had gotten the sores, but the breeder did not mention the incident. I firmly believe that if this colt's mother had not been so overly protective, none of the present problems would have happened.

I often find in animals, as in people, that when a trauma occurs during a lifetime, the person or animal stops growing emotionally from that point until the trauma is dealt with. This was true in this colt's life. The motion he was making with his mouth and the lowered head was actually a re-enactment of the nursing position. I suggested a nursing bottle to ease the desire to nurse. I also taught the owners how to visualize to him the actions they wanted and expected from him, such as allowing them to enter the stall and handle him safely. They were also instructed to promise to take him out into the pasture again where he very much wanted to be, as soon as he allowed them to place a halter on him and lead him about. Five days later, the owner called to tell me that the colt had responded to the therapy. He was allowing them to handle him and lead him. After the nursing bottle was offered, he quickly rejected it and stopped the head-down, nursing motion with his mouth. He was then well on his way to racing, something many of them love if they aren't told by their mothers to hate it. I felt in this instance that it would be good for him to race. He had the competitive spirit that is so essential in a horse that will spend his early life running.

Observing and learning from these animals, it was obvious that the mothers will teach not only their good qualities to their children, but their bad qualities as well. One such example occurred in Las Vegas, Nevada, where I was working for a dog club. Four different people brought dogs to me for consultations, but did not tell me that the dogs were related. It seemed strange that four dogs would have exactly the same emotional problem of shyness and told me similar stories about their mother's shy behavior. Finally, I realized they were talking about the same mother. When I asked my host if the dogs were indeed related, he said they were not only related, but they were littermates. I then met the mother dog and realized that she was very shy and insecure and since the puppies had communicated with her in their nonverbal intimacy, they had learned to think and feel as she did, shy and insecure.

IMPRINTING

My personal experience with my animal family and as an animal counselor is clearly responsible for my conclusion about animal behavior: it is *learned* behavior rather than instinctive and that it is learned primarily from the mother. She is the first object the newborn animal feels, senses and observes. This theory is reinforced by recent studies in imprinting done by Konrad Lorenz, the pioneer of this concept. According to the dictionary, imprinting means to "impress" or "mark on," an idea "in the mind." Technically, in psychological terms, it is the discovery that the animal identifies the first object it sees as its mother and will thereafter copy the behavior patterns of that object, whether it is human, a like animal, or another animal species.

A case involving ducks was described in a film in my psychology class, and again in my biology class. A couple decided to do a controlled experiment with ducks hatched in an incubator. The people waited for the eggs to hatch and were on hand as the first objects the new ducklings saw. The ducklings then perceived these humans as their parents and followed them about as they would a regular duck parent. They copied, as much as possible, the behavior of the humans who even had to teach them to swim.

A similar case involved a duck in Cincinnati, Ohio, where I appeared on the Nick Clooney television show, except that this duck's fate was an accident. When I appear on TV shows, the producers usually arrange to have local animals there for demonstration purposes to show how I communicate with them. I ask the animal if there is a problem and what caused it, and then relay the information to the audience. One lady brought a duck to the show to find out why the duck laid her eggs in the winter, in the snow, and refused to mate or sit on the eggs. The duck, told me, *"The humans are my family. They were the first ones I saw when I was born and they raised me in the house. It is nice and warm in the house so I lay my eggs in where it is warm. That is what I'm supposed to do isn't it?"* It is biologically correct for a duck to lay her eggs in warmer weather. This duck laid her eggs because it was in the warm house in the winter; she associated this with the proper conditions to lay her egg. However, she was often let outside to enjoy the air and since she had to lay the egg somewhere and really didn't know what to do with it, she laid it in the snow as well as in the house; wherever she happened to be. She had been raised by humans and not by ducks, so she felt the natural instinct to mate with a human and not a duck. She was utterly unable to relate to her own kind, especially since she had been raised as the only duck, depriving her of any contact with her own species from which to learn. Since she had been raised in a warm house, her biological timetable was also confused and off-balance.

Another case of imprinting which I find particularly interesting, involves two animals of different species. Several years ago, I was addressing a group of animal owners and counseling their pets in Omaha, Nebraska, where I met a lovely old French Briard dog and her friend, a kitten. She was so old that her owners kept an old T-shirt on her to keep her warm. (Circulation decreases in the older animal as it does in the human.) This dog had rescued an abandoned kitten from the barnyard before the kitten's eyes were opened and then had proceeded to raise the kitten as if it were her own, cleaning and protecting it from danger. When the kitten opened its eyes, the first thing it saw was the dog. The kitten told me that she thought the dog was her mother and wherever the dog went, the kitten also went, riding on the dog's back, clinging to the t-shirt. The kitten walked and acted like a dog, not a cat, because it copied the dog's actions and thought patterns.

CHAPTER 9

THE EMOTIONAL NECESSITY OF RESPECT

Now that you have selected your pet and brought it home, you know its background and are pretty well prepared to meet its demands, you will need to set aside some quality time to help it adjust to their new lifestyle. Adults, as well as very young animals, need your attention and special love to help them through this change. But does that mean spoiling it? No! You are just helping your new family member to know how to "fit in" and learn its new boundaries.

Life with pets can be fun and very rewarding, but pets can act up in some pretty frustrating ways and do a great deal of damage, whether it is to our furniture, our other pets or us. Most acting up behaviors is symptoms of frustration and/or lack of discipline. I am talking about behavior that occurs in the adult animal, not the normal baby behavior animals grow out of.

In this chapter, I deal with some of the daily life problems most pet owners face, as well as how to establish a good owner - pet relationship. Such a relationship is based first and foremost on the emotional necessity of respect, taught by enforcing discipline that is both reasonable and understandable to your pet. You may face problems of rivalry among your pet family or the larger and more complex conflict, between human and animal needs. You may also face problems stemming from animal insecurity that can express itself in over aggression or shyness and fear. Animals can also be subject to frustrations. The symptoms run a wide gamut that can include barking, chasing, furniture scratching and chewing, biting, hole digging, wetting, spraying and other "anti-social" behaviors. In this chapter, I will attempt to help you resolve some of these problems as well as prevent them.

One interesting observation that emerged from the growing awareness of my animal's behavior was the similarity of their difficulties to the behavior problems I encountered in my study of child psychology. Once I recognized the similarities, I was quick to begin applying some of the principles I had learned from children to the animals, and then to those animals I was called on for consultation. It is a deeply rewarding experience to help produce a harmonious relationship between owner and pet, and between pets.

Discipline leads to respect and respect is essential to any relationship. This first lesson was taught to me by several mother dogs as I watched them train their puppies. One day, Honey Bear, a neighbor's long haired, black Chihuahua, was staying at my home with her three puppies. When she started eating, her puppies came racing over to see what looked and smelled so interesting. I was shocked when she snapped at them, fearful she would hurt them. She responded with a very strong, *"Stay out of it, I'm teaching them to respect me. I'm not going to hurt my own babies."* When I questioned the puppies, they told me they were not hungry, just wanted to see what she had.

Some time later, when Princessa had her babies, I observed her teachings and they seemed remarkably thought out and premeditated. In one instance, the schedule took several weeks and considerable plotting. For about two years, I had watched her bury her bones in the avocado grove, and then apparently seemed to forget all about them. When the pups were old enough to be out in the pen, unattended by their mother, she proceeded to retrieve the bones and pile them in a heap, just outside the pen. She made no attempt to chew on them, but just left them there in a pile. Later, when I let the puppies out for their romp, she laid down by the pile and started to chew. The excited puppies bounced over to her treasure and attempted to grab some of the bones. Princessa promptly attacked them. Terrified she would hurt them, I raced to protect the puppies, only to have Princessa emphatically tell me to stay out of it. She had brought the bones there to teach them to respect her right to her possessions. Watching her, I realized she had planned the whole affair to teach them a valuable lesson. Several times after that, when I was petting her and the puppies tried to interfere, she also showed a snarling reprimand to their invasion of her right to be loved.

In these cases, the mother animal uses food and attention to teach respect. I began to realize that these were the two most important areas in the domesticated animal's life. When either of these is violated by another animal, fighting begins. I allowed them to be dominant over the babies until they reach four months of age, then I apply my own principles of equality to prevent the pecking order problem.

THREE RULES FOR THE HOME

I have found that when I apply the following three rules to my animals' relationships, it prevents conflict in the home.

First rule, each animal should have its own personal food dish for special meals, and this dish should never be violated by another animal under any circumstances. If there are leftovers you wish to give to another animal, switch it to that animal's dish, without being observed by the other animals. Even when one of my dogs, Loverboy, would leave his food, and see another dog checking his dish, he wouldn't get angry, but would ask me to make the other animal leave it alone. It was *his* dish and it hurt his feelings when I allowed this violation to go uncorrected. If you free feed dry food for dogs or cats, it usually doesn't bother them to share, but the wet food or meat meal is precious to them and they don't want to share it. Horses show the same possessiveness about their grain buckets and hay racks. Water is not important to them and none of them has ever complained about sharing a water bucket or trough.

Each dish should be as distinct as possible in shape, size and color. We used to be told animals can't see color, but they communicate color all the time to me. Scientists have learned that the rods and cones in animal's eyes are in different places from people, thus they now realize that dogs possess the same ability to see color that we do until that discovery. Animals communicate four basic colors to me - bright yellow, blue, green and red. Some animals can even distinguish between brown and black, but orange, red and pink all look red to them. All pastel colors look white.

The second rule concerns attention. When you are giving attention to one animal, never allow another one to push his nose in between the two of you. Many people think this act of jealousy is cute, but it isn't. It is an intrusion and shows disrespect. When you pet the initial animal, push the intruder back and, using a positive statement, say, "Wait your turn." When you set aside the first animal, and then give the second animal some individual attention. Animals learn that by pushing each other aside, they get their own way. They tell me that they are not aware of time, such as the difference between ten minutes and thirty minutes. They do not care if you spend an hour with one and then a few minutes with the other, as long as each one gets individual, uninterrupted attention.

Princessa snarled at her puppies when they interfered with me caressing her. But when they were four months old, I pushed the puppies back and visualized what I wanted and then said, "I am the boss now and I will make them respect you from now on." She finally accepted her equal position and we had no more problems.

Sometimes, when a pet sees two people embracing each other, it senses the good feelings and wants to share them. The pet, however, should not be allowed to push between the two people and interrupt this affection because it could cause the pet to become jealous and foster disrespect for one or the other people involved. It is usually best to curb this kind of behavior.

Third rule: There is one boss in the home, one dominant figure - the pet owners. In the wild, where the survival of the fittest preserves the best of the species, a dominant animal is necessary. This is also true in a domestic situation, but the dominant one should be you. People often tell me that their animals have lived together for years with one as the boss and have never had a fight. This may be true, but somewhere along the line I find that the dominated animal gets tired of being pushed around and will suddenly fight back. After having been bullied for so long, its anger has built up to the point that the ensuing battle is ferocious and nearly impossible to stop.

People can fight with words or through a court of law, but animals fight with teeth and claws. It is just not worth taking a chance of injury to allow rivalry for pack position. Stop it before it starts. You, the owners, are the boss, the alpha of the pack. Your animals are equal in your sight - loved and protected equally. Giving each animal its share is both fair and rewarding to you and to them.

Another reason for insisting on animal equality in the home is to prevent the obstruction of the dominated animal's personality. In almost every case, when the dominant animal dies, the dominated animal becomes different, with a personality it was never able to express. The dominated animal may also express joy at the death of the domineering animal that made its life miserable for many years. You should never allow one animal to rule over another. The hurt is intense.

Animals experience frustration just the same as people, but they express it differently. People show it by nail biting, overeating and pacing, whereas animals show it by excessive scratching and chewing their feet or digging in the yard. Before you do anything to correct or curb a behavior, try to find the source of the frustration first and then correct it.

If the animal chews its feet or scratches excessively, first check for fleas and it that is not the problem, it may be because it has allergies or is not getting enough exercise. A friend of mine couldn't run with his dogs and really had no place to go in the city, so he took his bicycle to the local school track and rode around with them until his Samoyed were tired or he would hang the lead out the window and drive VERY slowly with them until they were worn out. He made sure the lead was long enough to allow them to run at a safe distance from the car and made sure they didn't get too close to take a chance that they would get hit by the car. He was careful that the lead was tethered in such a way that if they saw something and tried to give chase, he could hold onto them safely. They loved these outings. For me, I sat on the back of my open station wagon, holding the leads of my three German Shepherds, while a friend drove me slowly around a large mall parking lot after it was closed. The dogs came home too tired to scratch and chew, giving their skin time to calm down and heal. We now have a special shampoo and spray put out by Micro Tek called "Eqyss," which can help with itchy skin; but, if the problem is a lack of exercise, then no shampoo will cure the problem.

Another common expression of frustration can occur while two dogs are in the back yard and an intruder tries to get in, or a meter reader looks over the fence. They couldn't get to the intruder, and in their excitement, they turn on each other. This is especially true if one animal has been allowed to dominate over another. The bully will fiercely turn on the underdog. Be careful about taking the advice of someone untrained in animal psychology. I once heard a

Veterinarian tell a pet owner to reinforce the position of the bully when the dominated one tried to fight back. Great! That's like telling the teacher to step in and help the school bully beat up on the smaller kid. That won't make the dominated one feel better or correct the problem! Animals feel the same way humans do in these instances. That veterinarian needs to stick to medicine and leave behavior training to the experts.

Some animals throw tantrums to release frustration, such as overturning waste baskets, tearing or chewing papers, and pulling things off the bed or couch. If the cause of frustration cannot be eliminated, then the behavior must be controlled or curbed. For instance, if the dogs are digging all over the yard, especially in hot weather, be sure they have one moist spot that they know is theirs and teach them the rest of the yard is off limits. Provide plenty of sticks, bones and chewable toys to give them the chance to work out their mauling and aggressive behavior, and then when damage is done to the home, discipline them.

One of the biggest mistakes many people make is based on the assumption that they must catch the animal in the act to administer discipline. This is not true. An animal can remember incidents in its life that date back to birth, as well as remember what it did a few minutes or a few hours ago. Take the pet back to the damage, visualize what it did and tell it this is why you are disciplining it. Then go ahead and punish it. When I speak of punishment, I mean that you should use whatever makes the animal uncomfortable. For instance, if an animal loves people and insists on jumping on them, tell the animal "off." They can learn the difference between off and down. When you say "down," it means put your body on the floor, and "off" means remove your body from the person or piece of furniture. These two words "off" and "down", have different connotations and they understand the difference. If they keep jumping on people when you tell them "off," then isolate them, which is the exact opposite of what they want. If they don't like people and show aggression towards them, then put them on a leash and make them behave in the presence of people. I had a very distinct case that exemplified the wrong training.

A client brought a Labrador to me to find out why this normally mild - mannered breed was biting everyone, including his owner.

The dog told me, *"When I was young, I didn't really*
When they came to the house to visit, I showed thei.
snarling and threatening them. My owner became afraid .
me outside, just where I wanted to be. I like it like this." ┗ .╻ur
years, this pattern of behavior became so deeply ingrained that the
owner was now helpless to correct him. Each time he showed
aggression, a groove was established in the brain patters, and each
time he showed aggression and got his own way, the groove became
deeper and more permanently set. In this particular case, it would
have taken a tremendous amount of work and time to undo what the
family had done. Although quite unintentionally, they had actually
taught the dog to attack people. Since the dog didn't like people
anyway, his basic, underlying attitude wasn't going to change, and
since he had progressively become more dangerous, the dog was no
longer safe to give to someone else. They didn't have the time,
money, confidence, or ability to correct the problem, so I
recommended the dog be put to sleep. This was one of the few
cases in which I have recommended the dog be put to sleep. This
was one of the few cases in which I have recommended such drastic
action. I find that most problems can be solved or corrected with
effort, intelligence, know how, and patience. If the animal likes
people to start with, half the battle is won; but in this case, the dog
never liked people, so his desire to behave wasn't there.

Cats pose three common problems: scratching furniture, spraying
- both males and females, and eating house plants. Usually they are
all easily corrected. One of my cats was making a mess of my
couch with her claws, so I made her a special scratching board. I
bought a piece of carpeting and nailed it, hemp - side up to the board
to keep her from getting her nails caught in the carpet fiber. Then I
nailed the board to the wall near the door, hung an elastic string to
the top of it, and attached a catnip ball. She loved playing with the
ball, pulling it back and letting it go, only to attack it again. It cured
her of scratching on the furniture. The board was more fun.

Never declaw an outdoor cat or you will take away its only
defense against predators. Indoor cats, however, tell me that when
declawed properly, it is relatively painless and doesn't bother them.
They can do the instinctive scratching motion and no one yells at
them. Declawing has saved thousands of cats lives as many people

.... not tolerate a cat destroying their furniture. Instead, they will dump their cats in already overcrowded shelters where their chances of being adopted are very slim, or drop them in some rural area thinking they can fend for themselves, or have their cats euthanized. Personally, I would rather see them declawed than destroyed.

As for cats that spray, I have tried methods other than those described in earlier chapters. The first method I used was on my cat, Snowbunny. She was really mad at me for keeping my three German Shepherds, and whenever she came in the house, she would look at them, back up to something, and spray. She told me she hated the dogs and wanted to "eliminate" them from our house. I told her they were going to stay, but that she was the one who would have to go if she kept spraying. One day, when she sprayed, I put her out and made her stay out even though she sat on the windowsill at night and cried and cried. I visualized her spraying in the house then being outdoors. A few days later, I let her in. I visualized her spraying in the house, and then being thrown out. I knew she got my picture because she never sprayed in my house again.

The second method is using a crate. Once you have found out why the cat is spraying, you then need to correct the basic problem and teach them that spraying is no longer needed or accepted. When you know they've sprayed, take them back to the area, shake them by the back of the neck like the mother cat does - be careful as you are bigger and stronger than mama cat, and then put them in a cage for a few hours. Soak up what urine you can with a paper towel, put it in their litter box, and then put the litter box in the crate with the cat, along with food and water. Don't be nice to them while they are in there because they are in detention. When you go near the crate, tell them in pictures what they did and why they are in the crate. Remember, only positive statements or pictures, no negatives. When you see them use the litter box, let them out and praise them for being such a good kitty. If they spray or mess again, repeat the caging for even longer periods of time, maybe for a day or two, remembering to feed and water them, and only let them out when you see them use the litter box. If the cat has any brains, he will soon associate freedom with using the box, and confinement with spraying.

Be sure to completely saturate the area the cat sprayed with rubbing alcohol, all the way down through the padding below the carpet to eliminate all the odor or they will keep going back to area where they find their scent. In some cases, you may have to remove the carpet, sand the floor underneath and Varathane the wood, or if it is concrete, bleach the flooring to remove the odor completely. If it is at all possible, avoid using carpets on the floor. When you own dogs and cats, carpeting harbors fleas, odor, dirt, and bacteria. If you clean the carpet and the cats or dogs insist on returning to the spot, to urinate again, you can place mothballs around the area, then cover the spot and mothballs with a throw rug. This will usually keep them from going back to the area because they will no longer smell their scent.

Cats tell me they love to urinate on the soft quilts on beds because it is like a nice litter box. Once they start using the bed, the only way I know of to stop that behavior, is to block access to the bedroom.

Indoor cats eat plants for bulk and minerals. You can divert them from your plants by buying cat grass from your local pet or farm store. The grass comes in small boxes that can be placed on your counter or windowsill, away from the dogs. Alfalfa, ground up, can also alleviate the problem, if they will eat it. Cats are fussy little creatures, so you can't force them to eat alfalfa or cat grass. When they do eat the grass, praise them, but if they continue to eat the house plants, chase them away with a squirt gun and a simple one word verbal command, "no." Sometimes cats will also use house plants like a litter box. That can easily be stopped by putting a few mothballs around the plant and they will leave it alone.

INSECURITY, SHYNESS AND AGGRESSION

One of the most common problems I deal with is insecurity. This emotional root may surface as either over - aggression or shyness. Insecurity usually has one of two causes. Either the animal has been deprived of exposure to new situations when it was young, or its mother, littermate or some other animal friend, has been allowed to dominate it or told it to be afraid of the world. I have already discussed ways of helping the young animal grow normally, but if your animal has already developed this problem, there are definite ways to help them over it.

Aggression is normal and good, but when it results in unprovoked attacks on humans and other animals, it is no longer healthy and must be unlearned. There is a strain of natural aggression inherent in some breeds, which can or cannot be trained out of them, depending upon the individual animal. However, the overly aggressive animal must be taught to curb its aggression and acceptable behavior.

I find that over - aggression is more common in males and often can be curbed by neutering. Spaying the female, though, does not seem to help this problem. Another way to deal with aggression is to use an instrument of discipline, such as a flyswatter because it is associated with "killing something". They don't know who you are going to kill, so they are going to be afraid of it no matter what, making it an effective discipline tool. All you have to do is smack the flyswatter against the wall and it works. Sometimes, I have found a wide plastic belt will do the same thing. Give one word commands like, "quiet," "no," "leave it," but don't hit them with the belt or flyswatter. If you do, they will find out it doesn't hurt and they will learn to ignore it. WARNING: DON'T USE YOUR HAND TO DISCIPLINE THE ANIMAL. It will not know whether you are going to hit it or stoke it when you reach for it, and the animal will become "hand shy." Do not use a newspaper either, because when you pick up a paper or magazine to read, the animal will become "paper shy" and turn away from you, afraid help it will be hit.

Another form of discipline is tying an animal up when it has been bad. Most animals hate restraint. Let your pet know you are angry and that it is being tied up, or shut out of the house, until it is ready to ask forgiveness. Never approach your pet to forgive it, or let it know you feel badly because you had to punish it, or it will feel it has gotten away with the bad behavior. They must make the first overture by approaching you with their tail down, head lowered in a submissive position, and sort of sidle over to you. You can then tell them you forgive them, but tell them they must be good or you will punish them again. Visualize the bad act connected to the discipline so they will know why they have been punished, then visualize the good behavior with praise. Correct the bad behavior, but reinforce the good.

An animal can become overly aggressive because of genetic programming, because it has learned to be that way, or because it is insecure. No matter what the reason, it must be corrected. When an insecure animal attacks another animal or person because it is fearful, it is called a "fear - biter." I am not talking about an animal defending itself when cornered by someone intent on hurting it, but about the insecure animal that shows aggressive biting when it is cornered, perhaps by a child who only wants to pet it. Insecure pets feel they need to get on top of a situation before it gets on top of them. If the behavior has become so ingrained that you can't get it corrected any other way, I will sometimes, <u>AS</u> <u>A</u> <u>LAST</u> <u>RESORT</u> <u>ONLY</u>, use an electric shock device such as a shock collar or cattle prod stick, to break the pattern. It may seem harsh, but if you can't break the patterns the alternative isn't attractive.

The cattle prod stick, which looks like a long flashlight powered by flashlight batteries, is a very handy gadget that should only be used by AN EXPERIENCED, RESPONSIBLE PET OWNER AND ONLY AFTER ALL ATTEMPTS TO RETRAIN THE PET HAVE FAILED. It is activated by pushing a button on the side which causes an electrical current to shoot out of the prongs when contact is made with a person or animal. It is extremely helpful for people who walk their dogs and are bothered by other animals trying to attack your pet. Like the shock collar, the remote shock collar, when the button is pushed, the prod makes a buzzing sound. This is usually sufficient to stop any attack animal. It seems to instinctively understand that the "buzz" is a warning to back off. I have only used the prod twice with my animals. The first time was with Princessa when we lived on a ranch in Duarte, California. We had several chickens, and leased our pastures to the local dairies to keep their pregnant cows until they were ready to deliver. Princessa had been trained to respect the livestock, but the neighbor dogs, a German Shepherd and a Samoyed, had not. They would slip under our fence and kill the chickens or chase the cows, causing them to abort. We tried numerous ways to keep them out, but without success; we finally taught Princessa to chase every dog or coyote that came on the property. This she did with great gusto, but we soon learned that she now believed she was to chase every dog, whether on or off the ranch. I tried to teach her the difference, but she just didn't get it.

When we moved to the city, the situation became dangerous because she wanted to attack every dog in sight. I tried the discipline methods I have mentioned, but they failed. The brain pattern to attack was now so deeply engrained that she just blanked out when she saw another dog and went for it. She became so intent on the chase that everything else got tuned out, including the sound of my voice calling her. She never heard me. After the attack, she would realize she was wrong and come back, knowing she would be punished. She was so perfect in every other way that I had to resort to harsh methods, or have her destroyed. I obtained a cattle prod stick, and the next time she went after a dog, I caught her and shocked her with it. At the same time, I sent her the image of the attack so she could clearly understand why she was being punished. The treatment was applied twice and the third time she started to attack, I called her, she heard me and stopped. Each time she responded favorably, I praised her excessively. Gradually, the pattern of reaction changed and she was no longer a danger to anyone. Always remember to reward good behavior and punish bad behavior, but never use food as a reward. Food is just a common part of life and if used as a reward, it can cause problems. Animals will only respond the way you want them to if you have food, instead of because they love you and enjoy the reward of your praise and pats.

If you have two pets that do not get along, separating them will only increase the problem. One time Princessa and her daughter got into a terrible fight over a ball. One had her chest ripped open and the other lost part of an ear. I decided that this could never happen again, so when they came home from the vet hospital, I got the cattle prod stick out. Boy, they were ready to finish the job, so with the help of a friend, I brought them into the same room on leashes. When they started the glaring, rising up on their toes and growling towards each other, I zapped each one, starting with the first aggressor, and visualized the fighting again while saying, "You want to fight? I'll show you how to fight!" And then zap them. It only took two zaps before they realized the fight wasn't worth it. They became so paranoid that for awhile they would look the other way when passing. Gradually, with lots of praise for being good, they stopped the fighting and lived together for another 10 years without a problem.

No sign of aggression toward the owner or the veterinarian should EVER be tolerated. It could cost the animal its life. When I worked for a veterinarian, I watched him sedate animals before he could treat them. However, in the case of an emergency, when time is of the essence, waiting for the anesthetic to take effect so that the vet can safely treat the animal, could be fatal. I am appalled by the people who laugh when the animal bites the vet trying to treat it. I just cannot understand this illogical attitude, and am constantly amazed at the wonderful veterinarians who continue to care for these animals under these circumstances. This aggressive behavior is not necessary as I have proven with my own animals. I have taught them that it is forbidden to even lift a lip in a threatening manner. They know better than to even try and most vets will comment on how nice and easy it is to work on my animals. They call it good temperament. I call it "plus training."

Many people wonder how their animal knows when it's near the vet's office. Well, it is because the animal can read your mind, and you are thinking that you are nearly there. You are also anticipating a problem, or anticipating its fear and subsequent biting, and it does what you expect it to do. It reacts because of your mental attitudes, so if you will relax, expect obedience and calmness with no problems, your pet's visit to the vet can be a relatively pleasant, trouble - free experience for all involved.

Dealing with insecurity in a shy dog that fears strangers, noise or any unfamiliar situation, demands forced exposure. (That doesn't work for cats, so don't waste your time.) Dogs do not like the forcing process, but they tell me how grateful they are to be over the fear. Place the dog in a choke collar attached to a leash so they cannot slip out of the collar and get away. If they can break loose, it will only reinforce their fear. As you approach what they fear, think of them being happy, friendly, and approaching easily. Your mental attitude is the key here. Hold the leash firmly and do not allow the animal to back off even as much as an inch. Then lavish it with praise every foot closer it gets to what it fears, and tell it how wonderful and friendly it is, and that everything is just fine. The more you can treat the event casually, as though nothing is wrong, the better they will, too and the faster they will conquer their fears. Hold the animal until it relaxes and then lavish more praise on it. Also, they must stand alone or be held away from you in order to gain self-confidence, because if they are allowed to lean against you, you become the security blanket. I don't know why it works like that, but it does. People have a tendency to speak softly and pleadingly to a fearful animal, saying words like "it's all right, come on baby," or "its okay". This only increases their fear. Just act and speak confidently, saying, "knock it off, you're fine," and go on like it is, and they will recover faster.

Philea, for example, was very afraid of people. When I asked her why, she told me she was afraid they were going to take her away from me again. I had sold her because I realized her mother and brother were dominating her to such an extent she was becoming painfully shy. When I got her back a year later, she would not let anybody near her. I took her with her mother and brother on short trips. At first, she was so afraid she would be left again, that she wouldn't leave my side to play, eat, or even urinate. She gradually gained some confidence, but still would not let people touch her. I took her to busy, crowded places and held her on a tight leash, forcing her to bump against people in passing. I forced her to stand still while people petted her and gave her special treats I had brought with me. I took her to a boarding kennel and left her for a day or two at a time, so she could learn to trust me when I told I would be back. Gradually she began to believe me, but she still refused to allow people near her when she was off the leash. One day, I realized how much she loved to be scratched on the rump. Whenever anybody reached out to her, I asked the person to scratch her rump first. Soon she associated people with this pleasant experience and when she met someone new, she turned around and waited for her scratch. This may seem funny, but I would much rather she back up to someone in a greeting than run away. After two years of socialization, she was finally over her shyness. It was a relief to know that should Philea get lost, she would now allow someone to pick her up and bring her home.

Philea also had to overcome her fear of fireworks and sudden noises. Many pet owners face this dilemma during the holidays.

Their dogs become so frightened they may tear through screens, barricades or jump fences to end up hopelessly lost. Tranquilizers don't really help them cope because they merely dull their reactions and do nothing to remove the fear. Sometimes we find that fear of loud noises like thunder and fireworks gets worse with each Rabies vaccination because the vaccination attacks the nervous system. We now have a "Love Your Pet Herbal" calmer that seems to help them deal with the noise because it works on the emotions as well as helping to heal the nervous system.

I have found that the animal is afraid because it doesn't know what is causing the "sudden" noise, and their first instinct is "flight" to safety. They don't know where they are going, just anyplace far from this terrible "thing" that is after them. They must actually see the gun or fireworks or whatever is causing the noise. I took Philea to Mexico during fiesta. The campgrounds were bursting with noise and fireworks, day and night. At the first sound, she took a nose dive for the car floor, closed her eyes and lay there trembling. No amount of coaxing would bring her up to eat or play. After twenty-four hours, I felt sorry for her and took her for a ride into the quiet country to get her to relax. This she did, and as we returned to the campsite, she felt calm and happy again. She was sitting in the back of the station wagon, looking out at the crowds, when she happened to see the next fireworks shoot off. She had no chance to close her eyes and hide, but literally froze until it was over. When nothing else happened, she turned to me and asked, *Is that all that noise is?* She realized the flash of light caused the noise and that that was the end of it; it had nothing to do with her in any way. After facing her fear, she willingly left the car and never again showed any fear of noise. The problem was completely gone.

Another incident that exemplified this point happened to a German shepherd that Annmarie Tipton was training. The dog's owner had moved to the beach with her dog, but couldn't understand why, all of a sudden, the dog became so frightened that it went through plate glass windows. They brought the dog to me, but all the dog could tell me was that the big, noisy birds that flew overhead were scaring him. No matter how much we thought, none of us could understand why birds would suddenly start scaring him so much he would go through windows and run away. Annmarie kept the dog and slept on the floor next to him, but never anticipated what was about to happen. In California, a parasite called Medfly, was destroying valuable fruit crops. Every Wednesday night, they flew over our kennel and sprayed Malathione on everything in the area in the hope it would kill the flies. On Wednesday night, when the helicopter went overhead, the dog went absolutely ballistic. In the morning, Annmarie called the owner to ask if there were any helicopters flying over their home. She wasn't surprised to learn that the Search and Rescue people in the area had built a heliport on the beach to aid in water rescues. Voila! The mystery of the big, noisy birds was solved. Annmarie then took the dog to the airfield where helicopters came and went all day, and made him face the "NOISY BIRDS!" Once he saw them and realized what they were, his fear of them was gone and he never attempted to escape from his home again.

Disciplining a nervous horse that spooks on the trail must be done immediately. First, stop. Don't let your horse back off, but wait until it ceases its nervous prancing. When your horse and you are calm, ask it to proceed along the trail. If you take it back to the barn instead of making it face the fear, the fear becomes more deeply ingrained. The horse then becomes what we call "barn sour," trying to return to the barn or "place of safety" all the time. Many horses tell me they really enjoy going out, but it has become such a habit to turn and go home, they can't control the urge to run. If they are allowed to gallop or rush home, back to their friend (horses tend to become very herd bound), it becomes such a habit they don't even know why they are rushing home. Only make the return journey home when the horse is relaxed, and at a leisurely pace. Spooking is also a bad habit that many tell me they don't understand why they do it, they just do. The more they get away with it, the worse it gets, so don't try to baby them out of that behavior, correct it and they can get over it.

OTHER BAD HABITS

There is nothing more irritating than a constantly barking dog. Chronic barking for no apparent reason is a badly engrained habit which the dog cannot help, and which you must stop. The habit often starts as an attention-getter that then becomes neurotic behavior. Animals tell me how miserable they feel when the habit takes over and how sore their throats become.

To correct this problem, first try the milder forms of discipline such as the flyswatter or wide, noisy, plastic belt hit on the wall. If this does not work, you may have to resort to the bark or sonar collar. The dog's bark activates the collar to produce a light shock or beeping in the dogs ears that breaks the brain pattern surprising them into stopping temporarily. The dog quickly learns that barking hurts, so it stops barking. For defense, a dog can protect itself or your home by growling and biting. This is still possible with the collar because only the high pitch of the bark will activate the shock. BE SURE THAT THERE ARE NO OTHER BARKING DOGS NEARBY BECAUSE THEIR BARKING CAN ALSO ACTIVATE YOUR DOG'S COLLAR. I knew someone who owned a Samoyed dog and took it to a dog show. The owner put the bark collar on the dog and left. The poor dog went into a state of shock within a few minutes because all the other dogs around him were barking, activating his collar. He just couldn't understand why the shocks kept coming! Those of us nearby took the collar off him and calmed him down until the owner returned. You can imagine the reprimand awaiting that person! After your animal is trained, you can get a collar that looks and feels like a shock collar, but without the batteries. This is usually sufficient to keep your pet under control. Some breeds of dogs just love to bark, such as Collies, Shelties, and Huskies, to name a few. Since they do it for fun, it is harder to break them. Many of the owners will "debark" them, which is a process of cutting the vocal cord nearly in half. They can still make noise, but not the loud barking noise that sends neighbors "up a wall" and gets you evicted. I had a Dalmatian and a French Briard and they both barked incessantly. Out of desperation, because I had already had to move twice after the neighbors complained, I finally had them debarked. Afterward, they told me they didn't really mind because it didn't hurt and they could bark all they wanted to (it was now a quiet whisper) and no one yelled at them any more. They were actually happier than before the operation.

Car chasing is a danger to your dog and any child who may run after the dog, as well as to the driver who may brake or veer to avoid hitting your dog and become involved in an accident. You may also be liable for injuries if this happens. For everybody's safety, YOUR DOG MUST NOT BE ALLOWED TO CHASE CARS.

There are a couple of ways you can break them. First, get a squirt gun and fill it with plain water or a combination of water and vinegar diluted in a ration of three-fourths water to one-fourth vinegar to insure that the mixture is not dangerous to the animal's eyes. A liquid soap bottle carefully cleaned of ALL soap residue, is a larger and more effective squirt gun. Arrange a ride in a friend's car. As your dog begins to chase, squirt it directly in the face. Two or three of these squirt-gun treatments should break your dog because it will learn that the thing it is chasing "bites" back. If this doesn't work, you may try something I did one day. I took a metal frying pan and a large wooden spoon and set it on the seat beside me. There was a dog that lived on the corner of our block that ALWAYS chased every car and his owners never attempted to stop him. I decided to teach him a lesson. As I started slowly around the corner, he came after me. I slammed on the breaks, grabbed the pan and spoon, jumped out of the car banging the pan and yelling as loud as I could, and chased him home. He was so shocked he never chased another car because he learned that they "chase back."

If all else fails and it is your dog, you may have to resort to a remote control shock collar. This is used by hunters training their dog to come back when called. It may seem harsh, but a good trainer will only use it as a last resort when the dog's safety is at stake. Hide some place where the dog can't see you and when he starts after a car, give him one sharp shock. You control the length of the shock with the button, but it will automatically shut off after a few seconds so you can't do them any harm. The voltage is very low, just enough to get their attention. Don't let the dog know it is you shocking him; he needs to find out that what he is doing is bad and just the action will cause him the shock. This is also useful in breaking the dog from climbing or jumping fences when you are not there, or so he thinks. Attacking other animals or other bad behavior must be curbed. The remote control collar is rather expensive, but could save you much more in vet bills or possibly save your pet from getting killed.

GROUP DISCIPLINE

Group discipline is a very interesting concept. Mary Roberts of Covina, California, owner of German Shepherd Champion, Gauss Wikingerbluet, clued me in on the unusual practice. Mary's first two Shepherd studs were trained not to leave the property, but not Gauss, who was new to the family. The first time they were in the front yard, Gauss promptly ran off to investigate the neighborhood. The other two shepherds followed Gauss to the edge of the property and waited. When Gauss returned, the other two dogs were so angry that he had been allowed to leave the property while they were not, that they attacked him, snarling and biting. This, Gauss told me, made him stay home. He had no intention of getting another beating from them.

I decided to use this theory of group discipline on a problem I had with Loverboy. Loverboy sometimes barked incessantly for attention and sometimes just for the fun of it. When I explained to him that he'd have to stop this barking because he disturbed the neighbors and me, he continued making a racket. I tried the standard forms of discipline previously discussed, except for the shock devices, without success.

It was definitely time for a chat. I sat down with Loverboy, Princessa and Philea and told them the next time one of them began barking needlessly, I would discipline them all. Later, Loverboy began to bark. First, I made sure there was no reason to bark, and then I smacked the plastic belt next to each one individually to scare them. As soon as I did that, I mentally showed Loverboy barking and them all getting in trouble. They got it. Later that evening when Loverboy barked again for no reason, Princessa promptly attacked him and put him in his place. After a lesson or two of that type, he learned to bark only when something was present. I make a point of praising him for that necessary bark as well as disciplining him for the foolish, unnecessary barking. Group discipline is a fascinating parallel to what we in human circles term as peer pressure.

All these training methods must be administered with love and concern for the good of your pet, as well as respect for your neighbor's rights to privacy and quiet. Remember, always discipline the bad behavior, and reward and praise the good behavior, and accompany the training with the proper visualization so they fully understand what is going on and why. Using the mind will make the training far more effective.

FRUSTRATIONS AND FUN

CHAPTER 10

This chapter also deals with discipline, but on a more sophisticated level that involves showing your dog, obedience classes (how to know if the trainer is good or not), how to train reliable protection dogs and gently guard duty training. I also discuss neutering and spaying because it is not only basic to an animal's personality and health, but in many cases, the animal's ability to obey commands without distraction. Finally, because it is such a rewarding experience for me and my pets, I suggest rules for traveling together. Discipline and good manners are even more essential on the road.

SHOWING YOUR DOG

You do not have to be a professional breeder to enjoy showing a good animal. When you obtain that purebred puppy, be careful about going to too many puppy matches or you could be in danger of boring them with the whole activity before they get to the important AKC shows. You always want to keep the real show as special and as much fun as you can. A few handling classes, plenty of socialization, and maybe a match or two to become familiar with the more formal ring procedure, is generally enough to get them ready. If you need more practice, then try to take different dogs to handling classes, even if it is a pet, just to get your training. The object here is to get you the training and practice, not bore your show dog.

As you gain confidence in what you need to do, you will be able to project that same perfect image to your dog using visualization, your dog's language. Visualization is very important in showing because you want your dog to know, in their language, how you expect them to perform Be positive and confident and he will respond accordingly.

Also, keep an ace or two up your sleeve. Find something special that your dog loves to eat or an activity they love, such as playing ball or swimming (if you are near water). He should only be given that special treat at the show, either in the ring or right after you come out, so he will connect the show ring with that treat. Many times a dog will do well until he gets to those last few points needed to finish his championship. This is when the owner becomes very serious, anxious, and stressed. A dog will pick up on that and start to act up, or just plain want to get away from what is now no longer fun. When you see them shying, pulling back or trying to leave the ring, that's probably what's happening. This may be the time that you yourself need to take some herbal "Calmers" and pull out that other special treat or activity you have been saving to re-ignite your dog's interest and sense of fun. A dog's happiness and temperament count very heavily with judges.

A final tip. If you have a male with strong hormones and want to show him, you may have problems. He may become distracted in the show ring when he smells the presence of females, especially a bitch in season. Ask your veterinarian for female hormones or give him our "herbal female balancer" about half an hour before he enters the ring. This will make him feel as though he has had the mating experience and will relax him. These hormones do not cause cancer nor create problems later if and when you wish to breed him.

Now, go have fun at the show and make lots of friends who enjoy the dogs as much as you do. For my husband and I, it is our main social life and a time for us to get away from our busy schedules and relax. We love it and have a great time visiting with friends who are like-minded.

OBEDIENCE CLASSES

Obedience classes can be fun and can help you develop a better relationship with your dog. This is especially true for the dog that doesn't want to settle down in the show ring or when you travel. It teaches them what to do to please you, but most of all; it is an important safety factor. In obedience classes they learn to *halt* and *come* immediately when called. This is especially important when in unfamiliar environments, not knowing these commands could cost them their lives, and you a great deal of grief.

A good class can be defined as teaching obedience through kindness. A good trainer knows that you don't just correct bad behavior, but reinforce good behavior as well as with praise and treats. Nothing is done to hurt the animal and nothing more than a jerk on the choke collar is allowed to get its attention. Training should be fun for you and your dog, but unfortunately there are some bad "trainers" who use brutal training method.

Here is what to look for and what to avoid. Watch the animals that are already in the trainer's class. If you see most of the dogs walking with their tails between their legs, head drooping, or body trembling, this is not the place to bring your dog. Subdued behavior usually means a bullied dog, not an educated one. Educated animals, who enjoy their training, will have their tails wagging constantly, be eager to run to obey the commands of their master or trainer, carry their heads high and have a bounce to their gait. That's the class you want to attend.

Some examples of authorized abuse took place in an obedience class where I took Princessa, ONLY ONCE. What went on during that one evening I would not have believed unless I had seen it with my own eyes, and the saddest part of all was that people were being told that that was the way they should train their dogs. The trainer was abusing the Bill Koehler method of training guard and attack dogs and adding some innovations of his own. A young, ten pound Miniature Schnauzer was being taught to heel. This is when the dog is supposed to move forward at the word "*heel*" as the left foot is also moved forward. The dog is to stay by the trainer or handler's left side until that foot comes to a stop, at which time the dog is to stop and promptly sit. The trainer took the small Schnauzer on a six-foot leash and choke collar, and said the word "heel" as he stepped forward with his right foot. This delayed the dog's start because the dog was following the left foot movement. When the dog did not move immediately, the trainer gave the leash such a hard jerk, the dog was flung forward like a whip, flipped over on its back, and landed on the hard cement. Strong jerking on a choker like that can damage the cartilage in the trachea, resulting in severe breathing problems often requiring surgery to correct.

r that incident, when the trainer said *heel,* the dog shot forward to keep from being flipped again. The dog was not being educated, but abused and bullied because he ran forward out of fear instead of learning to follow the left foot as he would need to do in an obedience trial.. Needless to say, that trainer got a piece of my mind as I left and so did the owner for allowing his dog to continue to be subjected to that kind of abuse. .

Another example involved an Irish Setter that was being used to teach the class how to stop a dog from jumping up on people. The trainer was told in the presence of everyone, that the dog had just been spayed the day before the class, so she was pretty sore. This didn't phase the abusive trainer who took the dog into the center of the ring and said, "Up, up" pointing to his chest. The dog obeyed by jumping up at which the trainer grabbed the animal's front paws, held them tight and kicked the dog in the stomach with his knee. This action sent her reeling backward until she too landed on her back on the cement. She staggered to her feet in pain and confusion. She had just been horribly punished for obeying. What she learned was to obey commands was painful, but never learned not to stop jumping on people. I also observed this particular trainer using the hot-shot stick for the slightest infraction of any obedience rule. This is against everything I believe about animal training. The only reason I am relating these horrible experiences is so you will know what to avoid. Electrical devices should never be allowed in the hands of such sadistic people, and this trainer was definitely very sadistic. I reported him to the authorities, but don't know if anything was ever stopped as I never went back with my dogs.

Lastly, but most importantly, use visualization in your training. If you want the dog to sit, think of him sitting next to you in the correct position, with his butt on the ground. If you look at the dog and say "sit" and think of him standing there not moving, he will think the word sit means to stand up. They learn the same way children do, by word association. You tell the child to sit up at the table, while pointing to the table. Before they even learn to write, they learn that when you say "table," you mean that flat thing that is usually in the kitchen with food and stuff on it. Animals learn the same way. You must tell them to sit, picture them in your mind sitting, and they will learn that putting their butts on the ground next to you, is what that word means. If you will do this with each command as you go through obedience training, your dog will progress much faster.

Even though your dog gets the training, remember, they still have a mind of their own. I was in an obedience trial one day with one of my dogs, Mark, when I noticed how fidgety he was getting during the "sit stay"exercise. This is an exercise where you leave your dog in a sit position, move to the opposite side of the ring, face the dog, and then wait for one full minute before returning to your dog. He must not move from where you left him and he must stay in the sitting position until you return to his side and the judge says, "Exercise finished". Only then is he allowed to move. This procedure is also applied to the "down-stay" exercise, but for three minutes where they must lie quietly. I was already thinking Mark was restless during the sit, so what was he going to do in the "down-stay"? When I stood opposite him in the "down-stay", I closed my eyes and kept thinking of him being quiet. The other exhibitors knew what I was doing as most of them knew me or had attended my classes on communication with animals, so when I heard them laughing, I opened my eyes and sure enough, Mark had pulled another one of his tricks on me. He hadn't gotten up, but had rolled over, stuck his feet out of the ring, and looked back at me, saying, *Thought I was going to do it, didn't you? Well, I stayed in one spot!* That is the time you want to choke them, but can't. Some dogs will pull tricks on you and you just have to roll with the "punches," so to speak.

Another time we were doing an obedience trial on one of those sweltering, 110 degree days at the Pomona, California fairgrounds. The blacktop was blistering hot, but that is where they put us to do the trials. Caesar, another one of my Shepherds, was pretty good until we got to the off-lead healing exercise.

When I reached the end of the row, he stayed with me, but as I did the about face turn, he suddenly disappeared. Since we aren't supposed to stop and look back, I kept going until the judge told me to go get my dog. Well, I couldn't really blame Caesar, who, as I made the turn, had spotted the duck pond next to us, and had just kept on going right outside the ring instead of turning with me.

vas, cooling his feet in the water. Oh well, such fun.

the cutest scenes I ever saw in an obedience ring, was a very tiny, miniature Dachshund, and his handler who was about 6 foot tall and pretty hefty. (When a dog stops on command, he must sit immediately and wait for the owner to move forward again as I have described earlier. If he doesn't sit, they lose points). In order for the judge to see if this particular Dachshund sat, she had to get down on her hands and knees and look from the ground. The dog was so close to the ground, you couldn't tell if she was sitting or standing any other way. When the Dachshund got to the exercise where the handler must leave the dog, go to the opposite side of the ring, call the dog, have the dog come to him, and sit in front of him, she was then given the signal to come around and sit at his side as he finished the exercise. As I watched this dog perform, I have never seen a happier animal. When the handler said "come", the dog ran as fast as she could, and skidded to a halt in front of him. When the handler gave the signal to the Dachshund to return to his side, the dog leapt into the air, spun around as she did so, and landed beside her handler with tail going in a blur. She was literally smiling as he praised her. That is the kind of response you get with good training. That dog loved pleasing its handler. I once saw a cartoon that really exemplifies how people treat their pets in training. Two dogs were sitting in the yard asking each other what the other's name was. One said, "My name is bad dog, what is yours?" The other one responded, "My name is Good Dog. Obviously one was reprimanded far too often while the other one was praised frequently during training.

By the way, does your dog believe his name is "Good Dog" or "Bad Dog". That choice is yours.

BOARDING PETS

Many pet owners cannot get away because they don't know how to travel with their pets and boarding costs can sometimes be prohibitive. Likewise, there are those animals who just can't handle being in a kennel, so this section will help you with some of these problems.

First, if you choose to board your pets, there are a few steps you can take to get them used to being in a kennel and to adjust to your absence while they are boarded. To prevent separation anxiety, you may want to follow the process explained in the previous chapter of how I conditioned Philea to the kennel by taking her for short, overnight stays, gradually lengthening those stays to reassure her I would always come back for her. In addition, you need to be aware of what you are thinking while you are away. As I previously related in the story of the two boxers whose owner worried about them not eating, also applies to your worrying as well about anything that might be going on in your absence. Be sure you have your pets in a safe and highly recommended kennel, and then go enjoy yourself and by all means, do not worry about them. Just send them thoughts of being fine and that you will be back, then relax and focus on your trip.

TRAVELING WITH PETS

A psychologically sound animal can travel anywhere with you, a companionship we all enjoy. For me, with so many animals, when I choose to take a few with me, they all want to go. I used to travel all over the world showing my dogs. When they saw both the crates and my suitcases come out, I had to keep their crates closed and I would find it jammed with dogs, all wanting to go. It was a special one-on-one time for them, and they loved it. I have a friend in Texas who used to send her Belgian Tervuren, Rowdy, with me to the shows. I flew from California to Dallas, Texas, spent the night there, and flew out the next morning for the shows. Rowdy loved going and he knew I was going to take him. We put his crate by the door and every time I got up during the night he made a beeline for his crate because he didn't want me leaving without him. He was a delight to travel with, got along with everyone, a perfect gentleman in the hotel, and just a wonderful traveling companion.

To prepare your animal for traveling, use the crate as a reward. Always give them some special treat that they only get when they are in it. Take them for rides in the crate so that they get used to being in it while the vehicle is in motion. Be sure, when you check them in at the airport as excess baggage, that you have a current health certificate. If traveling to other countries, find out ahead of time if there are rules that may be different from your country. For instance, when we went to the dog shows in Bermuda, we had to have a rabies shot within a year of arriving on the island. When you get to the airport, watch to be sure your dog is loaded. If it isn't, contact whoever you need to until you are sure it is on board. As you board the plane, remind the Captain to turn on the air circulator as he has a very precious cargo below, your beloved pet. Now, sit back and enjoy the trip. If you have any doubts at all about your dog being stressed, you can give them herbal "Calmers" that will help them through it (you may need to take some too), but don't use a tranquillizer. They will still be afraid, but because they are physically paralyzed by the tranquillizer, they can't do anything about it. Herbal "Calmers" work on the emotions as well as relaxing them physically, and are much safer. Your pet may have had a tranquillizer several times before and had no reaction, but you never know when they will. I have seen it happen, so I won't use them on my dogs. The herbal products we make are much safer and more effective.

Check ahead of time to be sure you can get a rental car or van that will allow animals, and the same for a motel. A lot of them won't, so check ahead to avoid sitting on the roadside with a dog, crate, and suitcase. That's no fun. If you are traveling to dog shows, the dog clubs will often give you references of those who will take you and your pet. Be sure you clean up after your animals as no one wants to walk in your dogs droppings and track it into their car or motel. Because people do not honor the grounds where they take their pets, many hotels and event facilities are shutting us out. Recently, when we went to a dog show in Las Vegas, the only hotel that would take us was Motel 6 and the American Motel next door to it, but they charged us $25.00 extra for the dog. The other motels that allowed animals, charged $50.00 extra per pet, so be aware that you may have an extra charge. Please, clean up after your dogs, or even these won't be available in the future. Many motels won't allow big dogs, only small ones. The funny part is that I find the people with small dogs are worse than the people with big dogs because they are more prone to allow the dogs to soil the room and not clean up after their wee pets. Don't try to reason with the desk person, unless it is the manager, because they don't have the authority to change the rules concerning pets. If you know the hotel you wish to stay in, you may want to write them a letter explaining to them that you understand their position and that you sympathize with them, but that you will respect their property if they will consider letting you stay with them. List the rules you intend to follow, if allowed to stay there, and THEN FOLLOW THEM. Here are some rules you may want to express.

1. Whatever you do, please, please, please, do not leave your pets in the room while you are gone. Strange noises, people constantly walking in the halls and the unfamiliarity of the surroundings may frighten them or cause them to bark or chew furniture. Leave them in your car if it is cool enough, in their own familiar crate, or arrange for someone to care for them. Some kennels and veterinary hospitals will do day care only, but you must make arrangements ahead of time. Boarding facilities and veterinary hospitals are safer, more familiar surroundings for your pets, and it will be easier for them to deal with your absence better than leaving them alone in an unfamiliar hotel room with the sounds of people walking around outside or overhead on the second floor.

2. Always carry a disposable bag and/or pooper-scooper of some kind. Pet owners, who allow their dogs to defecate on motel property and not clean it up, cause considerable resentment for obvious reasons. This hygienic act should be applied to public parks and beaches, too. No one wants to be running down the nice sandy beach in their bare feet and step in your dog's mess, or allow their children to play in sand that contains your dog's feces. Be considerate of what others must face from your visit.

3. If you are traveling with a bitch in season, please don't allow her to stay in the motel and sleep on the furniture. In fact, you should have her wear dog panties with pads that will prevent the scent or blood from getting on furniture because the next person renting the room may have a male who will instinctively mark any place where that scent is left. Be considerate of the motel owner who has to clean the mess up and who may decide to refuse the next dog person a room. It may be the next time you come

through; you won't get a room either.

My stay in a hotel once provided the staff with a valuable learning experience. We were traveling from California to the dog shows in Bermuda. We had a long layover in New York so we decided to stay in a hotel that allowed animals, and would shuttle us to and from the airport. After a good nights rest, we took the dogs, the crates, and all our paraphernalia down to the shuttle, but because there were so many people dressed in business suits getting on, the concierge wouldn't let us board. He said that it would disturb the other patrons needing the ride, and he wanted us to take a taxi. We told him no, that we had stayed there because they promised us a ride back to the airport, and we were holding him to that agreement.   Finally, he relented, and put us on an empty shuttle that would take us back to the JFK. The funny part came when we were loading. Most of the people getting into the other shuttles got off and came over to ride with us and the dogs. They had a great time petting them and fussing over such beautiful, clean, well-behaved dogs-Borzoi, Dalmatian, German Shepherd and Belgian Tervuren. The concierge was astounded. I still have pictures of my German Shepherd lying on my suitcase in the suitcase rack. It was priceless.

When traveling in your vehicle, of course, it is easiest when in a motor home because it becomes familiar. The animals feel just as much at home in it as they would in their own house. Take along an exercise pen that you can set up when you stop to give them exercise and security. If you travel in a car, be sure you NEVER leave them in a car in hot weather. On a hot 85 degree-day, the temperature inside your car even with windows slightly opened, will reach 102 degrees in 10 minutes and 120 degrees in 30 minutes. A dog's normal body temperature is 101 to 102, and if left in a car for more than a few minutes, their body temperature will reach 107 to 108 causing them to die from heat prostration or cause irreparable brain damage or death. A rule of thumb: if you wouldn't sit in there with the windows barely cracked, your animal shouldn't either!

If your pet is old, it will require extra consideration. At fourteen, Blacky had certain physical disabilities, but he so loved to go, that I decided that even if it cut his life short to travel, I would rather his life be full and happy, than shorter and unhappy being left home. I always made sure his basket and bedding were accessible because these familiar comforts gave him a sense of security.

I consider one safety precaution essential: microchips. There have been dozens of incidents were animals were separated from their owners and returned later because they were found and traced through their microchip available from your veterinarian or Micro Chip clinics. I had three incidents where dogs we had placed in pet homes had gotten out and the new owners hadn't informed us they were missing. We got them back, however, because when they were taken to a vet clinic, they found the chip and tracked it back to us. A family, who had purchased a beautiful Chinese Crested from me, was dumping it in the pound when the pound workers found the chip. They called me to tell me it was being dumped, but did I want it back. You bet I did. They made the person return it to me and would not accept it for adoption. Most animal shelters are very good about that sort of thing. Had I not chipped these dogs, no telling where they may have ended up? Besides, I understand that animals being sold for research will not be accepted by legitimate labs if they are micro-chipped. The labs are afraid the animals may be stolen because anyone who would go to the trouble and expense to microchip their pet probably didn't dump it and they could be liable. It's a wonderful safeguard.

An animal's main requirement is exercise, so on a long trip, plan to set aside some time each day for a good run. Teaching them to fetch will get the jitters out, or if they like to swim, find a nice, clean place where they can take a dip. Carry towels with you and a good blanket to place in the crate or on the seat of the car afterwards.

Cats can also be good travelers. Just be sure to keep a litter pan handy at all times and don't be upset if they seem nervous and vocal for the first few rides. They usually associate car rides with going to the vet because that is usually the only place they were taken in the past. As that fear subsides, they will look to the vehicle as a security too. When I first began traveling with my cats, Snow Bunny and Tigger, I kept them on leashes. A few times, they escaped the camper, but very quickly came back to what had become their familiar secure home. I knew they would get restless, so I trained them and the dogs to come to a whistle I carried. When they finally got to the point of responding immediately, I found safe places to park, outside the city or suburban area, left the side window open, and let the cats go. They loved it. They always returned for breakfast because the only time they were fed was when I woke up. If they didn't come then, they were not allowed out for a few nights. They quickly learned that when they and the dogs were let out for a run and the whistle blew for everyone to come back, they got there fast and made sure they were in by the time the dogs were. It worked for us. When they saw me packing the camper to leave on a trip, they beat us to the van and hid up in the bed to be sure they got to go. Yes, I was taking a bit of a chance, but it worked well for us and they were very happy. My cats were used to living and running on a ranch, so I knew that they knew how to take care of themselves. But if your cats are not streetwise, active, outdoor cats, and you don't feel safe letting them run, they can still adjust to having fun on a leash and exploring new environments.

Well-adjusted pets can be enjoyable traveling companions because they see things so differently from us and they love to share their adventures with us. It was a growing experience for all of us; a new adventure for them and a new experience for me watching their enjoyment. I see the world as they see it and that is a revelation.

PART II

STORIES

THE ANIMALS

TELL ME

PLUS

PETS SAY AND DO THE
DARNDEST THINGS

Puffins & Nupkins

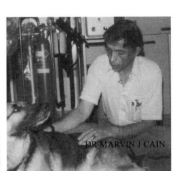

Princess Royal

Down on The Ranch

DR MARVIN J CAIN

Mr. Spunks

Blacky

Lady & Dawn

CHAPTER 11

PETS SAY AND DO THE DARNDEST THINGS

This chapter is dedicated to the many wonderful experiences I've had with the thousands of animals I have had the privilege of meeting over the past 37 years of "talking" with them. There have been some very funny moments, as well as just plain enlightening ones, that I hope you will also enjoy.

One of the most important lessons I learned early on in my career, is "Don't question when someone calls for an appointment, no matter how exotic the animal may seem to be." Case in point!

One day I received a call from a gentleman, asking for an appointment for his Unicorn. Yes, I am sure you just had the same impression I did when he called. I thought it was a joke, so I told him to call back because we were too busy to help him at that moment. About an hour later, he called again, asking for an appointment. When I asked him what he wanted me to learn from the Unicorn, he said, "I am trying to breed him and he won't have anything to do with the nannies." You guessed it. By now, I was really sure he was pulling my leg, so again I put him off. As I hung up we all had a good laugh about that one. He wasn't to be deterred, so he called again and again, insisting that he had to have the appointment. Now if you are anything like me, I didn't believe in Unicorn's. They were just legendary beings, right? Who ever heard of a horse with a horn coming out of its forehead? Well, finally we began to realize he wasn't a prankster, but was really serious. By then, we were becoming pretty curious, so made a time for the next day.

When he arrived in a van we were all absolutely surprised to see a white, angora goat, step out and sure enough, there was the horn protruding from his forehead. That goat acted like a dog, walked on a leash, was housebroken and came into the house like that was a normal thing to do. I was stunned. The owner explained that in legends of old, Unicorns were white, angora goats that sported beautiful white manes, not horses. Only in the last 400 years have artists depicted them as horses because it is more romantic than goats. Now my curiosity was really peaked. I had to know how these people got this phenomenon. Like most people, I surmised that they produced it surgically, but I needed to ask the goat to get the truth. That I did. Here is what he told me. *When I was a baby, I lived in the house with my people. They gave me a lot of baths and kept me very clean. I learned to do what the dogs did, walk on a leash, ride in the car and go outside to potty. When I was little, they put some pressure on my horn on both ends and messaged my forehead to make it soft and the horn just grew there. I am very proud of my horn and I know how to use it too.* This he demonstrated by pushing me with it.

He continued, *I love going to the fairs with them. We travel a lot and people dress up in long robes, tie things around their heads and walk me all around. I love to show off and everyone oohs and aahs about me and tells me how beautiful I am.*

"Where do you take him that fits that description," I asked the owners. "The Renaissance Fairs that are held all over the United States," he replied. "We live in the San Francisco area where we have an Angora goat farm and desperately want him to breed our nannies, but he won't have anything to do with them. Why?"

I turned back to the goat and asked him what was going on. *I don't know why he wants me to go out there with those things. They stink and I am not going to live in a barn no matter what they do. I belong in the house and the dogs and people are my companions, not those smelly things. I want to travel and be with people and show off for the crowd; that is where I am happy."* With that he turned and indicated he was ready to leave. I knew he was finished talking and sad to say, I had no advice to give them for this arrogant boy. They had taken him from his mother at such an early age that he was totally imprinted and bonded to people; (described in chapter 8) he was not going to act like a goat or a stud. No amount of hormones from him or from the females was going to change that attitude. To say the least, it was an interesting visit and a good lesson on how not to prejudge anyone who was asking for an appointment.

As a post script to that story, I saw that goat riding atop a float with a beautiful woman in the Ringling Brothers Circus. As he passed me, I asked him how he was doing and never have I talked to a happier animal that was having so much fun. He said his life was perfect. Sad to say, some idiot do gooder animal activists made so much fuss about how they were sure it was a fake, produced by surgery, and that this goat was suffering, that the circus finally just gave in to the pressure and got rid of him. No one would believe he had never been cut, but I did and still do. What a sad ending to a happy, happy animal living the life of fun and luxury, doing what he did best, wowing the crowds. He was one of the most delightful animals I ever met.

Of all the animals I have talked with, birds seem to be the biggest characters, and quite surprising, in the things they say and do, especially the African Gray and Cockatoo. I had a client visit one day with a Cockatoo. It was one of the friendliest birds I have ever met. It immediately jumped onto my arm and waited for me to scratch its neck. I had never done that before. It felt pretty weird, like handling a raw, but warm, chicken neck. After a few minutes I tried to stop, but every time I did, she looked me in the eye and waited for me to resume the massage. When I didn't, she took her claw, grabbed my finger and pushed it back towards her neck or under her wing. She was a cute character who never did give up trying to get scratched the whole time she was visiting.

The funniest and most intelligent ones I have met seem to be the African Gray. Judy Ebner in Southern California had one that was quite a character. It was plucking its feathers. I find this quite common when a bird is either bored, has thyroid problems, or is lacking in minerals in the diet. Too many people fail to feed their birds enough minerals, but feed a lot of sunflower seeds which are high in fat (even birds can develop cholesterol problems). Judy wanted me to chat with him to see if the bird would tell me why he was plucking his feathers or if he had an emotional problem, but she warned me, don't be surprised at what he says! When we entered the apartment, the bird was making quite an array of weird sounds and then broke into some pretty "fowl" language. Poor Judy was sooooo embarrassed. She told me that she had been trying to teach the bird to talk for years, but the only thing he would do was mimic the sounds in the room. As she opened the doors and cupboards, I recognized the sounds as what the bird was doing when we came in. She said that one day she became VERY angry and used some expletive words which the bird started to repeat verbatim and had been doing so ever since, but still wouldn't say any other word she attempted to teach it. He was just being a brat. That was purely mimicking, but the bird that belonged to another client, Mary, in Portland, Oregon, was a totally different story.

When I entered Mary's home through the living room, I was greeted by her Rottweiler, Ruby. She was a very sweet dog who escorted us into the kitchen area and waited for us to be seated. I looked up on the landing between the two bedrooms and noticed an African Gray parrot who was singing on pitch and in the proper sequence, *Old McDonald had a farm, e I e I o, and on this farm he had a pig, e I e I* at which he would stop singing and say *Ruby, you're a bad dog, Ruby be quiet, Ruby get in your crate* then he would resume singing again. We had a lot of fun laughing about how Mary's bird squealed on her as to how badly she was treating poor, sweet Ruby. I was a little surprised at the fact that the bird sang the song correctly and knew it was repeating what it heard as most birds do, but was not prepared for what was to come. As Mary went up the steps into the bedroom with some clothes she was putting away, the bird looked at her and said *I want an apple.* Mary ignored him as she went on about her business. You could tell the bird was not happy as he climbed down the side of the cage, looked into the bedroom and said *Weeeell?* After laughing a bit and more teasing of how mean she was to the bird not to give him an apple, she decided to give him some of her leftovers from her dinner. She put some newspaper on the counter, placed a plate of vegetables and meat on it and put the bird down next to it. He got the piece of meat, walked to the edge of the counter and proceeded, as is common for birds to do, to pull pieces off and throw them everywhere. Poor Ruby. She knew she wasn't allowed to reach up and take the meat away from the bird, so she patiently caught each piece the bird threw over the side. All went well until the bird decided to drop the meat on the counter and go back for something else from the plate. Just as he got to the plate, he turned his head so he could see what else was on the plate with one eye (birds see out of the sides of their heads and can see both sides at the same time), and with the other eye, he could see what was happening to his meat. All that was visible was Ruby's tongue reaching over the edge of the counter, looking for the meat. The bird bolted upright, yelled *Ooooohhhh shit!* and darted back to get his meat. Oh, where are the cameras when you need them! It was obvious this was more than a rote mimic, but thinking, while maybe not nice, appropriate response. This was the first time I realized that some birds do understand what they are saying.

Another bird I met in Minnesota, a beautiful Macaw, made me aware of another phenomenon animal's experience. I was there doing some lectures and consults when I was called to visit with a normally very friendly bird, who had some problems that were baffling the owners. As the owner entered the room where I was seated, he had the bird loose, sitting on his arm. When the Macaw spotted me, she immediately flew over and attacked me. After she was retrieved and held captive by the owner, I asked her why she had done this. She replied, *you tease me when I am in my cage. I hate you!* We were all stunned since I had never met the bird before! The mystery was solved when the owner's wife entered the room and remarked at how much I looked like their old housekeeper, same color hair, and same build and even had some of the same features. The housekeeper had indeed teased the poor bird and that is why they had fired her and now, because of the similarities, the bird thought I was her old tormentor.

This case of mistaken identity came through to me again when I visited with a horse I met during the same trip. An older man, wearing typical western clothes and large cowboy hat, had a horse he dearly loved. He wanted to know why his horse attacked him with teeth bared, every time he went into the corral. The horse told me *he beats me with a whip and I hate him. I want to kill him.* Everyone within hearing was floored because this man was one of the kindest and gentlest people in the stable. Knowing that animals can misinterpret what they see, I told him to take his hat off and try entering the corral again. Immediately, the horse trotted up to him looking for love and a treat. His demeanor had completely changed. We later learned that his trainer had been about the same size of this owner, always wore a large cowboy hat and had abused the horse with a whip. It seems strange, but something as simple as a hat can trigger such a different response.

I met a Dalmatian once who taught me a lesson. We were

standing outside the owner's home where I was trying to get the Dalmatian to tell me his problems. He didn't want to talk and kept evading my questions. Finally, he looked me straight in the eyes, walked over to me and lifted his leg on my pant leg, soaking it along with my shoe. I wasn't expecting it, so didn't get out of the way quickly enough. When I asked him why he did that to me, he said, *I don't want to tell you about it. It was traumatic so I'm telling you to leave me alone.* Believe me, I got the message loud and clear. Unfortunately, we still had to get him to talk about the incident because it was causing him some big problems and we needed to resolve them.

Sometimes it isn't always something that happens to the animal, but something they see that causes a problem. This came to my attention when I was called to the Alameda Race Track in Southern California. The trainer was having a terrible time handling one of the horses who had always been cooperative and gentle and easy to train up to this point. When I asked him what was wrong, he said *"I saw them taking my friend away. They pulled him out of his stall with a rope and dragged him up onto a truck. He couldn't move. I'm afraid they are going to do that to me, too."* The trainer did admit that they had had a horse that they had found dead in the stall the day before, just before this horse had acted up. He didn't know what had happened to him because they hadn't been able to find any marks or anything on the horse to indicate the cause of death. They and the vet had been totally baffled and yes, they had pulled the horse from the stall and hauled him up onto a truck just as this horse had related. He asked me to see if this horse knew what had happened to his friend during the night this all took place, so I did. He replied, *my friend told me he felt a sting on the neck and it hurt really badly, and then he couldn't stand up or breathe. I'm so afraid that is going to happen to me too that I am nervous and want to get away from here.* When we investigated, the only thing we could find in the stall was a couple of black widow spiders and a couple of brown recluse spiders. It seemed that the mystery may have been solved, for even when they performed a necropsy, they could find nothing else that could have caused his death, so we turned our attention back to the horse with the problem. After talking to him in positive statements, moving him to a different stall in a different shed row, he finally calmed down.

I had worked with this trainer before, so since I was already there, he asked me to chat with his pony horse (the trainer rides a pony horse and leads the race horse with a lead rope to and from the track). When I talked to the horse, it just felt weird, almost surreal. I knew something was wrong when everything the horse told me, according to his rider, was not true. Finally, I asked him what was wrong because the last time we had chatted, everything I had gotten was right on. The horse said, *I don't want to talk to you today so I'm just telling you anything to get rid of you.* Needless to say, the conversation ended.

Another cute one I had, was with a dog that belonged to a teenager I knew, named Michelle Ives. I was giving a lecture where her parents and many of their friends were present. At my lectures, I usually allow the owners to bring a few pets to chat with as a demonstration of how animals talk. When Michelle's dog came to the front, he was really happy. I asked him why, and he said; *I love going with my owner. We had a lot of fun coming here tonight. On the way, this car pulled up with "its" pretty lights blinking at us. We stopped and had fun visiting with the man who came over to our car. It was exciting and my owner was excited, too.* At that, her dad stood up and asked her if she'd been stopped by a cop and did she get a ticket? With a very sheepish look on her face, she admitted she did but hadn't intended to tell him. I guess you need to be careful what you do when your pet is present or they may squeal on you. This brings up a funny point. It seems that men are more conscious than women of this possibility. Men often tell me they don't want me to talk to their animals because they are afraid they will tell me what goes on in their bedrooms since the dog sleeps in there, too. Don't worry gentlemen, I don't ask and believe me, I don't want to know either. I have never had one animal volunteer that information and quite frankly, they aren't that interested either.

One of the cutest animals I ever observed was during a visit at my friend's house, Jackie and Marvin Happle. They had constructed their home to meet federal and state laws that enabled them to have exotic pets, such as Bobcats and Ocelots. Brandy, an ear-old Bobcat who lived in the home with them, adored Marvin, but never allowed anyone else to handle him. One day, several of us were sitting around Marvin's living room chatting. Brandy sat quietly, still as a statue, observing the situation and each individual from the security of the fireplace mantel. All of a sudden, Brandy stood up, stealthily leaped onto the television, walked across it, made his way to the back of the couch, where several of us were seated, walked behind us until he reached Ralph (who we later learned was an avid hunter), looked him in the eyes and smacked him, three times, on the face. Thankfully, he was declawed. He then flipped his stub of a tail, turned, and made his way back to his former perch on the fireplace mantel. We were absolutely dumbfounded, for Brandy had never done anything like that before. He wouldn't even come close to a stranger, much less smack him on the face! We knew something had happened to cause it. When questioned, Ralph finally confessed that he had been thinking of how nice Brandy would look as a stuffed animal sitting on his mantel at home among all the other animals he had killed and stuffed that were now sitting on the mantel or hanging on the wall as trophies. It was sure clear that Brandy had gotten the picture and had let Ralph know in no uncertain terms that he didn't like the idea. We all got a good laugh out of that, and I think Ralph got a lesson in how the animals he killed felt about what he had done.

One day I was attending a conference in Kentucky, for Veterinary acupuncturists. I was well known by this particular group as I had been one of their speakers a couple of times, demonstrating my ability to communicate with animals. Dr. H. L. Mitchell from Oklahoma, who had attended my lectures and demonstrations, approached me with an experience he had had with one of his clients. A lady from Missouri had brought her horse to him to be treated for a lameness problem. Since the treatment would take several days, she had left the horse at his clinic. A couple of days later, he said she had called him to tell him two things that sort of blew him away. She said that she had an animal communicator talk to her horse to find out how he was doing at Dr. Mitchell's clinic and if he was responding to the treatments. The horse had told the communicator that he was very tired and very hungry. It was so noisy he couldn't sleep at night and the "Little People" came into his stall and ate his food. She wanted to know what was going on and who was eating his food. Dr. Mitchell said he told her that there was a feed lot next to him and they had just brought in a new load of cattle that were restless, moving around all night and bellowing, but the "little people?" That was a puzzle. He then asked her who the animal communicator was. He said when he learned it was me, he had observed my abilities as quite accurate, and so he decided he'd better check it out. As a follow-up to the call, that night after dark, he slipped quietly down to the barn to check on who these "little people" were. When he flipped on the light, monkeys scattered everywhere. He couldn't believe his eyes for the "little people" were actually monkeys hiding in his barn in the rafters by day and feasting on the horse's food by night. The horse was right. Upon investigation, he found out that the exotic animal farm next to his clinic had had a breakout. The monkeys had gotten out of their compound and disappeared, but the owner didn't know where they were. The mystery was solved. They were retrieved by the owner, and all ended well. "I just had to tell you the story; I thought you'd get a kick out of it."

One of the joys of having two way conversations with animals has been knowing what my own animals are trying to tell me. For a couple of years, I had a dog and cat boarding kennel in El Monte, California. One day I was way up in the front of the house, as far as one can get from the kennels, which made it impossible for me to hear anything that was going on out back. Mr. Spunks, my French Briard, tore through the house looking for me. Finally he found me in the bedroom, stopped dead in his tracks and stared at me. Immediately I heard him say; *hurry, Annie is in the trouble and needs your help* Since I have learned to "listen" to what my animals tell me, I headed for the back yard as fast as I could, with Mr. Spunks hurrying ahead of me. Sure enough, a Great Dane that we were boarding had been in the grooming shop when another boarder came in through the gate. The Dane's owners had failed to tell us he knew how to open sliding glass doors and loved to attack other dogs. When the Dane saw the new dog coming in, he pushed the door open, tore down the drive and attacked the incoming boarder. Annie was by herself trying to break up the fight between the Great Dane and the Australian Shepherd. Had I not been there to intervene, no telling how badly it may have ended, but fortunately because of the watchfulness and caring of our "watchdog friend" Mr. Spunks, I was able to keep everyone from getting seriously hurt.

During the time I lived at the kennel in El Monte, I traveled often. One night Annie came to the airport to pick me up. Tipster, one of my German Shepherds was sitting sheepishly in the back seat. Curious, I asked him what was wrong. He told me; *the big blond dog bit my ear and I'm upset.* Big blond dog? I didn't have a big blond dog! "OK" I replied, "what big blond dog?" With that he turned to Anne and glared at her. *"Her"* In shock I turned to Anne, who at that time was a blond, for an explanation.

"Yes, I'm the big blond dog. I brought a rescue puppy into the kennel and he came up behind me, grabbed the puppy out of my arms and took off with it. I chased him down and for discipline, bit his ear, telling him if he ever did that again, I wouldn't just bite his ear with a pinch, but I'd chew it off." We sure had a good laugh over Tipster calling her a big blond dog, but I think he did learn his lesson because he never tried anything like that again.

After I moved to Oregon and got married, my husband Paul built separate runs for the little dogs. This is a safety measure as we live in the country where there are many hawks and Coyotes and 20 acres of tall grass in which they can get lost. One day while we were gone, Anne was cleaning the front yard and didn't realize two of the boys were missing. Yelky, Paul's favorite little Chihuahua who had been kenneled with two of the males, was spotted outside in the field. By this point in time, Anne had recaptured her ability to communicate with the animals, so she knew something was wrong. Yelky said, *the dogs are loose, the dogs are loose* at which she turned and headed for the open field. About the time Anne got to the tall grass, here came Yelky nipping at the heels of the two runaways, chasing them back home. Little did any of us realize that there was a tiny hole in the new fence? Those little escape artists had found it, thinking they were going on an adventure until little miss tattle tale, squealed on them.

CHAPTER 12

MOLLY AND THE MAILMAN

Through PART ONE of this book, I hope you have come to understand how wonderful all animals are and how much more you can share with them as you learn to "speak their language." I believe that it will become even more understandable if you also read the life stories of some of the animals from my second book, *Stories the Animals Tell Me.*

Throughout my career I have often been asked, "What is the most interesting animal you have ever communicated with?" Since they are all exciting and different to me, I cannot pick out just one, but am including a few to help you understand more clearly how they "view" their lives and feel about their relationships. Some of what they have communicated to me had to be written as an interpretation because there are no words to describe what I am experiencing, but I have kept to the truth of the idea as accurately as possible. I have also tried to give you a variety of animals so you can "understand" how they communicate, no matter what species it is. It is not the language they use, but how they relate to their environment and situations that make them different. I trust you will enjoy reading about them as much as I enjoyed meeting and chatting with each one.

I glanced at my watch. There were only twenty minutes left to go before I'd have to bring the class to a close and leave for the airport.

"I'm not sure I understand you," the elderly man to my right said. "When you communicate non-verbally, do you receive impressions of the conditions around the animal?"

"I'm not sure I understand your question," I replied. "What do you mean by impressions and conditions?"

"Well, when you were communicating with the Samoyed that the blonde woman brought with her today, for instance." He indicated the large, fluffy white dog that the class had just been practicing non-verbal communication on. "You said she enjoyed playing in the snow when her owner took her to the mountains to the dog sled races. How did you know she was in snow? Did you receive an impression of something white and cold?"

"There seems to have been a misunderstanding here," I said. "Perhaps if you practice a bit more it will become clear to you. To answer your questions, however, I saw snow."

"But how does an animal describe snow?" He persisted.

"An animal doesn't *describe* anything. Description is a function of vocabulary and animals don't have a vocabulary. What I *see* when I'm communicating non-verbally is what the animal *sees*. I also feel the emotions the animal feels; smell the smells and so forth. There are no words involved. When I want to share my perceptions of an animal's experience with another human, I have to use words because that is the major form of human communication."

He looked at me, perplexed.

"OK. Let's examine the word *snow*. What does it mean? It's merely a term we have designated to describe something that falls from the sky in certain climates at certain times of the year. It may be wet or dry – cold or white, and it can turn into ice under the proper conditions. We can ski on it, sled on it, build statues from it, or form it into balls and throw it at each other. The experience of snow has nothing to do with the word we use to identify it. We could just as easily call it *blurp,* if we agreed to do so, but the image called to mind would remain the same.

"Images are at the heart of the matter. If I say *snow* to you, a certain image comes to mind, composed of the properties I just listed. Stay with the image. That's how the animal is communicating, at the image or picture level of consciousness.

"Let's try going over the experience in the dog's life again. Look at her and try to see her in your mind's eye. Visualize her running through a snowdrift with her mistress. When you "*connect*" with her mentally, she will correct whatever discrepancies exist in your picture by returning to you a picture of what she saw. As you go on with this, you may also share the experience of her other four senses."

I watched the man with particular attention. He had made an earlier reference to a much-loved cat who was his constant companion. I assumed he was here to become better attuned to his pet.

I waited, hoping he could put aside his preoccupation with words long enough to do so. His brows knitted with effort and his eyes became smaller. Suddenly his face lit up. His features relaxed, his eyes glowed, and an expression came over his face that transformed his countenance in a way that I can only describe as beautific.

"I did it!" he cried. "I pictured the dog as you said to and suddenly the picture changed. She wasn't going through a drift, she was rolling in the snow, and there was a little blonde girl wearing a red cap and mittens standing next to her."

"That's my daughter," the Samoyed's owner said.

"And there's a group of children about to toboggan down a hill and a building - maybe a lodge, in the background...." His voice went on, enthusiastically describing to the minutest detail the image he'd received from the dog.

He stopped speaking and beamed at me. "Did I do it right?" he asked.

"You sure did," I replied. "Tell me, do you think the dog described all of that to you in words?"

"No!" he laughed. "She showed me!"

I glanced at my watch again. It was obvious there would not be time now to work with the one remaining animal, a stately Irish Setter whose kind and intelligent face had drawn me to her as soon as she entered the room.

"We had one more animal to work with," I said. "But I'm afraid I can't stay. I have to be at the airport in half an hour."

I looked at my class list to see who owned the setter. "Mrs. Mayer," I began.

"Estelle," she corrected in a soft, Appalachian drawl. I looked up and saw a pretty, auburn-haired woman with green eyes. She and her pet had their coloring in common. I wondered if that was part of their initial attraction for each other.

"Estelle, I wonder, could you possibly drive me to the airport? I'm unusually impressed by your dog's manner. Perhaps I could interview her after I check in for my flight."

"Of course," she said. "Molly can stay here with you for a minute while I bring my car around."

I said goodbye to the rest of the class and expressed my hope of hearing good progress reports from all of them soon. Then Molly and I went outside.

On the ride out of Norfolk, Molly sat between us. I asked Estelle how she'd acquired the dog.

"We got Molly almost by chance three years ago. She was sixteen and had been with a couple who lived near us since she was two. When they got divorced and moved away, the man took her for a while. Then he brought her back to her old neighborhood and left her there. Her first family had given her very good training, but I don't think she got much affection from them."

I looked at the lovely animal. She had about her an air of serenity one doesn't often find in setters.

"She wasn't an indoor dog when she came to us, "Estelle said, "and at first, she had difficulty letting us know when she needed to go outside. I don't think she quite knew how to go about it. Now she comes over to one of us and then walks to the door."

We pulled into the airport parking lot.

"I'll let you off at the entrance and we'll be in as soon as I park the car, "Estelle said.

I had just finished checking my luggage when they met me in the lobby. The three of us sat down near the ticket counter so that I could hear when my flight was called.

I proceeded to ask Molly about her life by visualizing a small frame house with a picket-fenced yard. I put Molly into the picture, just outside the front door.

A few seconds later, back came a corrected picture. I saw a large, red, two-story brick colonial house surrounded by pines and maple trees. Across the road, on the shore of a small lake, was a church. Two children, a boy about twelve with blond hair and brown eyes, and a brown-haired girl, evidently his sister, about fourteen, were walking from the church property to the front steps of the house. Molly was sitting there waiting for them.

Molly was telling me her story, which I will relate in my own words. For a nineteen – year - old dog, she had a remarkably clear mind.

I'm very content now. For most of my life I didn't know how nice it could be to have a human family.

I was taken away from my mother by a young man and woman. It was painful for me at first. I missed the warm milky smell of my mother's body and the comfort of sleeping with my brothers and sisters.

The woman fed me twice a day and taught me to walk on a leash by her side. She and the man were kind and gentle with me, but they rarely petted me. They were away from home most of the time.

We lived in a small place and I only went outside for short walks, always with the woman. Sometimes she took me to a nearby park and let me run. I lived for those moments when I could stretch my muscles and move freely. I could stop and sniff the bushes to learn which of the other dogs living nearby had been there recently. I could catch bugs in the grass and chase birds. Being in the park was much more fun than being at home.

I lived with them for two winters. Then one day the woman came home and started to cry when she looked at me. I sensed that they were going to move and wouldn't be able to take me with them, and they were going to find another family for me.

A short while later, another man and woman took me to their house. They made a bed for me in the garage, where I had to stay all the time. The garage floor felt cold and damp and very hard. I tried to get into the house at night a couple of times, but they caught me and put me back outside. I wanted to lie on a warm rug, but I never made it past the kitchen.

The garage smelled terrible, too. The man left his motorcycle next to my bed and it leaked gasoline onto the floor near me. Sometimes he started it up before taking it out to the driveway and the fumes made my eyes water.

I came to hate that garage. I still hate being confined and dark places drive me to frenzy.

Spring came. The warm weather brought with it a feeling I'd had before. I wanted to roam, to be with another dog. My body was never quite at rest. Even when I slept, I felt restless.

The man started leaving the garage door open, which gave me a bit more freedom. I knew I was supposed to stay near the house, but the urge to roam was strong. One day my urges got the best of me, though I was afraid my family would punish me. I waited until they had gone out and then set off myself.

I met another dog almost immediately. He was large and black with a tan muzzle and rough, curly hair. He seemed to like me very much. We played together for awhile, sniffing each other's scents and chewing each other's noses. He began to lick me lovingly. His musky smell made me giddy. I returned his caresses. Soon we mated. I wanted him to stay with me, but he left, so I wandered home alone.

That summer I was miserable. I had ten puppies, but I didn't have enough milk to feed all of them, and two died. I needed more food than usual because of the babies, but my family gave me only as much as I had gotten before. I felt hungry all the time.

I also felt tired. The puppies were never quiet. I'd just get through feeding or washing them and have to start all over again. There were so many that I never got any rest.

One by one, they were taken away by people who came to the garage. I was glad to see them go. I would have liked to keep one or two for company, but not all of them.

My strength returned slowly. I spent most of the late summer sleeping in the front yard. My people took me to the veterinarian's for a few days and when I came home they let me go outside instead of keeping me in the garage.

I was lying in the yard one cool fall morning when something happened that changed my life completely. I was watching the house next door when the mailman came walking down the street. I had seen mailmen before, but this one was different. He was whistling cheerfully. When he reached my house he stopped and spoke gently to me.

I was surprised. Mailmen didn't usually bother much with me. He knelt and scratched my ears. I turned my head sideways and smelled his arm. He smelled good to me. I wagged my tail furiously and licked his hands to tell him I liked him. He continued to stroke my head for a few minutes before going on his way.

When he came by the next day, he gave me a dog biscuit. Surprised and pleased, I ate it greedily. Then we visited awhile. This time I followed him as he walked away, but he told me to go back home.

I felt sad that my new friend didn't want to be with me as much as I wanted to be with him.

I began looking forward to his visits. I could see him in my mind's eye long before he rounded the corner near my house, so I was always on hand to greet him.

Some days another man came instead. I always knew when this was going to happen, because when I searched for my friend in my mind's eye, someone else's face would appear. On those days I didn't bother to be near the front door when the mail arrived.

Though my family didn't pay much attention to me, they noticed my friendship with the mailman. Even they could see that he meant a great deal to me. They wondered how I could tell when he would deliver mail and when someone else would.

One day, when my new friend made me stay behind in my yard, I sat down and whined. He turned and looked at me, and then he came back and rang our doorbell.

When the woman answered the door, I learned that the mailman's name was Bill Nelson. (Naming is a human practice; animals do not identify their human or animal friends by name. In some of these stories, however, I have added names for ease of reading.) He asked if it was all right for me to walk with him as he delivered the mail. They said it was. I could hardly believe my good luck!

From that day on, for ten winters, I went with Bill every single day he worked and I loved it. In the spring, the air smelled of flowers. In the summer, the pavement was sometimes so hot that it hurt my feet. In the fall, the red and gold leaves told me cold weather was coming. Sometimes in winter we were so cold that we shivered. Through it all, my friend and I delivered the mail together.

I met him at the start of his route each morning. He wanted me to wait on the sidewalk while he took mail to the different houses, so I did. When the sun was high, we shared the food he brought with him. Sometimes we had meat and cheese sandwiches for our lunch; other times, there were chunks of cold meat and potatoes. Often Bill brought us cookies for dessert.

Once in a while we ran into a mean dog who would threaten to bite Bill. I'd stand between him and the dog and growl, baring my teeth. The dog always knew he'd have to deal with me if he hurt Bill. I was an important part of Bill's work and I knew it.

We became well known in our town. People along our route came to their windows just to see us. I remember one very old woman who couldn't walk well enough to come out to the sidewalk. Every day she met Bill at the door to give him a dog biscuit for me.

Bill put a blanket over the seat of his truck. When it rained, we rode more than we walked. At the end of the day we got in the truck and Bill drove me back to my house. He always petted me before he left.

I felt more love from that man than from all the other people in my life put together. I felt needed and I had a friend who understood my needs.

His love meant more and more to me as time went on. My family began to be away from home more often and when they were home, they didn't pay attention to me. Some nights the only dinner I had was what I could forage from garbage cans in the neighborhood. Sometimes their voices were raised in anger.

Eventually, my family moved out of the house and the man took me to live with him in another small place. The woman went away.

I was miserable. For days I whimpered nearly all the time. Not only had I lost the company of my friend, I couldn't even go outside. I was alone most of the time and I didn't even know anyone who lived nearby; where I used to live, I had known everyone.

The man began yelling at me when I whimpered. One night I was whimpering softly in the living room. Suddenly he jumped out of his chair and told me to come with him. I was scared, because I could see he was very angry. He drove me back to our old house and put me out of the car.

I was thrilled to be back where I belonged! Now I could see Bill. Life seemed good again.

I didn't have a home to go to at night, so I took to sleeping wherever I could and I learned to rummage through garbage cans without knocking them over. The night after the garbage men came, I always went hungry.

Bill and I resumed our rounds. He was so happy to see me again that he whistled all the time. Except for the lack of regular meals, I was happy.

A family who lived down the street from my old house noticed that I was back and began to put food out for me. They had two children and since I hadn't been around children before, I was wary of them. They petted me often though, and I began to relax around them. We grew fond of each other. One night the boy coaxed me with food into the kitchen, where he had made a bed for me. Having lived in a garage for so long, it was hard for me to go inside.

I felt uneasy sleeping inside for the first few nights. It was warmer and much more comfortable than sleeping outside, but it was strange to me. The boy and his sister were kind to me, however, and I gradually came to accept them and their parents as my family.

Like everyone in the neighborhood, they knew about Bill and me. He delivered their mail, too. We continued making our rounds as usual and at night he brought me back to my new family. My life was complete.

Then a part of it ended abruptly. One day I sensed that Bill was unhappy. There were tears in his eyes as he pulled into my driveway after the day's work. He took my face in his hands and laid his cheek against mine. He spoke to me, sadly but with encouragement and I understood that he had to move away. I knew that I would see him again, but not often.

Not see him everyday? Not help him deliver the mail anymore? The meaning of our separation sank in slowly. What would we do without each other? My heart ached.

Bill held me close to him for a long while before he left that day. I've never felt such bittersweet love. His leaving was very painful, but I was grateful for the time and love we'd shared.

I felt lost and alone during the days that followed. I ate just enough to stay alive. Every day at mail time I thought of Bill, and saw him in my mind's eye walking down a strange street, alone.

The children did their best to console me. Nearly every day we went to a nearby field and played together. Their concern made me feel better and they became very important to me.

A river runs near our playfield. Often when the children were in school, I went wading in the river. One day the water dragged me from the shore. I panicked but fought hard against the pull until I got back on land. I didn't go in the river again.

I made friends with a man who worked in a large garden nearby. I kept him company and helped him dig in the flowerbeds. He liked me and I liked him, though I didn't feel about him the way I had about Bill. His clothes smelled interesting; I could smell other animals on them.

I made some dog friends as well. One soon went everywhere with me. We spent a lot of time hunting rabbits and chasing squirrels. One night as he was crossing the street behind me I heard a screeching sound and turned to see a car hit my friend. He didn't move afterward; I knew he would never move again. I missed him for a long time.

I had plenty to eat at home, so food was no problem, but I still checked garbage cans every so often. I enjoyed pawing through the trash and finding an empty can with a few bits of fish sticking to its sides, or perhaps an eggshell or two.

The boy played more with his friends than with me. After awhile the girl became my special person. She took me to her school several times. I enjoyed that because all her friends made a big fuss over me. We stood on a stage while she and the other children talked to each other. Everyone seemed to have a good time. The last time I stood on stage with the girl it was much different. All the children were nervous and they were wearing strange clothes. I was very nervous myself. When I looked out across the stage, I saw a lot of people sitting in chairs, watching us! When the children stopped speaking, the people in the chairs clapped their hands loudly.

I still see Bill once in a while, but we haven't delivered mail together in a long time. He comes to my house to visit me as I knew he would. I still miss him, but the girl is my special person now.

Next winter will be my twentieth. My joints are getting a little stiff. It takes me a little longer to get up and around in the mornings than when I was younger. People call me a wise old girl. I've seen many people come and go around me.

I'm very glad to have a loving family now, but some things are still hard for me. I like being inside, but I can't bring myself to go in unless I'm invited. I was made to stay outside for such a long time.

I have no trouble with being petted and hugged though. I love it.

As Molly stopped "talking," my flight was called. Passengers began lining up at the boarding gate. Regretfully, I rose to go.

The three of us said our goodbyes. I boarded the plane and the last thing I saw before it lifted off was Molly and Estelle, their red hair standing out in the crowd, waving me on my way.

CHAPTER 13

BIRD IN A YELLOW HAT

I had been looking forward to seeing my old friend and mentor, Dr. Marvin Cain. Marvin encouraged me in my work with animals during the first years and taught me much about practical veterinary work. I phoned him as soon as I arrived in Cincinnati, Ohio, on the last leg of my tour through the Midwest. When he answered, his voice echoed my own pleasure.

"I was hoping you'd be out this way soon," he said warmly. "Can you come by my office later today? I have a surprise for you."

"For me? What is it?"

"Oh, no you don't, Bea." He laughed. "I'm not saying another word about it until I see you. Will you be here this afternoon?"

"Marvin, I could hardly do otherwise now. I'll be there about two o'clock."

I checked into my hotel and called several people who had written to me requesting consultations. I spoke with a newspaper reporter who wanted an interview, unpacked my clothes, and had lunch. I called home to check on the latest litter of pups, yet all the while my thoughts kept returning to Marvin and his surprise.

When I walked into his office at 1:30, he was in an examining room with a patient. A black – and - tan dachshund puppy was having one of his front legs stitched as a result of an unfortunate encounter with a marauding tomcat. His owner, a worried-looking boy of about ten, stood by.

The poor animal was terrified by the proceedings. Two new and unpleasant experiences in one day were proving to be more stress than this young soul could handle.

The pup was crying piteously. I went to the examining table to reassure him. I told him I knew this was hard, but that he must lie still and let the doctor finish his work. My words appeared to comfort the pup because he quieted as Marvin finished his stitches.

I watched, amazed again at the deftness with which his large hands manipulated needle and thread. He completed the sutures and turned to the puppy's young master.

"Keep him quiet, now, Billy," he said. "Be sure he doesn't get the leg dirty and by all means, be sure he stays away from that tomcat!"

Boy and dog departed and Marvin turned his attention to me.

"Couldn't wait, could you?" he grinned, his brown eyes crinkling at the corners.

"Well," I said a bit defensively, "All my business was taken care of sooner than I expected and …."

"Never mind," he interrupted, "She's here early, too."

"Bea, I met a woman recently who has an absolutely fantastic rapport with animals, especially birds. She keeps a screech owl she rescued from the doubtful ministrations of two little girls who found him lying in their back yard following the tornado we had here last summer. I swear she reads his mind. The two of them are so well attuned they seem to share the same brain. Here they are now."

As he opened the door, I turned, half expecting to find a wrinkled crone with black gypsy eyes, wearing a garish scarf over her long greasy hair and holding an enormous bird in one hand as the other hand reached toward me, palm up, to be crossed with silver. What I saw instead was a slender, young woman in her 30's with a pleasant smile, dark blue eyes and an upturned nose. A tiny owl, no more than six inches high, was perched on her shoulder.

"I didn't know screech owls were so small," I said. The diminutive fowl turned to look at me. He was wearing the tiniest Mexican hat I'd ever seen, a miniature version of the ones people dance on at fiestas. Its pale yellow straw and bright cerise cockade set off the owl's gray and white tweed feathers. The contrast in colors was pleasing, but the overall effect was one of droll authority. He looked like a feathered version of a bandito, Hollywood B movie style.

His bright chartreuse eyes appraised me unblinkingly. His somber expression gave him an almost judicial air. I hoped I was going to measure up to whatever standard he seemed to be using to judge me.

Apparently I did, for when the woman lifted him off her shoulder, he flew immediately to mine where he continued his scrutiny at close range.

"His name is Sylvester," Marvin informed me.

"It fits," I said. "A natty name for a natty dresser. Who's your tailor, Sylvester?"

But Sylvester had turned his attentions elsewhere. He had caught sight of himself in a mirror behind my shoulder and was ostentatiously admiring his reflection. He began to dance on my shoulder, lifting his miniature feet in time to a tune only he could hear. He cocked his head to one side, then to the other, and became still again. Apparently the music had stopped.

I knew this bird had an interesting story to tell. His self-assured demeanor contrasted sharply with his history as Marvin had briefly outlined it. The majority of animals who undergo severe traumas at such an early age have about their bearing something which suggests their former pain, hesitancy, a poised-to-flee posture, a reluctance to subject themselves to new experiences or strange people.

Not Sylvester. Whatever methods the woman had employed in nurturing and training an injured wild baby bird, she had produced an emotionally healthy creature. I smiled at her, thinking how fortunate she and her small friend were to have found each other.

Curious to learn more about both of them from the bird himself, I asked Sylvester to tell me about his feelings during the tornado.

I began by picturing in my mind's eye a dark forest, carpeted by oak leaves wet with dew. Into that picture I put a tall tree, into the tree a nest, and into the nest a fledgling owl. The non –verbal question was "What happened to you here?"

The non-verbal answer came quickly as the picture began to change. I saw the tree bending almost double, leaves and branches blowing off wildly and heard the ominous rumble of a tornado-force wind. Sylvester was communicating with me.

The bad wind came up suddenly and I was afraid. My mother had left our nest to get food for my brother and me. She had been gone a very long time. I wanted her body between me and that awful howling sound. I pushed closer to my brother and buried my head in his feathers.

Our tree began to shake wildly. Branches creaked and groaned. Leaves and small limbs blew past us, tearing bits of straw from our nest.

158

I tried to cry out to my mother, but the fierce wind blew the sound back into my throat. Suddenly we were being thrown through the air. Rain poured on us and I couldn't see anymore. My head hurt terribly, then everything went black and I lost consciousness.

When the blackness lifted, the rain had stopped. The sun was shining again, but the light made my eyes hurt. I rolled to my side and looked for my brother. I saw him lying nearby and called weakly to him, but he didn't answer me. I pulled my aching body over to him. I snuggled up against him to let him know I was there, but he didn't move. His body was stiff like a stick.

I called out for my mother again. I wanted her to come and take me back to the nest. She didn't answer me.

I knew I needed to find shelter, even though the wind had stopped. I dragged myself to my feet, but was too weak to stand. As I fell, the blackness came again.

The next thing I knew I was being lifted once more, but this time it wasn't the wind. Something closed around my body and I fell into a large and very strange kind of nest. There was something thick and soft at the bottom, but the sides were smooth and straight. It was very different from the nest I had known before. It moved for awhile and then stopped suddenly.

I peeked upward. Four eyes in two small faces blinked back at me.

The faces had no feathers and looked like nothing I'd ever seen before. I was scared.

My mother had told me about creatures – humans - she'd encountered when she was hunting. These faces seemed to belong to them. My heart began to beat wildly. Maybe they would eat me the way I had eaten the bugs and critters my mother had brought to our nest. They disappeared.

They returned soon with something warm and wiggly - a worm, I think that they stuffed down my throat. It seemed I wasn't to be eaten, after all; the children were trying to help me. My mother used to feed me worms and bugs, but she always chewed them first. They were much softer than these.

My new friends even tried to help me swallow. I was still afraid of them, but I soon began to relax a little. Then I heard a strange voice call and I was alone again.

I looked around and saw that my new nest had been taken into a house. Darkness was falling in a way I didn't understand. Glimmers of light still shone in through the windows and though I could see leaves moving on the trees outside, the wind somehow didn't reach me.

I had never felt so alone. I called for my mother again. Soon I heard voices and the children returned. They had brought more food for me. When they picked me up and petted me I held very still; I knew they meant well, but I was still nervous.

They put me back into my new nest and went away. Sleeping by myself for the first time in my life, I longed for the comfort of my mother and my brother snuggling close to me.

Morning came and the children brought more food for me. I was starting to feel a little sick to my stomach; I felt too full-almost stuffed. The worms just seemed to lie there.

The children left me alone again. I was very lonely until dark, when they returned. I had lost enough of my fear of them to enjoy their company.

Another night came and went. I awoke as something covered my nest and shut out the light. The nest began to move, and I was frightened all over again. I slipped and slid and started to cry.

Suddenly the movement stopped. Whatever had covered my nest moved away? I looked up into a different looking human face that had something all over it which I later learned was hair. The children were there too, and one of them lifted me up and handed me to the man. He was so much bigger than me! I was terrified that he was going to hurt me. Instead, he spoke softly to me. I relaxed a little. He began to touch me all over my body. He picked up my wings and looked under them and ruffled my feathers. I stared at him as his mouth opened revealing large teeth. He turned and spoke briefly to the children, who then went away.

I looked around my new surroundings. Other animals were there too, lined up in rows of cages. The smell in one of the nests sent chills up my spine. I shivered and wanted to get away from it.

The man put me into one of the cages and made a nest out of something soft for me to hide in. I hunched down under it and felt better. Just as I was going to sleep, I felt myself being moved again. I looked up and the man was carrying my cage. I felt the wind blowing through my feathers and knew we were outside.

Soon we went inside again, somewhere else. A woman was waiting for us. She took the cage from the man and opened it, looking at me for awhile. Her eyes were dark blue and they blinked often. They shone with a warmth and gentleness that let me know I could trust her. I could feel her concern for me and I relaxed. She picked me up and petted me. I lost all fear of her.

When she put me down again it was in a large cage. I could see out of it on all sides. I saw other birds nearby. Some were in cages like mine, but some were not. It felt good being near other birds again. When I began to talk with them, I learned that the woman took care of them and that this was their home.

Later the woman brought me some food that tasted like what my mother used to feed me. I ate greedily and went to sleep feeling better than I had in a long while.

I stayed in that cage, in my new home, for a long time. At first, I didn't mind being confined, there were so many fascinating things to look at. I had never seen a chair, or a newspaper, or a lamp before.

Some of the other birds followed the woman as she moved through the house. They flew above her, landing on door lintels, then swooping down to follow her into the other rooms. It looked like fun to fly in a place with so many perches.

I wanted to follow the woman too. I called to her one day to tell her and she answered me. I thought that was fun, so I called her again. She answered again, and soon we were calling to each other every time she was near me.

Then one day she opened the door to my cage. I hopped out at once and stretched my wings. At last I had a chance to fly! I'd never tried it before, so I was wildly excited, and a little apprehensive.

The woman watched me closely. I sensed she was worried that I might fall and hurt myself. I wanted to show her how brave I was, so I stood very tall and flapped my wings several times before taking off.

I tried to swoop and glide as I had seen other birds do, but I landed on my bottom on the floor. I picked myself up and tried again, and this time my wings worked better. I flew around the room several times before landing on the mantel. The woman laughed and clapped her hands. I was terribly proud of myself. Now I could follow her with the others!

I discovered all kinds of things after that. A room where the woman kept our food, and a room where she ate her own food, newspapers that rustled and crackled when I landed on them, hanging plants I could perch on and hide behind, pictures to roost on, tables to walk across when I didn't feel like flying, curtains to climb, mail to rummage around in; and those wonderful keys!

Keys are my favorite things. I can carry them easily in my beak. They're bright, shiny, pretty to look at, and make nice sounds when I push then around. Best of all, I can tease the woman with them. They are pretty important to her, too. She takes them with her whenever she leaves the house. If I don't want her to go, I hide her keys so she has to stay until she finds them again, talking to herself as she searches. Sometimes when she wants to sleep and I want to play, I get her keys, fly over her, and drop them on her in bed. I do love keys!

I love the woman, too. We have our differences, though. There's an air - conditioner in a window in the living room where I love to perch. It's big enough to walk around on and I can see all the way into the kitchen from there. But when the woman turns it on it vibrates and blows cold air across the room. I've told her how much I hate this, but she won't leave it alone.

One day the woman brought a new bird into the house, a large one with a red comb on its head. I was sitting on the mantel and I flew down to introduce myself. I wanted to help show the new bird around. When I walked up to it, the stupid thing went wild! It jumped all over me, squawking and carrying on as it had no sense at all. I barely got away with all my feathers intact!

One day the woman put me outside. She said I should have a chance to live with my own kind. I didn't want to; I wanted to stay with her. I flew around the house and pecked at the windows until she let me back inside.

I enjoy going out with her, too. I like riding on her shoulder. Riding in her car is fun because I can look out the windows at trees and people, or at myself in the mirror. When we're out together, people always stop and look at us, especially when I'm wearing my hat. I love all the attention we get.

Every day the woman combs my feathers when she brushes her hair. She cleans my beak after she brushes her teeth. We do a lot of things together.

I'm very content with my life. I have plenty of food and a cozy place to sleep. I also have the friendship of the woman. She brings new birds home every so often and I have a chance to make new friends. Many of them are sick when they arrive here. The woman cares for them and sees to it that they're well when they leave. I don't know what they would do without her. I don't know what I would do either.

I smiled at Sylvester and his owner as the bird finished "speaking" to me. She had been watching him intently as I translated his thoughts and feelings into our language. It was easy to see the depth of her caring, and I felt that his imprinting to her instead of to his own kind had turned out very well for him. Sometimes imprinting, the process of identifying oneself with another, living by that other's ways, can be disastrous, because the animal may imprint too well and become frustrated at not being exactly like the other. Obviously, Sylvester enjoyed being himself.

CHAPTER 14

Arren and the Watchgoat

"Bea, this is Kay Kehoe. Do you remember me?"
The voice on the other end of the line sounded familiar, but I couldn't place the name. Finally it came to me. Kay was a young woman I had met while visiting my parents in Florida the previous winter. She and her horses had recently moved to Malibu, California and she was calling to see if I would come out to communicate with them. She wanted to be sure that they were having no problems in their new environment. We set an appointment for the following day.

I decided to take one of my German Shepherd show dogs, Arren, with me the following morning. I had been away from home a good bit lately and he had been traveling the show circuit with another dog handler. I thought we needed some time together to catch up on things.

Arren was raised on a farm and was quite familiar with horses. We were both looking forward to our visit as we left North Hollywood and drove along the Pacific Coast Highway toward Malibu. It was a beautiful day; cool from the night's rain. The ocean was exceptionally beautiful as it glinted and gleamed where the sun's rays struck it.

We reached Kay's driveway and turned into a narrow lane lined with tall trees. When we reached the house, Kay was waiting for us with her two dogs. She suggested that Arren accompany us to the stables, so we all headed up the hill. We reached the corrals first where Arren ran to the nearest horse, a dark bay gelding. Immediately, Arren turned, backed up, and asked the horse to scratch his back. The horse complied with his request, which pleased Arren to no end. Arren stood with his eyes closed in ecstasy. As the horse reached the itchiest spot on his back, Arren "zoned out" and didn't see the small red roan goat coming around the corner, his head lowered and pointed at Arren's side.

I became somewhat concerned, because Weedereater, so named in honor of his role in keeping up the grounds, outweighed Arren by about twenty pounds; I asked him what he intended to do. The goat responded:

I don't know if I should play with him the way I do with the other dogs. Maybe I should beat him up. I'm the watchdog around here. There are dogs and coyotes in these hills that bother us sometimes. One day some dogs from a neighboring farm came and made a nuisance of themselves. I butted them and put holes in their sides with my horns. They haven't come back again. I'm very important here.

Weedereater hedged his bet by going over and sniffing Arren, then pushed him around a little. I was amused by his behavior and intrigued by the mischievous glint in his eye.

I asked him to tell me more about himself and how he came to live with Kay and her horses.

I was born in a horse stable. I liked it there, it was nice to be around the horses and get attention from the people. I used to climb into the trailers with the horses, ate what they ate - sometimes hay and sometimes pellets, but all of it good. The only thing I didn't like was when the horses started running around the pasture. Whenever that happened, I ran back to Mother so they couldn't step on me. What I like best is having the horses chew on my horns. It feels good, like scratching an itch. I'm not afraid of horses stepping on me anymore. Now that I'm bigger, I can run faster than they can. I want always to live where there are horses. I like the grain and other things I can steal from them.

Kay and I stood chatting awhile, but I noticed that Weedereater was watching Arren from the corner of his eye. I asked him what he was doing.

I'm waiting. I'll get him when I'm ready.

Sure enough, a little while later Arren had had enough scratching and moved to a corner between two pastures to look at the horses on the other side of the fence. Suddenly the little goat charged him, butting him repeatedly. Arren couldn't get out of the corner and Weedereater knew it. Poor Arren went straight up in the air and over the top of the goat. He took off at a dead run and stopped some distance away. I called to him to come back, but he refused, telling me he wasn't coming near us again until I did something about that goat! I obliged him by putting myself between him and the goat, staying that way for the remainder of the time we were there.

Overall, I think Arren had a good time that day, but he's had a thing about goats ever since.

CHAPTER 15

THE PULL OF PLACE

I replaced the receiver and sat back in my chair, still laughing. The caller was Bonnie Dexter, a woman from Northridge, California, who had spoken with me a couple of weeks earlier to learn the history of two small mongrel strays who had shown up on her doorstep looking for a handout. They had gotten what they had come for and more. Bonnie is as soft a touch as I am when it comes to giving needy animals a home.

At the time, she had mentioned another pet, a cat that had been living in an old car in her yard for sometime. She suspected he belonged to the former owners of her house, and she called to say that she was coming over with the cat in a few minutes to find out if this was indeed the case. What she hadn't mentioned before was that the car was a 1959 Jaguar sedan that used to belong to Rocky Marciano, former heavyweight boxing champion of the world, and now also namesake to the feline who inhabited his old vehicle.

There was something about that cat using that car for his house which said it all. Here's this $20,000 super-engineered, high-powered, last-word-in-class marvel of automobile technology, a rolling cocoon designed to carry the rich and important of the world on their way in *ne plus ultra* leather upholstered luxury— being lived in by a cat; a beat-up black and white alley cat with a bad leg. It really doesn't do to assume that what we think a thing is, it is. You never know when a cat may come along and hand you an entirely new definition.

Bonnie arrived a few minutes later, a little out of breath from hauling her recalcitrant cat to my door. I suggested we give him a few minutes to recuperate from his trip; people may like riding in cars, but most cats hate it.

We arranged ourselves on the sofa in my office, with Rocky between us. A large white animal with black spots peppered throughout his coat, he had about him an air I've encountered before in animals who have triumphed over their circumstances. His one stiff, obviously bad back leg stuck out from under him at a sharp angle like a flag signaling to the world that the Marines have landed. He had a calm, determined face; he would, I thought, always have his way, people and events notwithstanding.

I asked Rocky how he had injured the leg by showing him a mental picture of himself when he was whole and healthy. Bonnie and I settle back in the cushions to await his answer.

I received a picture of Rocky sitting on the doorstep of a large, white wood and stucco house that was set well back from the street. A circular driveway curled before it and heavy black wrought iron gates closed off the property from the street. I asked Bonnie if this was her house; she confirmed that it was. Rocky went on with his story:

I've lived at this house since I was a tiny kitten. I love it here. My first family was a young couple. They took good care of me and petted me often, and sometimes I was affectionate with them.

I used to spend a lot of time in the tree by the house. I'd climb almost to the top and watch the goings-on in the neighborhood. Not much happened that I didn't know about.

I lived inside then. Someone was usually around to open the door for me when I needed to go outside, so I didn't bother using a litter pan. I don't like the feel of that grainy clay on my feet. The soft earth is much nicer, especially in the flowerbeds.

I had lived there for several summers when I learned that the man and woman were going to live somewhere else. At first I didn't think this would affect me. I assumed I would be staying on in my home.

I didn't know they would be taking all our furniture with them. One day, I went visiting in the neighborhood and when I got home, the house was empty. I was stunned! I didn't mind their leaving, but they were taking everything with them.

Late that night I was hanging around the front door, hoping someone would show up to feed me, when my people drove up. They seemed happy to see me again. They put me in the cat carrier and loaded me into their car. We drove for a long, long time.

I was upset by all the commotion. I tried to tell them to let me out, to take me home, but they seemed to think I'd be very happy in their new house. It didn't do any good to protest, the car kept moving on.

After what seemed like forever, we stopped in front of our new house. They carried me inside and fed me, then went to bed. I slept fitfully that night. The new place smelled strange to me. At our old house I had known every scent. If one of my friends had been by to visit me, I could tell by the scent they left. Here it was different. There were other animal smells around, but I didn't recognize any of them. Besides, our things were stacked all over the house in boxes. Nothing was where I was used to having it.

I felt unsure of myself and very frightened. I thought of my home with its nice safe smells and longed to return.

The next morning, I was left alone in the new place. I wandered around a bit and saw an open window, which I went through in a flash. The yard was as unfamiliar as the house, so I started to explore.

Within a short time, I felt something drawing me home, almost pulling my body. I walked on and on. Once in a while I recognized a scent I'd smelled when we were driving to the new place. That told me I was going the right way. Sometimes I turned and found that the pull had lessened. I'd stop, go back to where I'd turned and wait until I felt the pull again. I was going home!

Night came and went and still I kept moving. I was hungry by then, but there was no one to feed me, so I ate whatever I could find in garbage cans along the way.

The weather grew colder and sleeping outside became uncomfortable. Still I kept moving, drawn toward home.

At a time when I was feeling very low, I made a friend. One night I stopped near a large building that had lots of cars behind it. I was searching through the garbage cans when a small, fluffy, yellow cat came out of the building. I told him I was cold and hungry. He said his people always put out more food for him than he could finish, so he invited me in with him for dinner.

His people seemed nice enough, but they didn't like my dirty coat. I wanted to stay there awhile; at least long enough to gain back some of the strength I'd lost. When I cleaned myself up, they let me come inside.

I stayed with my friend and his people for several days. At first, it was wonderful having enough to eat and a friend of my own kind, but it didn't last. One morning the people went away and left me in the house with my friend. Soon I needed to relieve myself. I tried to wait for them to come back and let me outside, but I couldn't. I sprayed the curtains in their living room. When they return home and saw what I'd done, they were furious with me and threw me out. My friend spent time with me outside when he could during the next few days, but his family didn't allow me back into their house.

I considered trying to find my way back to my own people in their new house. Here I was, without enough to eat again or a comfortable place to sleep, but the pull which had started me on my way back home, just wouldn't quit. Soon I was traveling again.

I was famished most of the time and lost the strength I had gained at my friend's. One day, I discovered a large garbage can behind a restaurant. The smells coming through the kitchen made my mouth water. I was pawing through the trash when someone put a plate of meat out for me. Was I ever grateful! It had been a long time since I'd seen clean food and I almost choked from eating too fast.

Two big black cats and a clumsy gray dog arrived and chased me away, furious at finding me eating what they seemed to think was their food.

I kept moving. Late that night I crossed a railroad track. Suddenly I heard the sound of a car close by and as I began to run, I felt something strike my face. Pain shot through my head, something heavy crushed my leg and everything went black.

When I awoke, my head was throbbing. The pain moved in intense waves from my jaw to my eyes and back again. I tried to get up, but nausea made me dizzy. I looked down at my leg and found it was swollen and covered with blood. I tried to pull myself off the road, but I was too weak to move very fast. The sound of cars was all around me. I hoped I was far enough out of their way to avoid being hit again. My head felt as though it was exploding from the sound of the train that rolled by on the track next to me and things went black again.

The blackness came and went several more times. Finally I managed to drag myself into a building near the tracks, where I rested before looking around for something to eat. There were a few bugs crawling on the floor near me and I ate them at once. They weren't nearly enough, but they were better than nothing. I saw a rat lurking in a corner across the room. It saw me too, but didn't pay much attention, knowing I was injured. I needed to eat it to live, so I inched closer. Every time the rat looked my way, I pretended I wasn't stalking it.

It was filthy, as rats usually are. They're vicious creatures with sharp yellow teeth that can slash a cat's throat if given a chance. I usually stay away from them, but this time it was kill the rat or die of hunger. I timed my lunge perfectly and broke the rat's neck before it had a chance to see me coming.

I felt a little better after eating. I dragged myself to the door of the building to lie in the sun. My foot was still painful, but not as much as before. I rested there in the sun until I felt well enough to go on.

My journey home had turned into a nightmare of terror. There were a large number of dogs in the neighborhood near the tracks, so I had to be extremely careful. Whenever I saw a dog ahead of me, I hid in tall grass or behind a bush downwind until it passed. If the wind shifted at the wrong time, I had to run for my life as best as I could while dragging my injured leg. My heart thudded with fear at the thought of what would happen to me if I were caught.

Food was even more difficult to get now. I couldn't jump as well as I used to so getting at the garbage cans took everything I had. I felt desolate and desperately alone. I had almost given up when a woman with long brown hair found me.

She came out of her house as I was going through her trash. People often threw things at me—rocks or sticks—when they caught me looking for something to eat, so I was afraid to be seen. I started to run from her, but found to my surprise that she was calling softly to me.

I stopped and let her pick me up. She petted me and spoke gently to me. She took me into her house and gave me warm milk to drink and cleaned the dirt from my fur. She even made a bed for me in her kitchen. That night I slept peacefully for the first time in a long, long time.

The next day, the woman gave me a bath which got rid of my fleas. I felt much more comfortable then. She took me to a man who somehow made my leg numb. It was still useless, of course, but at least it didn't hurt anymore.

I stayed with the woman a long time. Having regular meals and a warm, safe place to sleep made all the difference in the world; gradually my strength returned, and I felt secure once more.

Oddly enough, the pull to my old home was gone. One day, as I was sitting in the living room looking out the window, I knew why. There, across the street, was my old house! When I had left it, the trees had been covered with leaves; now they were bare. It had taken me three seasons, but I had made it home.

I went to the woman and tried to thank her for the good care she had given me. Then I left her house and went home.

The people who live in my house now are kind to me too. They don't let me come inside. I went in once and had another spraying accident, but they have made me a room of my own in a car.

Things are fine now. I'm back where I want to be. I can visit with my friends in the old neighborhood. The smells are familiar. I have almost as good a view from the back of the car as I had from the tree. That's good because I can't climb anymore anyway. It doesn't matter. Being home is what's important.

Bonnie and Robert Dexter located the former owners of their house following this interview. They came to the Dexters' home and verified that this was indeed their cat Muffins. They wisely allowed him to remain at "his" house.

CHAPTER 16

THE CASE OF THE MISSING BUTTONS

Princessa's bark signaled the mailman's approach. I left my study and headed for the front door to meet him, but encountered an animal traffic jam in the living room by the simultaneous entrance of Philea and her pups. By the time I reached the hall, the mail was already lying on the floor.

I picked up the stack of letters, riffled quickly through them, and came across one bearing the globe and anchor insignia of the U.S. Marine Corps. Curious to learn who was writing to me from the military, I opened it at once.

It was from a Mrs. George Knopp of Oceanside, California. It read;

Dear Miss Lydecker,

We read about your ability to communicate with animals and are hoping you can find time to "interview" our dog Buttons. Two years ago my husband was assigned to the American Embassy in Poland, for a year's tour of duty there as Non-Commissioned Officer in Charge of International Security. Naturally, we were excited about the mission. Neither of us had been to Eastern Europe, and we were looking forward to the chance to experience a way of life much different from our own. We packed our "passport," and departed from Los Angeles airport. Buttons was on the flight with us. When we had to change planes in New York, we went to the animal hold to reassure ourselves that she was traveling comfortably. She had been given a tranquilizer to make the long journey easier for her. We wanted to let her know we were nearby and would be with her again soon.

However, when we reached the animal depot, Buttons wasn't there. An attendant informed us she had been taken for a walk and would be aboard the proper flight shortly.

Apparently, she was checked through without incident to Heathrow Airport in London, which was our next scheduled stopover. When we went to see her there before continuing on to

Germany, we were told we couldn't because of British quarantine regulations.

Concerned that she might be frightened by the airport noise and the several plane changes, we hurried to the animal hold as soon as we arrived in Berlin, which was our final point of departure. The attendants there couldn't locate Buttons, and we had to board our flight to Warsaw hoping their assurances that she would be found and shipped as soon as possible were justified.

She wasn't in Poland when we arrived, and to make a long story short, we spent ten very anxious days trying to trace her movements. Finally we were informed that she had been located and was waiting at the Warsaw airport for us. No one would tell us where she had been for all that time or where she was found.

We were somewhat apprehensive about this. Because my husband's job was of a sensitive nature, and because Buttons frequently accompanied him to his office wherever we were assigned, we thought that perhaps she had been taken so that a bugging device could be implanted somewhere in her body.

Now that we have returned to the States, we would like you to ask her exactly what did happen during those ten days. If it's convenient, we will bring her to Los Angeles one day next week.

Intrigued by the missing Buttons mystery, I called Mrs. Knopp and arranged for a consultation the following Tuesday. Buttons proved to be a slender black Cocker Spaniel with a completely white muzzle, which gave her a rather odd appearance from a distance. She had been freshly bathed and groomed for her outing, which made her coat glisten and shine. The Knopps and I waited while she sniffed around my living room. Eventually, with identification of the other animals in the house having been accomplished, she curled up on my sofa. I asked her to tell me about her adventures in the various airports of Europe.

My family was putting all our things in boxes. Everyone was very excited, including me. Each day when I went to play with my friend next door, I told him about our preparations. I was sorry to be leaving him. I hoped I would find as nice a friend where we were going.

When Vera took the suitcases from George's closet, I knew we would be leaving soon. I visited my friend for the last time when

George brought home the large wooden crate. Vera then took me to the veterinarian, who gave me a shot and some pills, and then we were on our way.

Vera gave me another pill when we reached the airport. She and George left me in my crate in a place with some other animals. It was terribly hot in the crate; I was very uncomfortable by the time the crate began to move up a conveyor belt into another, larger room full of crates and suitcases. The air was cooler there and I was able to finally relax and go to sleep.

The next thing I knew, I was in yet another room with even more animals and boxes. A man was walking around looking at pieces of paper tied to the boxes. When he reached my crate and looked at the paper on it, he opened the door. He fastened a leash, it was my leash! - to my collar and took me outside for a walk. It felt good to stretch my legs again. The fresh air smelled good, too. After I was able to relieve myself, the man took me back to the crate.

All my sleepiness had gone when the crate was moved again. I was frightened and started to cry. When the motion stopped, I found I was in another large area, surrounded by suitcases. I was nervous and wanted George and Vera to come and take me away from there, but instead, the room began to move again and a loud whining noise hurt my ears. I had to brace myself against a corner of my crate to keep from falling down. My water dish spilled and I was pretty wet. So this was air travel! Suddenly the whining noise stopped, but I had the feeling I was still moving.

A long time later, the whine started up again, then stopped suddenly. The door to the room opened and I was moved once again. I tried to watch where I was being taken, but I couldn't see much. When we stopped, a man carried me into a large place with walls around it. He put me into a fenced run near the entrance and brought me food and fresh water. He spoke a strange language, one I'd never heard before, but I understood him because I could see his thoughts. He was worried because the paper had come off my crate and he didn't know where I belonged. I felt desolate when I realized this. Evidently the paper had something to do with my family. If he didn't have it, how would they know where I was?

The man was kind to me during the days I was there with him. I found living in a run very hard, however. I had always gone to the bathroom outside, but now I was confined all the time. I held back as long as I could; finally, I just had to go. I was afraid the man would be angry with me for soiling the run. Instead, he cleaned up after me as though nothing was wrong with what I had done. I was grateful for that.

Another dog shared the run with me for a short time before his family came to get him. It made me feel terrible to see that dog go off with his people. I was lonely for George and Vera. I didn't think I'd ever see them again. I didn't know how to get back to them.

Then one day I saw the man watching me as he talked on the telephone. At one point he put the phone down and came over to look closely at me. When he went back to the phone, he seemed pleased. I perked up after that. Perhaps George and Vera had found me!

Later that day, the man put me in my crate, and a short time later, I was on the conveyor belt again. The whining sound and motion came once more. At times the room shook violently, my crate lurched into a stack of boxes, one of which came down on top of me, breaking the crate into pieces. I ran franticly to escape the wood and boxes crashing all around me. I couldn't find anyplace safe. Something hit my nose and made my head ache. Blood ran into my mouth. All around me boxes and crates were tumbling and crashing. The noise hurt my ears. I could feel my heart pounding against my chest. It was hard to breathe. I felt sick to my stomach; I retched and gagged on the vomit that rose in my throat.

Just as I thought I couldn't stand anymore, the room stopped moving. I looked around and saw that I had landed near a door. I stayed put, shaking, afraid that if I moved it would start all over again. I heard footsteps approaching, then voices. When the door opened, I dove through it, determined to get out of that terrible place.

I ran smack into a man's legs and felt his arms reach down and close around me. I struggled against him, terrified that he would put me back into that awful room. He spoke softly to me and stroked my head. I could see he meant me no harm and wanted to take me away from there. He carried me through a hallway, down a flight of stairs, across a large room filled with people and through another door.

We were outside! I could see sky and trees and breathe fresh air again. And then, wonderfully, I saw George and Vera standing near a car! Their faces broke into huge smiles when they saw me. Vera started to cry and so did I. I had thought I would never see them again.

The man handed me to George and I couldn't stop licking his face and snuggling into his chin. He laughed and held me close. The three of us got into the car and drove away.

We stopped after a few minutes, in front of a large stone building that George told me was an embassy. I bounded out of the car and relieved myself before we went inside.

That night George and Vera gave a party to celebrate my return to them. There were lots of people there - none that I knew - and I had a good time drinking wine whenever I could get at it.

I loved life at the embassy. There were always people around and George and Vera gave parties often. Their guests always fussed over me, petting me and saying how glad they were I'd been found.

We lived in a large apartment with thick red carpets. George worked there and I spent much of my time with him. I made one close animal friend, a shaggy black dog that lived next door to us. When my family let me out, he and I ran up and down the fence together.

The weather was much colder there than where we'd lived before. I didn't mind the cold too much, but when it snowed, the snow stuck to my hairy paws and I had to stand just outside the door while George and Vera cleaned my feet.

Other things were different there too. There weren't as many cars; instead, there were horses that pulled wooden carts behind them. I was fascinated by their smell. I loved to sit at the window and bark at them as they went by. Every time I heard the clopping of hooves on the stones below, I headed right for that window. I always wanted to go for a ride in one of those carts, but never got the chance.

EXPLORE

Sometimes George took me in his car to meet a lot of other men and all of us would run along the river together. I'd run with them for awhile, but then go back to the car because it was hard to keep up with them.

Living at the embassy was a good time for me. I was sorry to see Vera take the suitcases out of the closet because I knew it meant we were leaving. I got to thinking about the journey. I was worried that the same thing would happen going home. When George put me into another wooden crate, I started to shake.

Everything was fine this time, however. The trip home was long, but quiet. They gave me another pill before putting me on the conveyor belt so I slept soundly most of the way. When I awoke, George and Vera were standing next to my crate. We were home.

178

CHAPTER 17

HOME AWAY FROM THE RANGE

I was stretched out in a lawn chair in my back yard, soaking up the last rays of the late October sun. From my vantage point in front of the orange trees, on the west side of the property, I could see my house and patio and the swimming pool which lay between them.

The pool had remained in fairly good condition throughout the summer, despite the somewhat inconsistent attentions of my eleven-year-old nephew, Mark, whose job it was to maintain it during my recent cross-country tour. That crack near the pool steps would have to be repaired soon, however. Ah well, one was only eleven once and understandably Mark preferred swimming in the pool to working on it.

I turned my attention to the house. It appeared well tended, though the shutters could use a fresh coat of paint. These things notwithstanding, it was very good to be home. From early June to late September, I had covered nearly three thousand miles in my motor home. I'd taught more than twenty classes in nonverbal communication with animals, and consulted privately with dozens of pet owners curious to learn why their animals behaved as they did. I had met literally hundreds of interesting people and animals, whose sharing of their lives had considerably enriched my own. Everywhere I went I was well received, but now I was able to relax with my own family in my own home. I felt fulfilled and grateful.

I sighed contentedly and rolled over. My German Shepherds, Princessa and her son Loverboy, were lying patiently under the trees waiting for me to exhibit some sign of life. The change in my position was sufficient evidence that I was ready for some action so they jumped up immediately.

Loverboy brought me an orange to throw for them, so I obliged him by pitching it as far as I could. It thudded against the back fence and bounced to the ground between the two dogs. They immediately began a contest for possession.

I watched them play, amused at the mock seriousness of their struggle, that was rapidly becoming noisier than I felt was fair to my neighbors. I was about to intervene when Loverboy snatched the mangled fruit from his mother and tossed it into the pool. It plopped into the water like a fat orange frog. Loverboy yelped gleefully.

"You're getting old, Prinny girl," I told her affectionately. "Used to be nobody got anything away from you." She shot me a reproachful look and stalked off to the house, so intent on appearing dignified that she bumped into Mark as he came through the living room door.

"What's the matter with her?" he asked as he turned to watch her retreat. "She lose another orange?"

"Yes. They're getting slippier every year."

Mark sat down beside me and scratched Loverboy's ears. The dog left off cleaning the citrus pulp from his paws long enough to plant a sticky kiss on the boy's cheek. "He smells like a Minute Maid factory. By the way, Aunt Bea, there's a call for you. I think it's long distance."

"Mark! Why didn't you tell me right away?"

"I did. That's why I came out here in the first place," he said, looking puzzled.

"Don't forget to clean the oranges out of the pool before you come inside," I called over my shoulder as I headed for the house.

When I picked up the phone in my study, there was a slight crackle on the line. The voice on the other end sounded excited.

"Bea? Hi! It's Julie. Guess what! We finally got the horses, a mare and a gelding. Are you coming up this way soon? We're anxious to have you meet them. There's so much we want to know about their backgrounds."

The caller was my friend Julie Crawshaw, who lives in San Luis Obispo. Just before my trip, she and her friend Bradd Hopkins had applied to the Bureau of Land Management for two mustangs from the summer's wild horse roundup.

"Well, let me look at my calendar," I said. "I should be up in your neck of the woods soon."

I leafed quickly through the papers on my desk and found my November schedule, scanned it briefly and saw that I was to be in San Francisco on the fifth for a television appearance. Luckily the days before that were free so I could spend some time with my

friends and their new animals. I promised Julie I would try to
reach San Luis Obispo before nightfall on the third and rang off.

I sat for a few minutes thinking. Julie and I had known each
other seven years. She had an excellent instinctive rapport with
her animals and was progressing well with non-verbal
communication. For years she had supported the wild horse cause,
writing to her elected representatives on behalf of the country's
mustangs, who were, at that time, being killed by the hundreds and
sold to pet food processors. When the Wild Horse Protection Act
was passed in 1971, she was jubilant, and a few years later, when
the government began to cull the rapidly growing herds by
rounding up some of the horses and offering them for "adoption"
to private persons, she and Bradd had been among the first to
apply.

Difficulties in capturing the canny wild creatures had plagued
the BLM from the start. I wondered just how much these animals
had had to endure during their capture and transport to one of the
distribution centers. If their first contact with humans had been
extremely traumatic, it was going to be a while before their new
"parents" would be able to gentle them. I hoped my friends would
be successful in their venture.

A week later, I herded my canine family into my motor home
and made a quick nose count before heading north. Philea and
Loverboy were curled up on the back bed with their mother,
Pincessa. Mark Anthony, Caesar and Cleopatra, three of Philea's
last litter, were busy shredding a sock on the couch behind the
driver's seat. Blacky, my eighteen-year-old Pomeranian,
practically toothless and nearly deaf, but still an intrepid traveler,
was perched happily on the passenger seat next to me. I looked to
make sure I had remembered to load my clothes, waved goodbye
to Mark and my sister Florence and left.

The rich wash of color which normally covered the California
hills in autumn was subdued to pale golds and browns by the
year's scant rainfall. The harsh scent of dry grass was everywhere
as we drove up the coast highway. Occasionally, we passed a field
blackened by brush fires. The ocean flirted in and out of sight with
the curves in the road, and when the highway finally straightened

out next to the water, I couldn't resist its temptation. We took the next freeway exit and headed for the beach.

The dogs were delighted. They piled out of the motor home as soon as it stopped, like harried executives heading home after work. The tide was low, which left the beach littered with shells and driftwood. Here and there, a hermit crab made anxious by our approach, scuttled toward the receding water. The puppies spotted an exposed kelp bed and raced off to investigate its odd-looking bulbs while the three older shepherds and I jogged along the water's edge with Blacky bringing up the rear, desperately trying to keep up.

When we reached San Luis Obispo it was nearly dusk because our beach excursion had lasted longer than I had planned. I sped up guiltily, remembering I had promised to arrive in time to see the horses that evening. By the time I pulled off the highway onto the dirt road that led to the ranch, purple shadows had almost engulfed the hills surrounding Edna Valley. White pasture fences stood out in the failing light. As I reached the driveway, I could just make out the shapes of the horses in the corrals near the long, low house. Unfortunately, any further evaluation would have to wait until morning.

The smell of Chinese food came floating out when Julie opened the door. "You got here just in time," she said. "Empires come and go, but chicken with sweet pepper waits for no one. Put the dogs in the south pasture and let's eat!"

I hurried to comply and soon we were spread out around the long kitchen table, trying to eat and catch each other up on the summer's events at the same time. I told them at length about my cross-country tour and mentioned my plans for a second book.

"Oh, you've got to interview our horses and include their stories!" Julie exclaimed.

"Yes, they should provide you with some unusual material," Bradd said. "Being run off one's range by a helicopter is an experience most horses certainly never have."

"How old are the two you adopted?" I asked.

"The mare's about six and the gelding probably ten or eleven, judging as well as we can without seeing their teeth," Julie answered.

"Are you crazy?" I asked. "Why didn't you get younger horses? They'd be much easier to work with! Whatever possessed you to take these?"

"The fact that there weren't any young ones available for two years, and you know who wouldn't wait that long," Bradd replied. "Besides, I think we can gentle these. I used to work on a pack train over in the Kern River Plateau and a number of horses in the string that had been broken to ride, were taken from the wild as adults. There's a picture over there of one I used to ride a lot."

I peered dubiously at a photograph of a pinto gelding, apparently carrying his rider as though he'd been born under the saddle. "Well, good luck Bradd."

Julie grinned at me. "The people who run the distribution center for the BLM in Escondido have an 8-year-old stallion who's been out of the wild just under two years. They've been showing him for the past six months and he's so intelligent and well behaved, they nearly always take a first."

"Hmmmmmm. I can hardly wait until daylight."

The chill of winter was in the air when I rose at seven o'clock the next morning. I hurriedly pulled on jeans and a sweater and went to the kitchen where the welcome aroma of fresh coffee greeted me. Julie was already up and had started a fire in the black potbellied stove.

"Brrr, it gets cold up here," I mumbled through stiff lips. "Don't you hate getting out of bed on mornings like this?" I asked her.

"Oh, you get used to it after awhile," she said philosophically. "Anyway, one of the pleasures of country living is visiting your city friends who've got central heating."

I poured myself a cup of coffee and moved quickly over to the fire. "What's on the agenda for today?"

"After breakfast, which is in about ten minutes, whatever you like, as long as you spend some time with the horses."

"Fine way to treat a houseguest," said Bradd as he came through the door. "Bea spends most of her life working with animals, comes up here for a little clean air and relaxation, and still can't get a vacation!"

"I don't mind at all," I laughed. "In fact, I'm looking forward to meeting the horses. I've never interviewed a wild horse before - it should prove fascinating."

"Right now I'm more fascinated by scrambled eggs and hash browns," said Bradd as we sat down to eat.

By the time we had finished breakfast, the morning sun had dissipated the coastal fog. We headed for the corrals.

I saw the mare first. She was still munching her morning flake of hay, but looked up and nickered softly as we approached.

She was a lovely little thing, barely fourteen-and-a-half hands high. Mustangs generally fall into two categories, those who retain enough of their distant Spanish and Moorish blood to be recognizable as descendants of the conquistadores' horses, and those who don't. This one was definitely the former. She was a pale bittersweet color, neither really bay nor buckskin, with the broad forehead, large eyes and pale muzzle common to the wild horses of Spain and Portugal. She had a short coupled back, narrow withers and a nicely set head. But for the shaggy winter coat grown for the freezing winters of her native northern California Mountains, and the fact that her mane and tail were matted and full of burrs, she looked like she could have stepped out of a sixteenth-century painting of Cortez's expedition to the New World. She was also very thin.

"What's her name?" I asked Julie.

"Astarte. I named her after the Phoenician goddess of the new moon. She's only been here a few weeks, but she already leads well, and I can pet her face and neck. "

The mare finished her breakfast and moved to the side of her corral. She propped her chin against the top rail and stood watching us curiously, flicking her ears back and forth as we talked.

"Ask her about her life when she was wild," Julie said.

"OK. Let's see…how about if I start by asking her to tell me what she did when she was a baby?"

We sat down on the grassy area near the corral. I asked Astarte to tell me about her life as a foal. I could sense her puzzlement at encountering a person who could communicate as she did. After a few minutes she began her tale, which I translated into words for Bradd and Julie.

I was standing in my favorite meadow, idly watching a bee move from one patch of flowers to another, when Toby came over and suggested that we follow it. The bee stopped at almost every other flower between where we were and the forest, but we didn't care. We munched happily on the sweet yarrow heads as we walked along, content just to be in each other's company. Toby was my best friend, the only one of the colts who knew how to play without being too rough for me. Although his curiosity often got us into trouble, I felt safe with him because he always looked out for me.

We lost sight of the bee just after we entered the cool pine barren. The wind, blowing from behind us, carried the warm scent of the meadow. Ahead of us we heard an unusual, loud hum that quickly became an angry buzz. We walked cautiously around a large stand of trees. We knew whatever was ahead of us could smell us first.

We entered a small clearing and almost ran into a bear! He had one paw thrust in a hollow tree and there were bees flying furiously all around his head. We were terrified by the sight of the huge black beast. He was standing on his hind legs bellowing at the bees, but when he saw us, he dropped to all fours and growled. We turned tail and raced back to the meadow, to the safety of our herd. I told Toby I wasn't ever going back to the forest without the others in the herd!

I have known worse terrors since then, but as far as I can recall, that was the worst experience of my young life.

For the most part, my early life was very happy. Winters were hard, though. I remember being cold much of the time, huddling close to the others to keep the winds from my body.

My first winter was especially difficult. I was smaller and younger than the other foals in our herd. All the mothers took care of us together; we could go to any of them and be treated equally. Our own mothers were special to us, of course, but we were a family. When freezing weather came, we had a close circle of warm bodies around us all the time. Still, I spent a lot of time that first winter trying to keep from shaking.

When I was very small, my mother guarded me all the time. Sometimes when I would rather have played with the other babies, I had to stay by her side. When I got bigger, she let me go more often. I was never afraid to be away from her. I knew if I got into trouble I could go to one of the other mares and they would protect me.

There were times, though, when I wanted only her. Once when we were going down a steep hill, I slipped and fell on my chin, hurting my neck.. I went to my mother and she chewed on it to make it feel better.

Even though our herd was large, we always had enough to eat; there was plenty of tall grass to feed us. I do remember one winter when it snowed so much we couldn't leave our circle for a long time. The whiteness hurt our eyes and made looking for food impossible. We were all very hungry by the time the snow stopped.

The only other thing that scared me in my early life was the stallion fights that happened when another herd would come into our range. Their stallion would always challenge my father to fight. I remember standing behind my mother and trembling at his answer. I knew it meant noise and violence would follow. I was always too scared to watch very much of what happened. Sometimes I'd peek out from behind my mother to see my father and the other stallion biting and striking at each other, squealing furiously the whole time. My father was so strong that he drove all the other stallions away. For a long time my life was secure. I had food, I had the herd for protection and I had Toby.

Things changed in the late part of my third summer. A large bay stallion entered our meadow and challenged my father to fight. It was a long and bloody battle and the mare and foals of both herds mingled together in our fright. Suddenly, the dust cleared and the herd began to run. I ran with them a long way from the meadow before I realized I was in the wrong herd. Each time I tried to stop and go back to my own herd, the bay stallion forced me to stay with his mares.

I was scared and lonely and very unsure of my position with this new herd. I had to stay with them, I knew the stallion would bite me if I tried to leave. He was much bigger than I and not gentle with me the way my father had been.

He led us out of the trees and across the hills. We went over some very rocky ground; pieces of my hooves chipped off. My feet hurt badly, I'd stand in the cool water as long as I could whenever we found a stream to drink from.

Eventually we stopped moving and settled into our new range where I was terribly unhappy and homesick. I missed Toby and my other friends. This place was very different from the meadows I'd lived in before. We had gone above the tree line. Instead of the tall pines and lush grass I was used to, there were only small, scrubby plants that barely provided us with enough food.

After awhile I relaxed a little and began to make friends with others in this herd. I was still lonely for my old friends, but I needed to be close to another horse.

In time, I felt restless. It was almost as if something I couldn't quite hear were calling to me. I recognized the feeling it had come before, when I was in my father's herd. The first time I felt that way, I danced around my father to show him how pretty I was. I wanted him to share my feeling, but he swung his head at me and told me to get away from him.

This stallion acted much different. When I pranced for him, he joined me and began to nuzzle my neck. I was excited by his attentions and he seemed to be excited too. He mounted me and my longings were satisfied.

We moved more often than my first herd had. The stallion lost most of his fights, and we had to take whatever range was left to us by the other herds. Because of the sparse food supply, I was hungry much of the time.

My body had been changing gradually. I was swollen and thick by the time we headed down out of the hills into a hot, sandy area. Suddenly I felt the muscles in my belly pull. It hurt. I cried out to the others, but they paid no attention to me. The pain came again and again and many times again. Then my first foal was born.

Right away, I knew something was very wrong with him. His back legs were twisted. I nudged him to try to make him get up, but he just couldn't, no matter how hard he tried. I felt terrible, seeing him so tiny and helpless. The stallion came over to see him, but he couldn't get the baby to his feet either. I stayed with him, licking him and lying next to his little body. I tried to get my

EXPLORE

nipples close enough to his mouth for him to nurse, but I couldn't. He became weaker and weaker.

Then a terrible thing happened. From a helicopter circling overhead came sharp bursts like thunder. The other horses jostled around, agitated. Panicking for my foal's safety, I tried to protect him from their hooves. The thunderclaps came faster and louder; someone was shooting at us! The others began to run. Frantically trying to escape, they trampled my baby to death as I stood helpless and full of pain. I remember looking down at his tiny mangled body and feeling an awful sense of loss. I knew he would never rise to his feet.

The stallion rushed up and bit my rump because I wasn't running with the others; finally I did. One of the mares in front of me fell and I jumped over her, intent on getting away from the noise from above. A bullet, hard and hot, seared my neck and blood ran through my mane. I was racing so fast that my heart pounded violently in my chest, my stomach churned and my lungs felt as if they would burst.

Finally, the noise stopped. Covered with sweat and shaking with fear and exhaustion, I found shelter under a rock ledge above a dry creek bed. Two of the others in my herd were with me; the rest had fallen to the ground. They too, would never rise to their feet again.

The three of us hid together under the ledge for a long time. Finally, we began to walk down the riverbed. Though the riverbanks became steeper, we were too frightened to leave their cover. My neck, hot and swollen and very sore, hurt terribly. Soon I could hardly move my head for the pain.

We came to a small waterfall. I stood under the water and let it wash over my sore neck. It seemed to take the burning away. In awhile I felt better.

We wandered along for a long, long way. There was little to eat and we were becoming weak. Then we heard the sound of horses on the ridge above and struggled up the steep hill toward them. One of the mares slipped and fell just before we reached the top. Her body crashed to the bottom of the incline and she never moved again.

The two of us who got to the top soon found the horses we'd heard from below - mares and a few burros. I was nervous at first, unsure of them, but they were friendly, so we joined them. We soon met a stallion with a small herd who took us in.

We moved on to the low hills where there was more food. Having a family once again, I began to feel a little more secure. We found some food—not much, but more than where we had been before. I finally stopped being hungry all the time. The weather was colder here than in the sandy place we'd left, and it rained much of the time.

Winter passed and spring arrived. My second foal was born, a filly. She was healthy; soon running by my side as our herd moved along through the low hills.

When she was still very small, I heard another helicopter in the sky. I felt panicky. I was sure we would be shot at again. I saw some shelter and started to run for it. I thought my baby would follow me, but she stayed with the herd, which was running away from the shelter. I was desperate. I called to her, but she wouldn't come to me, so I ran back to the herd. We raced across the hills. My heart was pounding loudly, my body covered with sweat. This time no horses fell to the ground.

We crossed a rocky ridge and came into a small valley enclosed by hills. It was too late to turn back. We had to keep running— into a place we couldn't leave. We milled around, all of us terrified. There was a lot of dust and for awhile, I couldn't see clearly. I called for my baby and found her by her answering cry.

When the dust settled and I was able to look around me, I found that we were in a corral. On the far side there were large trucks that people were herding some of the horses into. Soon, we too, were forced into a truck that soon was on its way. This was my first close-range experience with people, and I found it terrifying.

A long, long time later we arrived at a place that had large corrals, most filled with horses. My filly and I were put into one together. After we had been there only a few nights, I felt a terrible, wrenching pain in my belly. My body hadn't swollen with foal, but I knew I was carrying another baby. The pain continued until I passed a large bloody mass onto the ground. I knew I had lost my baby, but the pain was gone.

Several days later, we were loaded into another truck with several horses and moved again, this time to a place where we had a large corral to ourselves. The people who lived nearby came often to visit us. I wasn't very afraid of them, because they spoke very gently and brought us food.

From time–to-time other people came to our corral and watched us. I didn't pay much attention to any of them until one day a man and a woman stayed by us for a long time. The woman kept calling softly to me. She told me I was beautiful and that I was going to live with her.

I was herded into a small chute, where someone put a halter on my head. Then my filly and I were loaded into a trailer and it began to move.

When we stopped, darkness had come. The woman opened the trailer gate and we backed out into another corral. The moon was full and I could see large pastures and a few sheep, but no other horses.

The next morning, when the woman brought us hay and grain, she stayed and talked to us. She wanted to be friends. I liked her, so I took some food from her hand. My filly didn't like her at all though. She bit and kicked at the woman and even kicked at me. I knew it was time for her to stop nursing, so I kept pushing her away, but she always came back for more. I was getting tired of her demands on me.

Things went on unchanged for awhile. Then one day we were loaded into a trailer again. The first time it stopped, my filly was unloaded. When it stopped a second time, I was home.

I like it here. I still think about living with the herd sometimes. I still miss Toby once in awhile, but I feel much safer here than I have ever felt before.

I'm very fond of the woman and I'm coming to like the man. They both pay a lot of attention to me, petting me and bringing me food.

I'm doing many things I never did before and never thought I'd do. I walk on a lead next to the woman and stop when I hear her say "Whoa." It gets a little boring sometimes, but I have my fun as well. Often, when I know my people are coming with my food, I dance and buck around the corral; it always makes them laugh. I think I'm going to be happy here.

"I don't think you're going to have much trouble gentling this one," I said when Astarte finished. "She wants to be friends."

Bradd had been standing silently behind us while Astarte was communicating with me. Now he spoke. "Let's see what my horse has to say for himself."

We got up and walked around the hay shed that separated the two corrals. I stopped short on the other side, stunned by what I saw. There, in the center of the second enclosure stood a dark bay gelding. His head was up, sniffing the wind. He caught my scent and turned to face me. I caught my breath sharply. Rarely have I encountered such charisma in anyone, man or beast. My eyes slid over him, noting the white star on his forehead, his powerful neck and shoulders, and finally his long fetlocks that hinted at some draft blood in his ancestry. His mane and tail were a mess and his coat even shaggier than the mare's. It didn't matter. He could have been completely bald and still kept his dignity. This was an animal to reckon with. The defiance he projected told me that though gelded, he possessed all the sovereignty of a stallion and he fully intended to keep it.

The three of us settled ourselves once again and I asked my friends if they'd had any success in touching him.

"Very little, only when we've been feeding him grain from his bucket," Bradd said. "I think we will, eventually, but it's going to take some time. They geld these horses cowboy style, which is the one thing I object to. His first contact with humans brought him instant physical pain and we've got to overcome that somehow and gain his trust."

"Let me see what he has to say about his capture. By the way, have you named him?"

"Yes. We call him Houdini. He got his lead rope off his halter the first night he was here. We found it outside the corral, about twenty feet away."

I watched the wild horse as Bradd spoke. Houdini met my gaze for a few seconds and then turned to look toward the hills. I asked him how he had come from the hills to this place. His objections to people and to his captivity seemed to make him, if anything, more eager to "talk." He had a lot to get off his chest, his story began:

The sound of Roxanne's anguished cries began to fade. I drew on the last of my strength and lunged against the mass of bodies around me. I would reach her. I would kill whoever was taking her away from me. Somehow we would get out of this place together and find our way back home.

The air reeked of urine and sweat. It was the smell of too many, too close, too long. It was also the smell of fear.

I felt panic; I was losing ground faster than I could gain it. I called to her and she answered. By the time I reached the edge of the canyon, she was gone. I tried to get through the barbed wire, but fell, exhausted.

They had succeeded these people who came to take our land. They had chased us into a box canyon, diving at us in helicopters for several days. They had separated families. Some of the most frightened of us had tried to climb the steep cliff sides and had fallen to the rocks below.

There was no way out for the rest of us. We could only give up and die or live as captives. I am a survivor, but I'll live on my terms, not theirs.

They came for me eventually, too, and herded me into a truck. The ride wasn't as bad as being in the canyon had been. We were very crowded, but there were fewer of us and at least it was clean. We rode for hours and hours. The top of the truck was open so we could see the sun and eventually the stars. The trip gave me time to think about my life before I first met man.

There were lots of wild animals in the semi-desert where I was born. Some were dangerous and frightening to us. Once I saw a coyote eating a dead horse; every once in awhile we'd see a cougar and run for our lives. We lived in harmony with badgers and squirrels.

My favorite creatures were the little lizards that lived in the rocky crevices and scrub brush in the low hills. When I was a foal, I loved to chase them into their homes and wait for them to come out again. Sometimes I spent the whole day playing that game.

My mother was a chestnut mare with one white front foot and a big belly. Her milk was sweet and plentiful. My mother was good to talk with. *She always knew what to do. She loved me very much. Once, when I was too young to know better, I tried to eat a cactus. I knew that none of the other horses ate cactus, but this one smelled so sweet and wet, I decided to taste it anyway. I got my lips full of painful quills and had to run to my mother for help. She pulled most of them out with her teeth, though some broke before she could get them out. I had to spend two days with my lips in the watering hole to bring down the swelling. My mother stayed with me the whole time.*

I can't remember feeling much hunger during my early life. My father always knew where there was food and water. During the summers we lived in the lowlands, eating sagebrush and desert herbs. We spent our winters in the hills. There was deep snow there, but the trees kept the icy winds from our bodies. We ate the bark and needles and what leaves were left when the grass was covered by snow.

We had bad times too, of course. There were sometimes dust storms on the desert. I remember one in particular, we walked for three days without knowing where we were going. My father moved around the outside of the herd to keep us together. Sand blew into our eyes and stung our bodies; it was hard to breathe. During the worst part of the storm, my father made us stand in a circle with our heads to the inside of the flanks of the horse in front of us. Finally, the storm ended and we were able to move on.

One winter was very hard. There had been little rain that year and there was hardly any grass at all. We had to eat to stay warm, so we ate bitter bark off trees, and moss from rocks. For water, we ate snow.

In spite of the hard times, we were happy. There was plenty of land for range, so even though there were other herds in the area, we had enough food.

Sometimes we joined another herd of horses for awhile. We'd travel together a ways, but even then my father was always the leader. He was a handsome black stallion, agile and strong, with a fine and beautiful head. I loved to watch him stand guard for us. I can see him now standing on a hilltop, the wind blowing through his mane. He watched for anything that might harm us. Knowing that, we felt very safe.

The other colts and I loved to play tag. One of us would graze behind the others until there was enough distance to take off at a dead run. Then we'd run up and nip the rump of the nearest colt, then he'd run and nip the colt in front of him. Soon we were all running in a circle trying to keep from being nipped. Sometimes we fell and bruised our legs or bumped our heads, but that didn't stop us. We got back up, shook ourselves off, and started running again.

One evening, when I came back to my mother, she seemed in pain. I wanted to tell her what I'd done that day, but she pushed me away. I couldn't understand why she was behaving that way. When I tried to get close to her, to nurse for awhile before going to sleep, she told me I was too old to nurse, that I should be on my own and away from her. The next morning, she had another foal by her side. I stayed as close to her as I could after that, but she wouldn't let me touch either her or the foal. I wandered back to my friends and found that some of them had been pushed away by their mothers, too. It seemed that things were supposed to be this way. My friends and I began to range farther from the herd during the day, only coming back to them at night.

Some of the young mares began to have an exciting smell. I started to see them as something other than playmates. There was one filly I particularly liked, a beautiful bay with lovely eyes and a soft voice. She seemed to like me, too.

I wanted her to be my mate. I pranced up to her one day, dancing around her, shaking my head and trying to impress her with my strength and grace. Just as we were about to touch noses, my father charged over to us and bit my sides and rump. I ran to a hilltop and stood looking down at them. I couldn't figure out why he had attacked me. I waited awhile before going down the hill to court Roxanne again, but the same thing happened. After I tried several more times, my father forced me to stay out of the herd altogether. He wanted Roxanne to stay with his herd. I had to follow the others at a distance, along with several other young stallions.

I knew Roxanne wanted to be with me as much as I wanted to be with her, so I stayed close enough to keep her in sight. One day, she held back as the herd moved down their range valley. I stood on a rocky hilltop above them, careful not to let my father see me. Roxanne kept her head down and tried to look as though she were intent on grazing, letting the rest of the herd move ahead of her. When they were well past, she turned and dashed toward my hill. My father raced after her right away, but she had enough of a head start to reach me before he reached the bottom of the hill. He called to her angrily, but didn't come after her; that would have meant leaving the others in the valley without protection.

We were finally together! Roxanne was badly bruised and lame in one leg from where she had fallen a number of times in her race up the hill. This meant we had to stay put until she could move more easily. When we eventually moved on, looking for new range, two of the other stallions from our herd joined us. We now had our own small herd.

Some time later we encountered a strange animal. It wasn't quite like anything we had known before. though it looked like us, it was neither a mare nor a stallion. We wanted to kill it because of its terrible smell. We finally realized it was a horse like us, but one that was very ill. I went up to him to see what was wrong.

He told me of being moved in a trailer that had been hit by something and turned over. He was badly hurt. He had wandered away in a daze, his wounds had become infected, and he was so weak he could hardly move but didn't know where to find food or water. We began nudging him in the direction I knew he had to go to reach the nearest stream, but since he could only take two or three steps at a time, with a rest in between, it took us a long time to reach the water. He drank deeply and then lay down in the stream to let the water wash over him, resting his head on a flat rock. We stayed with him all that night to keep the coyotes away. The next morning, he lay still and stiff and cold. We moved on, sad that we had been unable to save him.

One day we came upon a herd of mares with no stallion and joined them. The other two stallions with me took some of the mares and formed herds of their own. Three of the mares joined Roxanne and me and we stayed together for some time. Roxanne and two of the new mares had my foals.

When the weather became colder, I knew I had to lead my herd to a sheltered range. One of the mares was so old she couldn't travel well. I coaxed her again and again, but she refused to come. One of the other stallions brought his herd along with us; the other stayed down in the valley with the rest of the mares, who were afraid to leave the range where their former stallion had kept them.

The rains came when we were still looking for a range with enough food and protection for all of us. We formed a circle with our backs to the wind and put the foals in the center so they would stay warm. Sometimes, I lay down next to them to shelter them from the wind. I loved my foals dearly.

Eventually, we found a place with forage and a cave formed by the boulders overhanging a dry streambed. We could range during the day and return to the cave at night. Several deer joined us in the cave. That winter was long and cold with very little food, but we made it through.

Toward the end of that winter, I was out scouting the area when I heard a horse nearby. I thought he might be coming to try and steal my mares from me, so I ran out to challenge him. I stopped as soon as he came into sight. It was another horse like the one we'd helped in the stream. On his back he carried a creature with the same terrible smell. It was my first meeting with man.

This man was hunched over, his head bent against the wind. His horse seemed to carry him without fear, though I couldn't understand why. I tried to ask him about it, but since he didn't understand fear and caution of everything new as I did, he couldn't answer me clearly.

In the days that followed, we saw more men on horseback. Soon cattle came and began eating our range, so we had to move on. Our bad time had begun. People and cattle were driving us from our land. There simply wasn't enough food for all of us. We had to move to higher ground where there wasn't as much food and water. We lived among sparse scrub and an occasional pine, instead of grass and tall trees. We were hungry most of the time.

There were other problems, too. One day a foal slipped and fell as we crossed rocky ground. We tried to help him walk, but each time we got him to his feet, he fell again. We knew the foal needed us, but we had to move on. As we started to leave, the foal called miserably to his mother, who went back to him. I never saw him again, but she later rejoined us. She was thin and weak and scarred from coyote bites. The coyotes had eaten her baby.

Our real trouble came with helicopters. Flying much lower than we'd ever seen them, they swooped down at us like hawks, herding us toward the canyons. Other horses, too, were running in the same direction. We were so terrified; we couldn't stop to eat what little food there was.

We all ran together toward what we thought was safety. We entered a large canyon that quickly filled with horses. When we tried to leave, we found our way blocked. Some of the horses braved the steep canyon walls and fell. They lay with broken legs and necks until the men guarding the canyon entrance shot them. Others became so discouraged they simply lay down and gave up.

We were there for what seemed like a very long time, though only one night actually came and went. The men threw hay on the ground for us, but their smell covered it so completely that I couldn't eat it. Pretty soon it had been trampled and covered with urine and manure from the other horses.

Then the men herded some of us out of the canyon and into big trucks, which took them away. Most of my mares were taken very early, though Roxanne and I managed somehow to stay together for awhile. Then one day they drove me and the remaining stallions against the canyon wall and took Roxanne and the other mares. Then they came for us and forced us up a narrow ramp into a big truck, just like they had done to our mares.

After the long truck ride, we came to a place that had people around, but they didn't seem to want to hurt us. They gave us hay and fresh water often and even cleaned our corrals every day. More horses arrived in more trucks. I frantically looked in each one for Roxanne, but she never came.

A woman came to the corrals often and spoke softly to us. She seemed to know how terrified and angry we were. She told us there was nothing to fear anymore, that she loved us. We knew she did, but we stayed as far from her and all the humans as we could anyway.

EXPLORE

A foal in a nearby corral had an injured leg. The woman took him out and washed his wound. She brushed and petted him every day. Soon he was following her around. I couldn't see how that foal could stand to have her touch him much less start nickering and calling to her softly whenever he saw her coming. There were several other horses there that let her touch them too. I was confused at that.

One day I felt very sleepy after eating. I vaguely remember a rope around my neck, hands on my body and a sharp pain in my groin. I clearly remember feeling hideously sick to my stomach later.

From time-to- time people came and looked at us; sometimes one or two were taken out and never returned. One day, a man stood for a long time looking at me and later came back with a woman. They spoke gently to me and went away again.

One morning soon after that, a man came and drove all the others out of the corral. When I tried to go with them, he blocked my way. When I was alone with him, he opened the gate to the smaller corral next to mine and drove me into it. Then he drove me into a chute. I was furious and tried to back out, but he had closed the gate. Then he put a halter on my head and released me back into the small corral.

A truck with an enclosed trailer backed up to the corral gate. The man forced me to move closer to it. I faced him and threatened to fight, but he kept coming toward me anyway. Finally I could stand it no more and just bolted past him. He moved behind me again, edging me closer and closer to the trailer until finally I went into it to get away from him.

When the man tried to close the trailer gate, I kicked at him, driving him back for the instant I needed to shoot out of the trailer again. I went in and out of that trailer several more times before he got the gate closed!

Then I was trapped. The trailer began to move. The roof covered it completely, so I couldn't see the sun at all. I decided to fight my way out and started kicking and thrashing around. I managed to turn completely around, wanting to jump out the back, but there wasn't enough room to get through.

198

Finally the trailer stopped. I heard the voices of the man and the woman who had last spoken to me when I was in the corral. The gate dropped and I bolted out, ready to fight.

I found myself in another large corral, in this pasture. There were several people watching me. I was angry, terrified and very sick. My body was covered with sweat, my head ached, and I was exhausted. The woman spoke quietly to me when she brought hay for me and the mare in the next corral, then all got quiet as everyone left.

After I calmed down, I learned from the mare that she was glad to be here because there was enough to eat and the people were good to her. She had had a bad time when she lived in the hills and was happy to be in a place where she felt safe, though she hadn't been here long.

The people here are kind enough. They give us plenty of food and fresh water and keep the corrals clean, but for days I refused to even look at them. No human is ever going to dominate me.

I became ill, my nose filled with fluid, and I was feverish. I refused to give in. Fresh herbs were added to my food along with something I hadn't tasted before. Gradually, I got well again.

The man and the woman spend more time talking with me now. Sometimes they hold my food in their hands, instead of placing it in my manger. I know they love me, but I'm having a hard time accepting them. I want to be friends with Astarte, though, because I want to be close to my own kind.

It isn't easy for me to reject these people; they're so kind to me. Sometimes when the man feeds me, he touches my cheek. The first time he touched me, my flesh crawled. I don't react that way to human touch anymore, but I don't enjoy it; I don't understand why Astarte does.

It feels good to be full again after having been hungry for so long. When I see the woman bringing my hay, I'm happy. She sings to me sometimes and tells me that I am beautiful and noble and that she loves me. She understands me. Once in awhile, I think I'll give up and become friends, but then I look out across the pasture to the hills and remember my early life and I can't.

I miss Roxanne bitterly. I long to run free in the hills again, in spite of all the troubles I had there. Sometimes I'm so homesick my heart hurts. I want to go home.

A hen clucked noisily, announcing to the world that she had just laid an egg. The rooster crowed. The sound shook us from the almost hypnotic spell Houdini's story had woven. I rose slowly, brushing loose grass from my clothes. We walked silently and sadly into the house.

As I drove out of the ranch later that day, the last thing I saw was Houdini's head silhouetted against the horizon, looking north, and felt such sadness for him. He was in good hands, but I could still feel the pain and loneliness he had for his mate and freedom.

I have seen both Astarte and Houdini several times since then. Astarte is progressing as I expected she would. She is now completely gentled. Julie can bathe her, clean her feet, and handle her with confidence. She is also learning to be a saddle horse. She even told me she enjoys her lessons on the lunge line.

Houdini, surprisingly, has lost most of his anger and his homesickness. His will is still extremely strong and probably always will be. He may never have a saddle on his back, but he has come slowly to return Bradd and Julie's love for him. He still has his sovereign attitude. No one will ever dominate him, but I think he just may come to cooperate with his people. At any rate, he is alive and well, if not entirely happy, at least not ragingly miserable anymore.

Both horses are allowed the run of the pastures now. Julie has only to call for them to come running to her, eager to be with their new friends.

CHAPTER 18

MAINE COON MENTOR

Cuesta Grade is the second steepest grade in the state of California, its summit topped only by the Donner Pass. It runs between San Luis Obispo and Atascadero, but from the bottom of the hill on Highway 101, it doesn't look like much of a climb.

As you go up the mountain road, the scenery stays pretty much the same—live oaks and chaparral. The old road cut by Chinese laborers more than a century ago, winds in and out around the lower side of the mountain.

Suddenly, you are at the top of the grade where everything changes. The highway heads inland. Instead of the temperate climate touched by the Pacific Ocean breezes, you now enter an area that is either blinding hot or bitter cold. Ranches and livestock dominate the flat land, while houses built by people trying to get away from the changing weather, dot the hillsides.

The land has a feeling of harshness about it, a stark beauty that refuses to be transformed into gentility by the activities of contractors who see it only as an avenue to profit.

Driving through this part of California always exhilarates me. It is this very refusal to acquiesce, to be molded by someone else's idea of what it should be, that I find so satisfying.

I pondered these thoughts as I headed toward Paso Robles, jockeying my motor home around curves designed before anyone ever thought of building a vehicle to live in, even for a vacation. The traffic around me was an odd mixture of Middle America and the working cowboy. It was a lovely weekend day that allowed the vacationers who drove late-model station wagons, to haul motorboats behind them for a day's recreation on Lake Naciemento. They passed the working cowboy who drove his pickup full of hay and grain, to feed his livestock that needed care every day. No weekends off for them! I wondered how much longer the pickups would outnumber the wagons.

The road veered sharply east, then flattened and narrowed. I turned north again, drove for what seemed a very long way before coming to the bottom of the hill that Gail and Chris said would be my marker that I was just about there. Sure enough, the sign that read Paso Robles Boarding Kennel stood at the entrance of a narrow drive that ended at a long brick house. Immediately, five dogs and a burro announced my arrival.

Chris Riley ran out from the kennels, obviously very pleased to see me. She and her friend, Gail Carey, had missed the class I taught in this area ten months earlier, but they were anxious for me to interview their various animals.

Chris reached the motor home a little out of breath, her blue eyes laughing beneath curly black bangs. "Hi, I see you found us!" she exclaimed cheerfully. "Come on inside where it's reasonably cool and quiet."

"OK, just let me make sure the parking brake's set on this thing first," I responded.

Soon we were inside the dining room where Gail was waiting for us with a variety of critters waiting for their turn to "chat". Chris introduced us. Gail said, "I think if we leave the animals here for now, we can bring them into the living room one at a time when you're ready to talk with them. I thought I'd get them all in one place to save hunting them up when their turns come."

Chris looked around. "Where's Willie?" she asked.

"I don't know where he is right now, probably off someplace hunting. He'll show up before Bea leaves, I'm sure. You know how curious he is."

"Willie was Gail's cat when we met," Chris said to me, "but now he's mine. Or rather, I'm his—one is never really sure which way it is with a cat."

"From the cat's point of view, I'm sure it's the latter," I laughed. "I've never known a cat who didn't believe in his heart of hearts that the people around him were there for his convenience."

"Chris, who do you think we should take first?" asked Gail, as she adjusted her glasses that had just been knocked askew by the affectionate attentions of a handsome young Doberman pinscher.

"Let's do Mahoney first. I want to know if she meant to kill our lamb or if it was an accident."

I settled into a soft, comfortable sofa in their living room as Gail brought in Mahoney, a pretty black and silver German shepherd with an inquisitive face.

Mahoney told me she had only been playing with the sheep when the silly thing started to squeal loudly. Afraid she'd be blamed for hurting it if its cries brought Chris from the barn she had tried to make it be quiet, but ended up killing it by mistake. Eat it? What for? There was always plenty of food here. Besides, the wool had left a bad taste in her mouth. She was glad it was gone; now it wouldn't get her into trouble anymore.

Mahoney was followed by Mike, the Doberman. He was a gentle thing, but very self-conscious. Still a puppy, he told me he was sensitive about his clumsiness which had apparently reached a peak when he accidentally knocked over an antique vase. He was also annoyed because he said that people made fun of his ears which still tended to flop now and again. I reassured him that he was just going through a phase and that soon he'd be a grown dog who fit into his paws. He was so cheered by the knowledge that someone sympathized with his adolescent woes, that he sat next to me during all the other interviews.

A small mixed terrier named Squeak was next, obviously the grand old man of the group despite his tendency to sound like a mouse. He was much beloved by the other dogs who regarded his occasional crabbiness with indulgence.

Following Squeak was "Smilin' Sullivan who immediately showed me the reason for his name by coming over and raising his lips in a welcoming grin. A Labrador/Irish setter cross, the color of late autumn leaves, considered himself an important part of the operation here because he loved to greet people as they brought their animals to the kennels. He also enjoyed wandering through the neighborhood at night looking for garbage. Chris and Gail were relieved to learn that that was all he'd been doing - they were afraid he might have been bothering the neighbors' livestock.

As I was finishing with Sullivan, Gail looked down the hall and announced that Willie was on his way. I turned to see a huge Maine Coon cat strolling slowly through the door. The Maine Coon derived their name because they showed up in Maine, the

northeastern part of the country, about two hundred years ago -
probably refugees from the whaling ships that docked there.
There was nothing of the refugee about this one, however. He
was a magnificent specimen, elegant in every regard except the dirt
on his coat. From his large round head with its level yellow gaze
to his erect thick tail, he was every inch lord and master of all he
surveyed. Nothing would faze him, I thought, not even an animal
ten times his size.

I asked him if he knew he needed a bath.

*Of course I know. I'm not going to do anything about it though.
I don't like the taste of dirt. Once in awhile I clean myself up, just
to keep in practice, but mostly I don't worry about it. It's hard to
keep clean in the country anyway.*

*I like living here much better than in the city. There are more
interesting things to do and much more interesting smells. I love
to stalk the barn and hills for rats and gophers. They are
everywhere, especially around the chicken house where there is
plenty of grain for them to eat. I'm an excellent hunter.*

*For awhile, something was getting into the hen house and
sucking the eggs dry. I knew Gail and Chris were worried about
it, so I decided to find the animal and kill it. I waited around the
corner by the entrance to the chicken coop. I was pretty surprised
at the smell I detected when it was approaching, a musty scent
unlike a rat or gopher. I got more than I expected when it arrived.
The egg sucker turned out to be a huge white weasel. I jumped out
at him, thinking he'd run, but boy was I surprised when he turned
and ran straight at me. He bit viciously at my face and I backed
off in a hurry. When I got over the shock, I sprang at him. I
couldn't kill him, but he finally left and hasn't been back since. I
sure taught him a lesson.*

*I don't eat my kill as a rule. Gail feeds me canned food which
tastes much better than a rat. The thrill for me is in the hunting. I
love outwitting another animal.*

*I do carry my prey back to the house where I give it to my friend
Denny. He likes his food raw but he's a very shy cat, too afraid to
hunt well for himself. His mother, who was wild, hunted for him
and his siblings when they were young, but he left her before she
had a chance to teach him the finer points of hunting.*

I look out for Denny. I let him sleep next to me at night because he's afraid of the dark. I'm always very gentle with him. I asked him once why he was so scared of everything and everybody, but he didn't know. It doesn't really matter though. I see to it that he's perfectly safe. If one of the boarders at the kennel threatens Denny, I tell the dog he'll have to deal with me first. So far, I haven't had to carry through.

I enjoy teasing the dogs on their way in and out of the kennel. They're always on leashes or being carried by their people. It drives them wild when I walk ahead of them waving my tail, just out of their reach. They bark their silly heads off.

I'm not the least bit afraid of dogs. Sometimes I let the ones Gail and Chris keep, play with me. Often, when Mike is doing guard duty at night, I go out and keep him company. He likes to have me there with him.

Gail and Chris got another pet a little while ago, a burro. I've become very fond of him. He was wild when he came here, didn't even know anything about people. I've made him feel as much at home as I could and we're good friends now. I spend my afternoons in his pasture with him, chasing the bugs he stirs up as he pulls up grass with his teeth. He smells good to me; sometimes I rub up against him just to get some of his smell on me. I don't worry about keeping clean. I don't have to. I'm in charge here.

CHAPTER 19

PAINFUL SEPARATION

Breeding show animals is not for the faint of heart, nor for those free spirits who wish their lives to remain unencumbered and uninvolved. It's grueling work, both physically and emotionally. You spend all your time as a midwife, worrying over the babies. Are they progressing as they should? Does that one over there, who was born last and is a bit on the runty side, show enough spunk to compete successfully with his brothers and sisters for food? What about their mother, how's she holding up under all this added pressure? She looks tired. When you pause long enough to look in a mirror, so do you.

You spend your money on dog food, vitamins and vet bills that arrive in the mailbox all too often. If you get through the first ten weeks relatively unscathed, you realize you're going to have to part with these small creatures who've become such a big part of your life.

That was the point, wasn't it? But how can you let them go? You screen all prospective buyers with an intensity matched only by the CIA interviewing double agents. If they pass all your tests for potential "parents," you sell them a puppy and cry a little as you watch them leave.

Breeding has its moments though, such as when you hear that one of your pups has become the preferred police dog in a large metropolitan department, or when you stand in the spectator's gallery and watch one of yours receive its first championship point.

My friend, Wilna Coulter, and I were sitting around one day comparing notes on our latest litters. She bred Samoyeds, those soft, white, furry canines who inspired the phrase "Three Dog Night." The people of the northern Siberian plains, who developed the breed, described the severity of the weather by the number of dogs they had to have sleeping with them in order to keep warm. Since three Samoyeds are about as many as one could comfortably have sharing one's bedroll, a "three dog night" became their term for the most extreme cold.

PAINFUL SEPARATION

We had just finished bragging about the show ring accomplishments of our respective young when Wilna's face grew suddenly sad.

Surprised, I asked "What's wrong, Wilna? You look like you're about to cry."

"Well," she replied, "it's this dog I placed with some friends of mine. He seems unhappy and I don't know why. They're lovely people, teachers, both of them. Even though the dog is alone during the day, I think he gets plenty of attention when they're home. Yu-Kahn of Whitecliff—that's the dog's name---spends most of his time moping about looking perfectly miserable. He was originally with another family, but was stolen. You know, there's quite a lucrative black market in pedigreed dogs. People snatch them and make a fortune reselling them under falsified papers. Since dognappers have virtually no overhead expenses as we do, all the money goes straight into their pockets. Anyway, this dog was recovered, thank heaven. He was stolen in California and moved to Dallas, Texas, but the younger brother of the thieves' supplier, went to school with one of the kids in the dog's family. Word got back to the parents and they called in the police."

"That sounds like a happy ending. Many people are not nearly so fortunate in locating their stolen pets."

"It might have been if the family had been able to keep him once they got him back. They live on a ranch and the dog began chasing the neighbor's sheep. They couldn't afford to fence an area large enough for him or let him continue his new activity, so they asked me to find another home for him. He's the grandson of my prize show dog, Champion Sho-offs Czar of Whitecliff."

"How old was the dog when he went to his first family?"

"Twelve weeks. Yes, I know what you're thinking; just the right age from him to imprint to the people. The question is can we get him to 'unimprint' long enough to learn to love his new family?"

"We can try. Maybe if I communicate with him, it will help. Lots of times, if animals share their grief, they can then let it go, so to speak."

"What an excellent idea! I'll call Maralyn and Barbara now. If they're home and available, maybe we could go over there today."

When Wilna called, we learned that they were home and definitely wanted us to come over. When we arrived, Yu-Kahn greeted us at the door with his owners Maralyn Clark and Barbara Gingher, two middle-aged women whose quiet, gentle manner gave testimony to Wilna's view of them as caring pet owners.

Yu-Kahn greeted Wilna enthusiastically. After he finished licking her face, I spoke to him and he turned to look at me. He was a beautiful example of the breed with a fine triangular head and well-spaced eyes. We went into the living room where we settled into our chairs. Yu-Kahn walked over to me, sat down and nestled his chin onto my knee. I asked him to tell me about living with his first family.

I loved the man best of all. I went to live with him, the woman and their children, when I was still very small. I remember being put in a crate that the man lifted into the back of his car. I had never been confined like that before and I hated it. There was no room to move around inside the crate, so I howled in protest.

Hearing my complaint, the man stopped the car and let me into the front seat with him. At that moment, I knew I had found a true friend. I sat quietly beside him, wanting to behave well for him.

I liked the woman and the children too, but not as much as him. They didn't play with me the way he did. He often took me for long walks on the beach or in the hills. Sometimes we'd wrestle; I could be rough with him. The women and children were much smaller than he -I knew I could hurt them, so I had to be careful when we played.

We lived in several different places. The first time we moved, it was to a colder climate. That was fine with me, I feel most comfortable when the air is cold. We lived in a house with a fenced yard, so I could go outside anytime I wanted to.

Sometimes there was snow. When it was deep, the man sometimes put me and the children in the car and took us to the mountains for the day. The children enjoyed the snow. They slid down the hills with me chasing after them. I was happy when they had such a good time. Sometimes they made snowballs and threw them for me to fetch. I tried awfully hard to carry the snowballs in my mouth, but they usually broke before I got back to the children.

My master and I took long walks in the snowy hills. Sometimes we walked from sunup to sundown, just the two of us, happy to be in each other's company.

When we moved again, it was to a house far away from other houses. There wasn't a fenced yard, but I had more room to run. There were lots of large animals nearby - cattle, sheep and horses. I was so fascinated by their smell that I spent much of my time roaming around looking for them. I made friends with a gray and white blue-eyed dog who also liked to smell the big animals. We met often to search for them together.

We liked the sheep best because we could make them run. We'd sneak up on a herd and scatter them in all directions, which we found amusing; it was a great new game. They sounded funny, bleating the way they did. I was shocked when one day a man who had been watching us play with the sheep, shot at us. The bullets missed us, but my friend and I were so frightened by the noise and the man's anger, that we ran away as fast as we could.

We saw a picture in his mind of us killing the sheep and eating them. We were horrified; neither of us had ever killed anything. We both had plenty to eat at home.

One day, my friend and I were running along the road when a green van pulled to a stop in front of us. Two big men jumped out and grabbed my friend and me. We fought hard enough that my friend got away, but they put a rope around my neck and hauled me, still fighting, into the van. There were other dogs inside, all with ropes around their necks.

Panicked, I kept trying to get away even as the van began to move. I knew my family would be worrying when I didn't get home for dinner. My stomach felt funny from fear; I felt so sick I couldn't eat when the men offered me food.

After what seemed forever, the van stopped where we were taken into a yard and tied to the fence. There were already lots of other dogs tied there, all kinds and ages. The yard was hot and damp - not at all what I was used to.

I stayed there many days while other dogs came and went. I was so upset at being away from my family that I couldn't eat. The place was filthy, full of fleas and ticks. My fur got very dirty; my skin was covered with bites.

One day the men came into the yard carrying some papers that I knew had something to do with me. I realized the people intended to clean me up and sell me. I wondered where I would be going and if I would ever see my beloved family again.

Suddenly I felt a familiar presence. Looking around, I saw the woman of my family! I pulled at my rope to get free, frantic with fear that she wouldn't see me.

She walked into the yard with a policeman, who carried a mean looking club. I have never been as relieved in my life as I was when she ran over and untied me from the fence. The policeman made the other men who had stolen me, get into his car.

The children were waiting for us in a car out front. I raced toward them faster than I'd ever run before and jumped into the car. When they hugged me, they cried at how thin and dirty I was. I cried too.

I was famished. On our way home, we stopped so my family could buy some of the food I like best. They gave me plenty of food and water, but I couldn't seem to get full. I was also starved for attention, so the children loved on me all the way home. People who saw us along the way told my family I looked like the happiest dog they'd ever seen.

When we got home the woman clipped my coat and gave me a long bath to get rid of my fleas. It felt wonderful to be clean again, but with most of my fur gone, people laughed when they saw me. I was embarrassed until it grew out again.

I was delighted to be home with my master once more. I played with my friend again too. As we ran and rolled in the fields together, it was as though the bad time had never happened.

We even started chasing sheep again. We had just sent a whole bunch of them running one day when we heard gunshots, the bullets breaking the air close to my head. I ran full out to get away from them.

The man who shot at us came over that evening and told my family about my friend and me chasing his sheep. After that, they kept me tied near the back door. I was miserable; I paced and cried for days, but my master thought they couldn't take a chance on my being shot and killed.

Then Wilna came to my house and took me away in her car. As I looked back, I saw the man and the family standing in the driveway, watching us. I could feel their sadness.

I whimpered all the way to Wilna's house and tried to make her know that I wanted to go back to my family. I was sure I'd done something wrong, but I didn't know what. If they'd just take me back, I would never do anything wrong again.

I stayed with Wilna for a few days before I came to live with these women. They're kind to me, I know they love me, but I want to go home. Since I like men better than women, I'd like to make friends with a young man who comes here sometimes but doesn't pay much attention to me.

The women take me to dog shows. I've won several ribbons, and I like feeling that I have done something well. But everywhere we go, I look for my family. I haven't seen them yet.

I was sad after hearing Yu-Khan's story. Often animals, particularly dogs, bond to one person and are unable to live contentedly with anyone else. When something happens to separate the animal and its bonded owner, it can be psychologically crippling for the animal.

Fortunately, when Maralyn and Barbara realized how unhappy Yu-Khan was, and that he preferred to be with men, they set out to find a more suitable home for him. He is now living in Cincinnati, Ohio, with the family who owned his mother. He and his master get along famously. He has been in a number of dog shows and is well on his way to becoming a champion. He's made a good adjustment and is now content.

CHAPTER 20

GREED CAN BE LETHAL

There is undoubtedly some truth to the currently fashionable view that animals kept in national parks don't benefit from their unnaturally close contact with humans, and vice versa. On the whole, however, I think most park animals are vastly better off than they would be if they were returned to some vaguely utopian "wild." Their lives are longer, happier and more secure when we exert some intelligent, positive control over their environment. Indeed, we have no choice in the matter. Our world has become so overpopulated with humans that there is insufficient natural habitat remaining for many wild animals. The problem, then, lies in making well-informed choices, and in educating the public. We need to accept our responsibility for the welfare of those entrusted to our stewardship by God, and not expect animals to act like people.

A good case in point is the animal life in Zion National Park, Utah. Recently, I saw ample evidence there, both positive and negative, of human impact upon the lives of the animal residents.

Zion Canyon was cut from the surrounding mountains by the North Fork of the Virgin River. It is a breathtaking vista that has led people over the ages, to see in its' buttes and crags, everything from angels to beehives. The highway comes in at the top of the canyon. On either side are peaks and cliffs of hues so brilliant they remind me of a rainbow tower two - to three - thousand - feet above. Erosion caused by water and wind has cut away the soft outer pink rock and left behind the harder substrata, colored magenta, lilac, rose, true red and every once in awhile, dazzling white.

I drove into the park on a warm summer morning. The air was still and contented. I stopped at Sunrise Point, one of nearly a dozen places which afford an excellent view of the rock formations. I sat for awhile soaking in the beauty and serenity of the surroundings. Soon I noticed a group of chipmunks scampering toward a group of sightseers. I asked one of them non-verbally why they were following the people.

I come close to people to be fed their special food that we love. All chipmunks do. That's why we're out here now, dancing and fooling around. Often when people see us playing, they throw crackers or popcorn or nuts on the ground for us.

We have more than enough to eat without people—there are plenty of nuts and berries here to feed us, but we like the taste of your food better.

Several nights ago, two of my friends died in our burrow. We'd been eating treats all day. The rest of us had a hard time pulling their bodies out of the tunnels. I was sad and frightened, partly because I don't know why they died.

One of them left a litter of babies. They were too small to be raised by anyone else and died soon after she did.

The chipmunk scampered away, intent on begging one last, preservative-filled, over salted morsel. His small system, accustomed to, and designed for, a much different diet, would undoubtedly suffer for whatever he received. It made me feel badly as I realized that I too had contributed to some of the problems when I threw a slice of bread to the Raven nearby. I was absolutely blown apart at how well he had adapted to what he was given. At first he had eaten the small pieces I threw, but realized he couldn't pick up the big piece and fly away with it. He studied it for a moment, took his beak and rolled it into a ball, then picked it up and flew away. That was one of the most brilliant displays of intelligence I'd ever seen in a bird. The only comfort I felt was that it was just grains, nothing on it, but after talking to the chipmunks, vowed I would never endanger the wildlife again. I had just been taught a valuable lesson.

Feeling saddened, I walked back down the trail to my car. As I approached, I noticed a number of people nearby with cameras. I quickened my steps to see what they were photographing.

I rounded a bend and came upon the object of their attention. There among the trees was a young mother deer, her tiny son a few feet behind her. I approached slowly to within about six feet of her and sat down to talk with her. I asked her why she was alone there, away from the rest of her herd.

We don't have to stay close together here. We only go back to the herd at night or in winter, when we need to keep warm.

I used to live in another place, dry and sandy, with little to eat or drink. When the nights grew cold, we often heard the sound of guns. We ran to get away from the hunters, but many of our herd were killed.

Then my mother and I found this place where I feel safe. There are no gunshots here, and what I like most is that there is plenty of grass to eat and water to drink.

One day I jumped so high that I hurt my leg badly when I hit the ground. No matter how hard I tried, I couldn't walk. A man came by in a truck and saw me trying to drag my leg along after me. I was terrified by his smell and size.

My heart pounded wildly as he walked up to me. He spoke so quietly and gently that I realized he wanted to help me. He put me into the truck and took me to an enclosed area. He gave me plenty to eat and put something on my leg. When I was walking again, he brought me here. He still brings me food when there's no grass to eat.

I'm not afraid of people now, though I don't like being touched. I'm safe here and I know it. Here there are no guns - there is no fear. I spend my time teaching my babies how to live and what to eat. I love raising them.

This baby here is always getting himself into trouble. Once he ran too fast when we were near the edge of a cliff and off he went. He cried until I found a path down to him and brought him back up. He loves to eat the small flowers on the bushes because they're sweet. I, myself, prefer grass.

The baby bounded off, evidently wanting to run and play. He stumbled and almost fell, but immediately his mother was off after him. She had her hands, or should I say, hooves full.

I could feel her happiness at being able to raise her young in such a secure place. Our national parks do more than just define land boundaries; they provide a safe haven for many creatures whose lives would otherwise be quite perilous indeed. I felt happy myself, knowing that this young mother deer would be able to raise her baby in safety.

This is what I mean about intelligent choices and educated public. The park rangers know what they're talking about when they say that human food is bad for wild animals - listen to them. It will eradicate one more peril from the animals' lives.

CHAPTER 21

MATHEMATICAL WIZARD

I was in the shower when the phone rang. Though I have heard that only one call in a hundred is worth trailing water as you slog soggily toward the receiver, I am totally unable to apply the information to my own life. I have always been inquisitive; an unanswered call leaves me spending the remainder of my day wondering who the caller was.

This time I was also in the middle of shampooing my hair. I yelled to my nephew Mark to answer the phone, but the ring persisted. Dragging my soaking hair from my eyes, I grabbed a towel and ran to answer it. It turned out to be that one in a hundred.

The caller was my friend Evelyn Appelt. She and her husband Stan had just returned from a trip to San Jose, there they had met a man named Jim Todd, who had trained his Dalmatian, Sonny, to count.

Stan and Evelyn know me well enough to realize immediately that I would want to meet this mathematical wizard. She gave me the Todd's phone number, and we promised to get together soon. As I hung up, I was so excited by the information; I didn't even mop up the floor. I was going to San Jose soon to see clients, and I was already looking forward to meeting Sonny.

I contacted Jim Todd the day before I left Los Angeles some three weeks later. He sounded delighted at the prospect of having his dog interviewed.

The weather was cold and wet as I drove north along the coast. I mused over Evelyn's description of Jim's dog as a "mathematical wizard." I had read about dogs with similar abilities, but had never met one in the flesh. I was especially curious to learn first-hand if Jim was communicating the answers to math problems non-verbally without realizing it himself. Usually animals who learn tricks do so from a Pavlovian training process in which the animal is asked to perform in reply to certain signals, then rewarded for each correct response.

I turned west just south of the city and headed for the Todd's house, hoping the incoming fog would hold off long enough for me to navigate the narrow road. It did, and soon I was parked in front of their home.

I knocked on the door which was answered by a tall, reddish-haired man of about sixty, whose warm welcome put me at ease immediately. Next to him, peering up at me was a black and white face, connected by a slender, sleek body and a rhythmically waving tail.

"Come in, come in. It's much nicer being near a warm fireplace than outside this time of year, isn't it?" Jim said heartily, leading me into his living room where there was indeed a large fire blazing away.

Halfway down the hall he stopped, turned to his dog and said "Sonny, close the door, please." The dog, still waving his tail, trotted back to the entrance, slid his nose sideways along the width of the door, and waited for it to slip shut quietly before rejoining his master and me.

Sonny and I arranged ourselves comfortably in front of the fire while Jim went to his desk to withdraw a large portfolio.

"I thought you might enjoy looking at some of Sonny's press clippings before you begin talking with him," he said, handing me the envelope. "He's been performing in front of audiences for a little over six years now. He's become quite the celebrity. Pretty soon I'll have to get him his own desk; my own is becoming crowded with his things."

I leafed through the folder, admiring aloud the dog's photogenic face. As I did so, Sonny sat looking over my shoulder at the pictures of himself and appearing pleased whenever I commented upon one.

"How did you and Sonny begin performing, Jim?" I asked when I'd finished scanning the folio.

"Well, you know, I just started Sonny the way most people do, with the usual 'sit, stay, down' commands. He picked them up very quickly. We progressed to tricks, sitting up and begging, playing 'dead dog' and so forth. I've always believed that animals are capable of doing and understanding far more than most people give them credit for. They're like kids - they tease and play, but underneath there's a very real desire to be helpful, to please the adults in their lives. When he had mastered an entire repertoire of tricks, I decided to teach him math. I started by holding up one finger and asking him how many it was. When he barked once, I gave him a cookie and a pat on the head. A lot of what he does is rote, of course; we practice his math every night so he doesn't get rusty."

When you were teaching him, did you hold a picture in your mind of Sonny 'answering' you correctly?" I asked.

Jim considered for a moment before replying. "Oh, I suppose I did. It wasn't something I sat down and planned, it just sort of evolved. I think there are many dogs who have Sonny's capability, but so often when the dog comes to his owner and asks for attention, the owner tells him to go lie down. In other words, the flow gets shut off. I believe Sonny is capable of learning anything I'm capable of teaching him. I simply made a point of looking at the possibilities which were there and working with them. Dogs love being helpful. If more people would realize that simple fact, we'd have fewer unhappy animals."

And how did you begin performing for other people?"

"Well, once Sonny had mastered enough math to work for twenty minutes or so at a stretch, I asked the fellows in my bowling club if they'd like me to bring him to one of our meetings. They said yes, so I took him to the next one. He had a wonderful time mixing with the members during the first part of the meeting. I wasn't sure if he'd perform with so many people there, but he turned out to be a real ham. From then on people began asking us to do our act for school groups, church fundraisers, what have you."

"Do you have any professional acting experience?"

"Nope, I'm just a natural ham, too."

"Would you and Sonny show me what you do when you perform in public, Jim? I'd like to watch first, and then ask the dog how he came to understand what you wanted him to do."

There was a blackboard in the kitchen with a small overstuffed chair facing it, both next to a counter on which rested a large pile of cheese scraps. Sonny immediately jumped onto the chair and faced Jim, who had moved to the blackboard and was writing two times two. He finished and looked at Sonny. "How much is two times two, Sonny?" he asked.

Sonny barked four times. Jim gave him a piece of cheese. Then Jim wrote on the board again. He read it to Sonny. "What is the fourth root of sixteen cubed, Sonny?" He asked. Sonny barked eight times. He got another piece of cheese.

I could see what was happening. Jim was visualizing in his mind's eye what he wanted Sonny to do. When he gave him the square root problem, he held a mental image of Sonny barking. When Sonny had barked eight times, he changed the picture to Sonny sitting quietly being rewarded with a piece of cheese. It didn't matter what was written on the blackboard, really, except that it cued Sonny he was about to be asked a question. During the several demonstrations of Sonny's math ability that followed, I projected the wrong number of barks to him in my own mind, but the dog was so tuned in to his owner, he gave the correct answer in every instance.

Jim turned to me, beaming. "Did I tell you Sonny has an honorary degree in math from Cupertino High School?" he asked. "He 'taught' a math class there a couple of years back. The students were so impressed with him; they made him one of them."

"Would you mind leaving the room for a few moments? I'd like to see if Sonny will respond to me if you're not around. "

"Oh, I'm sure he will, I'm sure he will," Jim said, making his exit. "By the way, he knows that two barks in reply to a question means no and three barks means yes. Take all the time you want. I'm certain he'll answer you correctly."

When Jim had gone, I asked Sonny, "Am I a dog?" Two barks. I asked "Sonny, are you a dog?" Three barks. "Sonny, am I a man?" Again two barks. I called for Jim to come back into the kitchen and told him I was ready to interview Sonny.

I wanted to know the whole story of his life to date, so I took Sonny back to his puppy hood in my mind's eye. He responded by beginning his story at about six weeks of age.

My mother, brothers and sisters, all lived in a laundry room when I was very small. I liked it there, it was warm and comfortable. I had plenty of company and the nice milky smell of my mother's body.

There was a barrier between our room and the rest of the house, but we could often hear the children playing in the next room. Sometimes their mother brought them in to pet us. I liked those times best. I love attention.

One day, I looked up and saw a new face smiling down at me. It was Jim. I liked him at once because his eyes were kind. His rough overcoat had a number of interesting new smells. I lumbered over—I was still tripping on my feet a lot then—to make friends with him.

He picked me up and put my chin on his shoulder. I buried my nose against his neck and sniffed him. He scratched my ears gently and wrapped his coat around me tightly, then took me away with him.

I was lonely for my family the first night I lived with Jim. He seemed to know this because he stayed with me most of the time. He made a warm bed for me with thick blankets in a large box. They weren't as soft to sleep against as the bodies I was used to, but they did keep me warm.

As time passed, Jim and I became good friends. He gave me nice chewy things to play with. One was an old sock stuffed with rags; it smelled like his foot. How I loved chewing on that sock! One day, chewing on it and looking up at Jim, I saw a picture of me carrying the sock to him, so I took it to him right away. He praised me, petted me and told me how good I was.

That made me happy. I started trying to understand him, to read his mental pictures. He seemed to sense that I was able to do what he wanted me to without his having to ask me. He knew how much I wanted to please him.

Then he began actually telling me what he wanted me to do. I learned to roll over, shake hands and play dead. He was so pleased with me that he gave me bits of cheese when I did something right.

One day, he asked me to count the number of fingers he was holding up. I had no idea, but he was conveying an image of me barking one time, so that's just what I did. He patted me on the head and told me how well I'd done. Mostly, I do what he wants me to by looking at his mental pictures. People think I'm clever because I can answer their questions this way. All the time, I'm just getting the answer from their minds.

Soon we were showing off for Jim's friends when they came to our house. One night, Jim took me with him when he went out bowling. I did all my tricks perfectly. I loved all the attention I got from his friends. Soon after that we started going other places together. Now we go out all the time. We do our tricks on a stage now and afterwards the audience claps their hands a lot.

Often we go to schools. I love that because the children always make such a fuss over me. They pet me and praise me a lot after I'm done working at the blackboard. I love the delicious smell of schoolrooms; a mixture of peanut butter, sweat and chalk.

One day, as Jim was loading some things into his car, I saw him wondering if I'd help him carry his clothes out. We were going to spend a few days in the mountains and he wanted his sweater to keep warm.

I wanted to help, so I ran back to the house and got it for him. Now, whenever we go someplace and have things to take with us, Jim leaves some of them in a pile for me to carry out by myself. It makes me feel important.

Last summer I helped him and some of his friends build a cabin in the mountains. I carried tools for them, from one to the other. I like going to the mountains in the summer, but in the winter the wind blows through my fur and makes me cold. The whiteness of the snow hurts my eyes too.

Sometimes we visit Jim's daughter. That's fun because she has a dog. We play catch, all of us together. It's nice seeing another dog once in a while, but Jim is the center of my life.

As I left the Todd's' house that day, I felt grateful that there are people in this world like Jim who can see an animal's potential and allow him to realize it. All animals should be so fortunate. Perhaps one day they all will be.

CHAPTER 22

CANADIAN CIRCUIT

Between the early September heat, and a blanket of smog that covered the Los Angeles basin like thick yellow death, breathing had become an exercise in self-torture. I maneuvered through traffic, exhaust fumes being the biggest contributing factor to the problem, and managed to find a parking place a block away from my destination, the travel agency.

Inside the building, the air was an icy shock. I walked to the counter with the shortest line. Evidently, everyone who thought they could swing some time away from the city was booking reservations to other places. A large table under the window to my left was littered with brochures whose color photographs made them appear almost garish in contrast to the understated dove grey interior of the place. As I leafed through one on Baja, California, I remembered the wonderful time I'd spent there over Christmas nearly a year ago. I had camped on the beach with my six German shepherds, Blacky, my Pomeranian and, of course, no phones, letters, lectures or the host of other demands my regimented schedule presented. We had run on beaches of pristine pale sand, explored the ragged, scrub covered sand dunes, and shopped in a marketplace where exotic cactus fruit was sold along with Coca Cola and olives. We had eaten when we felt like it, slept late every morning, and spent the cool evenings gazing at the stars. When we left for home, relaxed and happy, I promised myself I would return there every year to refresh my spirit.

I glanced at the calendar on the wall. That trip had been nine months ago but the upcoming three months were to be filled with work. Well, maybe next year we could go back.

"What can I do for you miss?" asked a tired-looking clerk in a slightly rumpled seersucker suit. "Will you need reservations or just information?"

"Both, actually," I replied. "I need to make hotel reservations in Toronto for the week after next. I'm flying up to meet one of my dogs. I'll make my own arrangements with the airlines, but if you have a flight schedule for the twenty-second, it would be helpful"

He stared at me disbelievingly. "I see. Will your dog be requiring a hotel room as well?"

"No. That is, I need a room in a hotel that would accept dogs. I'll have two of them with me, both German shepherds. I'm going to be taking them to the Metropolitan dog show."

The agent leafed through a large book of hotel listings and located one in downtown Toronto which would accept pets. I filled out the necessary forms and paid for two nights in advance as he stuffed a packet with tourist information, and handed it to me along with my receipt. I took it from him and was about to leave when he said, "One more thing, miss."

"Yes?"

"I hope your dogs enjoy the show," he added with a smirk on his face.

"Twenty thousand unemployed comedians in this state, I thought to myself, and I swear I've met every one of them. There's something about needing accommodations for one's animals that turns the dullest people into contenders for the smart aleck, comic hall of fame.

Later, at home, I perused the brochures the clerk had given me. I'd been in Toronto several times to appear on the television talk show, "Canada after Dark." The photos showed the city as I remembered it, beautifully clean, very cosmopolitan, its architecture obviously designed to accommodate people as well as please the eye.

When I arrived in Toronto in the early part of November, the weather was still sunny, but there was a touch of fall in the crisp air. I drove through the city slowly, admiring the landmarks I'd seen in the travel brochures. I checked in at my hotel with Angie, one of the shepherds I planned to show at the Met. I co-own both Angie and her brother Arren with a fellow shepherd aficionado, but this was going to be my first experience with them in the show ring. Since Angie was the newest at this, I wanted her here a day early so she could relax and get used to the atmosphere.

The Met show, short for Metropolitan Kennel Club, was being held this year in the Canadian National Exhibition Center, a huge complex of buildings and yards where a number of fairs and animal shows are held. This setup works out quite well because the people on the mezzanine level have a clear view of the action going on below them with easy access to the rings below if they want a closer look.

The following morning, Angie and I picked Arren up at the airport and headed for the Met. We arrived early for the show and made our way through the throngs of exhibitors, both human and canine, that crowded the main floor. I checked the schedule and saw that the German shepherd class was to be at two o'clock. I set up our things in our allotted space outside the building where we could leave the dogs while we strolled through the vendors unencumbered. After walking around the twelve rings of the main show section, I moved up to the mezzanine level to visit the pet care section, noting with pleasure the large number of chemical free products on display. Down the way from pet care was Atlas the German Shepherd Wonder Dog, who starred in the movie "Lions for Breakfast" with the young actor Jan Rubes, who did such a fine job in the Walt Disney production of *The Incredible Journey.*

I stopped to chat with Atlas's owners, Marvin and Barbara Kelso, who own Marvinsway Kennels in Woodstock, Canada. Marvin, a slender, dark haired man of about forty, told me he thought Atlas was enjoying the show, but that he seemed a bit tired today. I asked Atlas to tell me about his life as a performer. A handsome animal about six years old, Atlas came over and sat next to me while he communicated his views on life in the acting profession.

I love performing because of the praise I get. I can do lots of different tricks: I jump through a hoop while it is burning; I untie people when their hands are bound with rope; I climb ladders and walk on narrow boards above ground; I pick up trash and put it into garbage cans, and I walk backward.

Marvin taught me to do all these things and he is really proud of me. I do my best to give a good performance each time I appear. I work in front of children a lot—we're always going to schools. I like the children, but sometimes they are so noisy I can't hear Marvin's commands clearly. That upsets me when that happens. I loved working with Jan Rubes. I was glad that Marvin stayed with me the entire time though; I'd rather be with him than anyone,

We live in an open place with lots of farm animals. I usually stay in the house, unless my family goes away without me. Then I stay in the kennels with the other dogs. I enjoy being home with my family more than anything. The children and I often go for long walks in the woods. Sometimes we even sleep there at night. I love it when one of them builds a campfire for us to sit around.

I'm enjoying this show, but I'm a little bit tired. Our hotel room was so hot I didn't sleep well last night, but felt a little better this morning after we went for a walk along the waterfront.

It seems that food takes a priority in most animals' lives because *Atlas* broke off as Marvin and Barb's seventeen-year-old son Mike approached with snacks he'd purchased for everyone.

I rejoined my own Shepherds and groomed them until their class was called. I was more nervous than they when we entered the ring. They both behaved very well even though they didn't win.

We departed the show early because I wanted to call the Toronto Mounted Police Unit to see if I could visit them during my stay in the city. I'd always been fascinated by pictures of the mounted units; the horses seemed to take a genuine pride in their work. I was curious to find out if this was really the case.

"You're joshing me." The voice on the other end of the line carried a clipped British accent. It belonged to Inspector Edward Johnson of the Toronto Metropolitan Mounted Unit, whom I'd rung up to ask if I could visit the stables in Sunnybrook Park.

"No, sir, I couldn't be more serious."

"You're sure you want to interview the horses and not the men?"

"Well, I'd like to talk with the men too, but the main purpose of my visit would be to learn first-hand from the horses what it's like to work on a police force and how they feel about it."

There was a long silence before he responded, somewhat doubtfully. "I guess it will be all right. If you come about nine-thirty in the morning, you'll catch the horses before they leave for the first patrol. You can probably find me at the exercise

EXPLORE

paddocks—we're training two new mounts just now and I'll be there supervising."

"Fine, I'll see you tomorrow morning."

The following day, I took a taxi to Sunnybrook Park, an area of several square miles located in the northeast section of the city. The stables proved to be nearly a mile into the park. The cab traveled up a wide thoroughfare, through heavily wooded areas rife with falling autumn leaves, passing by a rushing stream whose banks were lined with weeping willows and sycamore, finally crossing a wooden bridge into the stable area. The taxi stopped in front of a long, white, two story building with a gabled orange roof. A large board which listed the horses stabled within and their locations of their stalls, hung just above the doors. I paid my fare and got out to take a closer look.

The board listed sixty-one horses. I walked around the immaculately kept building and came to the paddocks area Inspector Johnson had mentioned. Beyond it was another stable complex identical to the first.

There, men were inside the far paddock, working with two handsome dark bays, a mare and a gelding. A tall, distinguished-looking man in uniform was standing near the rail watching. I assumed he was Inspector Johnson, so I went over to introduce myself. I thought at first the Inspector seemed to be somewhat leery of a woman who claimed she could communicate non-verbally with animals, but he soon fell into discussing his charges with a good deal of enthusiasm.

I learned that the horses are purchased as three-year-olds from farmers in the area who cross draft mares with Percherons, Belgians or high stepping Hackney stallions. This produces a horse with the size, stamina and calm disposition of the working breed and the agility of the lighter coach horse.

The horses are remarkably uniform in size and coloring; and all are brown with darker manes and tails. They work under a full English bridle with both bit and bradoon, and a British Army trooper saddle that is similar to the American McClellan cavalry saddle in that the pommel and cantle are about equal in size and shape, giving the rider a flat forward seat balance.

226

The men are in their early twenties when they join the unit as recruits. They receive six-to-eight weeks of equitation training, during which they ride four hours a day, five days a week. Each man is assigned his own horse and does his own stabling and care for the animal. They spend two hours at the beginning of the day grooming, cleaning stalls and readying their tack; then four hours riding and another two, caring for their mounts to feed and settle them for the night.

The horses are trained in light dressage for six months to a year before being taken on their first patrol. Dressage is a French word for a method of training a horse in obedience and in precision movement in which horse and rider learns to work together as a unit. This requires quite a bit of effort as each must learn to read and respond to the other's signals, to the slightest shift in weight or tension of muscle. It's an exacting process, but the results are well worth the effort. Watching a "finished" dressage team is like viewing a centaur.

The horses and men in the ring before us had some ground to cover before they could be compared to those mythological creatures. Most of the men who join the Mounted Unit have never ridden before, which leads to some amusing gaffes.

One young man with an earnest expression and an obvious lack of equine experience had just dismounted on the wrong side of his horse. The mare seemed astonished by his lack of etiquette. She stared at him for a long moment before turning to the slender, brown-haired man in the center of the ring with a "did you see that?" look on her face. From her deference to him, I gathered he was their trainer.

The Inspector and I both laughed. He called for a break in the work session so that the trainer could join us at the rail. He was introduced as Jerry Haywood who listened intently as Inspector Johnson described my work and why I was there. He gazed at me appraisingly before speaking. Evidently, I met with his approval because when he did finally speak, it was to ask if I'd mind his company during the interviews—there were some things he'd always wanted to know about some of the horses and one in particular.

The three of us walked toward the stables and paused at the second paddock to watch a new horse being taken through his paces by an experienced rider. Another mounted policeman joined them, both working together at getting the youngster accustomed to turning and stopping on command.

We went into the stables. A large board inside listed the locations of the five stables under Inspector Johnson's jurisdiction. They were of varying sizes - one housed as few as eight horses, another as many as twenty-eight. The stalls were narrow so that the horses were tied and had to face forward toward the feed box, which is the way most barns in Europe and in America use to be. Today, horses in the United States are boxed so they can move about freely. Jerry explained to me that the horses received sufficient exercise every day not to require a box stall. They were tied into the straight stalls at night by means of a rope with a weight at one end which ran through a heavy iron ring, attached to the horse's manger. This allowed the animal to move freely but contained him in the enclosure at the same time. The extreme cleanliness of the quarters and the thick straw bedding in the stalls, told me that these horses received the best of care.. I asked Jerry how long they work on the unit before retirement. He told me they are retired at eighteen years of age and that there is a long list of people waiting to 'adopt' them at the end of their service. I could readily understand this. A savvy, well-cared for horse that can remain calm in almost any situation is a very desirable mount. He went on to explain their duties were mainly for traffic and crowd control in the city's parks and for locating lost children. Toronto has many large parks, some with remote areas in which children can easily lose their way.

Buck, the horse Jerry wanted me to communicate with, entered the stable with Don Vincent, a former member of the British cavalry who had been training horses and men for the Mounted Unit for nine years. I recognized the horse as the gelding in the first paddock. Don explained that he preferred to use Buck whenever possible for a new recruit's first ride because he is an extremely good teacher. Buck stood at sixteen hands, an attractive dark bay with a mischievous glint to his eye. I asked him if he liked his work.

I've trained a lot of recruits in my day. I make it as difficult as possible for them to handle me. I never do anything to harm them, but I love to tease them. I dance around instead of standing quietly when they're trying to mount, toss my head when we're supposed to be standing at attention, and pull the reins from my rider's hands. I like to keep the new guys on their toes.

I enjoy my job, but I'm a little bit lazy. I don't like going on patrol because it's too much work. When I train the new men, all I have to do is spend a little time in the schooling paddock each day. Then I can come back to my stall where I am pampered.

Jerry taught me to work under saddle when I first came here. There was snow on the ground then. Often he and I went out looking for lost children in the park. We usually found them. I felt important when I could carry them back safely to their parents.

I have a little trouble with my knees now. If I don't get out and work a bit every day, they swell up and get sore. Jerry knows this so he makes the rider sit well back in the saddle when we're going downhill; that way I don't have too much weight on my front legs.

There's a small wooden bridge I often have to cross. It sways slightly when my feet touch it and makes a hollow sound that scares me. I hate that bridge and often wonder if I'll make it safely to the other side.

When I do go out on patrol, I always hope we'll be working at making people behave themselves. I love standing my ground and telling people they'd better do as my rider tells them. They move back when I come around! I love children though. I don't like to frighten them. I'm proud when they come up to me and tell me how beautiful I am. Sometimes I can see they're afraid I'll harm them; they should know I'd never do that.

Jerry stroked the horse's nose affectionately as I repeated Buck's story. I could see the strong rapport between the two. Jerry had probably known of Buck's likes and dislikes before learning of them from the horse's mouth, so to speak

As a recruit and his mount entered the stables, I walked over to them. The horse was a sixteen hand, eleven-year-old gelding named Trooper.

I don't do anything right for the new men at first. They have to learn to make me behave. I wouldn't actually hurt any of them—I

don't buck much and I don't kick at all—but I know when I've got a green rider on my back. I love giving him a hard time. Sometimes I pretend not to understand a command. I stand there enjoying myself while my rider tries to figure out how to make me do what he wants.

I love keeping people in line in the park, I like pushing them back. The men have to keep me on a tight rein.

In the summers, I work at the island, patrolling the waterfront. The soft sand and the feeling of space around me are very pleasant; the long jogs along the shore let me really stretch my legs. I come home tired, but it's a good tiredness. Autumn is nice too when there's frost on the ground. Then the earth is firm and cool; it feels good on my feet.

I hate the parades we sometimes have to march in. I'm never allowed to look around to see what's going on. I have to keep my head straight the whole time. It's frustrating. There are all kinds of interesting parade smells I'd like to explore. I'm always curious about new things, especially smells.

I'm not like Buck. I love to be on the go and hate just standing here in my stall. Even if my feet are sore, I don't limp or move slowly. I know if I do, Jerry will leave me in the stables and I'll miss the day's work.

I'd rather have a rider who knows what he's doing than one who's learning. For a long time, I worked with one man who knew how to ride well; I didn't have to teach him anything. I loved him and I'm sorry he's gone.

After Trooper, there was Charlie, who turned out to be a woman hater. Maybe hate is too strong a word—Charlie had spent most of his life in the exclusive company of men and the different smell and sound of women was unpleasant to him. He'd had a bad experience as a youngster, which he shared with me and the men as I translated his thoughts for them.

I was raised in a windy area near a river. There was very little snow, but it was cold and damp most of the time. I lived on a large farm with people who treated me and my mother kindly. They always made sure we had plenty to eat.

Eventually they sent me to live with some other people. A woman at the new place hit me often, though I don't know why. I

did my best each time she saddled me, but it never seemed to be what she wanted. She always carried a whip and I grew to dread the sight of her walking into the barn. After some time, I was moved again and brought here. Finally I am happy again as I love it here. The men treat me well but most of all, they respect me. I have problems with my legs if I don't get enough exercise, but Don knows this and sees to it that I get out as often as I need to.
When I first knew Don, I was still afraid of people. I bucked him off every time he got on my back. I expected him to hit me, but he didn't; he just got back on. Finally I lost my desire to throw him; he was so patient and gentle. Eventually I came to trust and love him. I'm curious about the other men too, but I'm still not sure enough of them to feel safe.

I made a point of not touching Charlie after learning of his dislike of women. I don't touch the animals with whom I communicate unless they indicate to me that they'd like me to pet them, but I felt with Charlie it was more important to refrain because of his obvious insecurity. I was thankful that he had ended up with the Mounties. His life could have been very unpleasant, indeed, had he gone from one owner to another, misbehaving more and more with each new one, not understanding what was wanted from him. He would probably have wound up at the slaughter house as dog food. Fortunately, Don had the wisdom to see beyond Charlie's bucking and obstreperousness to the underlying fear, and had the patience too lovingly and kindly wait it all out.

Susan, an eight–year-old mare, was the only horse of a different color I saw there and the only one with whom I communicated who disliked her stall.

I detest being closed up inside. I'm used to being out in a large, open place like where I was born and raised. That's one reason I'm so eager to go out and work each morning. It gets me out of this stable. I don't mind all the other horses - there were lots of them where I lived before. I love the men here, especially the one who rides me the most. He brushes my hair every day and cleans my feet carefully. When my feet hurt and smell badly, he washes them with something that makes them feel better.

I enjoy my work. I love to jog around the park in the early morning, but I do tire easily. I'm ready to rest long before Trooper or Charlie has even begun to think about it!

The men finished their saddling and were ready to leave the stables for the day's first tour of duty. I said goodbye and watched them ride off, their dark uniforms immaculate, their mounts' coats glistening in the morning sun. I stood for a moment drinking in the sweet smell of clean hay, warm animal bodies and saddle soap before I too departed.

As the taxi that took me out of the park that day crossed the bridge, I paid particular attention to the sound of its tires on the wooden boards. I recalled Buck's reluctance to set foot on the structure. I thought about how surprised his rider had been to learn of that. Like a true professional, Buck had accepted the less desirable parts of his job and went on his rounds cheerfully. I wished that working animals everywhere could be as happy and well-adjusted as those who had just told me their stories.

CHAPTER 23

DOWN ON THE RANCH

Human relationships with animals becomes increasingly complex the further one moves from being simply a pet owner. Most people, who keep a dog or a cat, usually develop a parental attitude toward their pet, with good reason. Our pets are dependent upon us in the same manner our children are. We provide them with food, shelter, grooming, medical care, love and a certain amount of training. If our animal contact is limited to our own pets and those of our friends, it's easy to view all animals in the same manner.

However, there is a wealth of human and animal interaction that few of us ever experience. Consider mounted police horses: their riders ride not for pleasure, but because it is the most logical means of transportation for their job. The riders must be able to rely on their mounts as equal partners in their work. The animals sense this, and respond by accepting responsibility.

I think all animals are capable of far more intelligent cooperation than they are ever in a position to display. Working sheep or cattle dogs, for example, are the same species as dogs kept only for companionship. (This is not to belittle companionship. I would be the last person in the world to underestimate the emotional value of animal friends.) The difference between an Australian shepherd who works and one who is kept as a pet, lies not in the animal, but in the owner's expectations of him.

Another variety of human-to-animal experience is that of the people who raise our food. Whether they are Amish farmers who still use horses to plow their fields and pull their carts to market, or western cattle ranchers who walk a fine line between the best interests of their livestock and their wallets. These farmers and ranchers realize another basic fact of animal existence - we are as dependent on animals as they are on us.

During the past nine years of my work in non-verbal communication with animals, I have been privileged to share the thoughts and feelings of all kinds of animals. In this book, I have presented only a small fraction of them to my readers. One experience I would particularly like to share is my visit to the Buena Vista Cattle Company of Madera, California, which has since relocated to Bend, Oregon.

I received a call one day from R.L. Freeborn, who, with his wife, Susan, manages the ranch. They were anxious to learn why their prize bull, Hercules, was having serious skin problems. Their vet had examined him, but could find no physical cause for the problem. I was planning a trip to the area the following week, so I agreed to stop by and visit with their livestock.

I was eager to be on my way as I entered the Los Angeles International Airport and made my way down the long corridor to the boarding area. Deplaning in Fresno was like entering another world. Instead of having to walk through an underground tunnel into the airport, I stepped directly onto the runway. There was a light breeze blowing warm air around me. It was a beautiful sunny day. I stood for a minute or two, savoring my surroundings before going inside.

Susie was waiting for me with the ranch truck. As we headed through the city, I pondered on the contrast between the Fresno that was and the one which is coming to be. What had been a sleepy little cow town with a handful of residents was rapidly growing into a bustling city. There were still cowboys strolling down the streets looking much as their predecessors of a hundred years ago did, but there were also men in business suits, carrying briefcases, hurrying on their way.

During the forty-five minute drive to the ranch, Susie and I talked about her animals. I asked her how she felt about raising cattle for food and how she felt about the animals themselves. I learned that Buena Vista Cattle is a seed stock producer and that the progeny from its herd either stay with the herd or go to commercial operators for breeding stock, but only a very small percentage of its cattle go to slaughter.

The ranchers who raise animals that wind up on our plates may seem callous to some. There is something extremely endearing about a baby of any species, a newborn calf, a just-dropped lamb, or a baby chick brings all our protective feelings to the fore. It is difficult for many of us to think about their eventual destiny. Unless we all become vegetarians, some of us must not only think about their slaughter, but actually carry it out. For those people, there is little room for the kind of paternal affection in which the average pet owner indulges.

As we turned into the long driveway leading to the ranch house, Susie asked me if I knew how slaughter animals feel about dying. I told her that, in my experience from communicating with some of them, most animals raised for food do not fear death. The only thing that frightens them is the possibility of a painful death. As long as their end is quick and humane, they can accept it. If they are well cared for during their life and dispatched from it with concern for their feelings, I don't believe we need to feel guilty for killing them. I do, however, feel very strongly that people should be aware of the conditions under which their meat is raised. Veal is one meat I will never eat because most veal calves are confined to small pens in a dark barn, for their entire lives. It is an extremely cruel method of producing meat. The rationale given for this inhumane treatment of animals is that the calves put on weight faster if they are not allowed to run in a pasture and burn up some of the calories they take in. Since shutting off the lights in a barn reduces the electrical bill, many ranchers force these poor animals to live in total darkness. Susie assured me that all the calves at Buena Vista are pastured, not stalled, and lead very free lives until they are sold for slaughter or breeding. I was comforted by that as I saw many calves in the fields on either side of the driveway, some just dropped, others a bit older. All were with their mothers in the larger herd, living in the manner most natural for them.

R.L. Freeborn came out to greet us as the truck pulled to a stop. A tall man with a long stride and a cowboy's habit of using few words, he was obviously concerned with doing the best for the animals in his care. It was a little hard for R.L. to accept the idea of non-verbal communication with animals, but he was anxious to learn if his cattle were content with their lives and what, if anything could be done to make them happier.

The three of us stopped briefly at a paddock near the house in which a gentle-looking, soft-eyed, brown and white cow was suckling a calf. R.L. explained that she was a nursemaid cow, one who cares for orphan calves. I asked her how she felt about not having any babies of her own. She expressed perfect contentment with taking care of the other cows' offspring. She liked having a paddock to herself and being close to the house. Susie wanted to know if the cow was pregnant, as she had been covered by one of their bulls a few weeks earlier. This would be her first offspring since coming to the ranch. I asked her if she felt she was carrying a baby, but she didn't know.

We turned away and headed for the bull pastures on the other side of the house. On the way, we stopped at another paddock where a two-year-old bay gelding quarter horse was waiting for his trainer to work with him. I asked the youngster if he wanted to be a race horse or a cattle horse. He replied that he was excited about learning to work the cattle and wanted to stay on the ranch.

There were several cowboys coming and going as we continued on our way. The bulls that are with the cows for only a few months each season were being separated and brought back into the paddocks near the barns. R.L. wanted me to check with the brood cows to see if they were content with their lives. I did and found that most were. One or two didn't want any more babies, but most accepted their role on the ranch with no resentment.

We arrived at the bull paddocks. The cattle at Buena Vista are a cross between Brahmas and Black Angus, called Brangus cattle. On the average, the bulls weigh in at about twenty-one hundred pounds. Cows weigh about eleven to thirteen hundred pounds after calving and heifers, which are young females, weigh about seven hundred pounds. They are large, impressive animals, especially the bulls.

The first bull had a physical problem - he was tired all the time. I could feel that his body was functioning very slowly. R.L. said they couldn't figure out why this one kept stumbling over his own feet, hurting himself. I told him it was because the animal had some sort of energy problem and was too tired to look where he was going.

We came to their best breeder, a son of Hercules, with a very aggressive disposition. He definitely didn't want to be petted by people. He knew he gave the ranch hands and R.L. problems with his often fractious behavior, but told me he wouldn't intentionally harm them. He just didn't want to be too close to people. He was a marked contrast to his father who was in the next pen.

R.L. and Susie were very concerned over Hercules's skin problem and his apparent unhappiness. I learned that he had been hand-raised, and then shipped to a place where he was with a large number of other bulls. At that time, his skin trouble started. I questioned the bull about his situation.

I'm afraid of some of the older cows. They know what we're supposed to do, but they frighten me. The younger ones are all right though. I'd much rather be around people than cattle. I grew up living near a house and people were always coming by my paddock to pet me. I miss that. When I'm down here, away from the house, I don't see enough of people. I like to watch them, to see what they are doing. I'm unhappy being out here near the pastures and away from them.

I could see that Hercules had imprinted to people at an early age. Sometimes that can be a good thing if an animal is destined to be a pet. Sylvester, the tiny hoot owl with the yellow hat, had imprinted to his owner. It wasn't what she would have chosen for him to do, but he came to her at an age when he was looking to the creatures in his immediate vicinity for a model, so he turned to her. Hercules had evidently done much the same thing and was now far away from his original owner and even people. I was sure his skin troubles were from stress. I asked him if he was rubbing his hair off and making his skin sore.

Sometimes I rub against the paddock because my skin itches. I know it worries R.L. and Susie. One time, I knew they were really worried when they cut a piece of my skin out that they said a doctor was going to look at. It hurt a bit, but it's ok now.

I liked the weather better in my former home because it was cooler and damper than it is here. I don't like being in the hot, drying sun. There was a little girl there, too. I liked to watch her play on the swing near my paddock.

I like the woman who feeds me; I even like birds, horses, dogs and the cats that come around often, but I don't like these other bulls.

I don't mind being with one cow, but a herd is too many for me. Sometimes I snort at the people here; I think it frightens them, but I don't intend to. I'm only talking to them the way I would talk to other cattle. I'd be happy if I never had to look at another cow again.

Sometimes the men ride horses into the pastures and chase us back to our paddocks. I don't mind that at all. It's just that the herd confuses me. There are just too many of them.

When R.L. and Susie heard this, they said they would move Hercules closer to the house again. He is so thoroughly imprinted to people that he really doesn't have any interest in breeding the cows they bring to him. Life was a bit tough for him in his state of mind. I put myself mentally into Hercules's body to see if his hair loss was being caused by a parasite of some sort. He did not seem to have any infection, nor did I feel any parasites biting him, all of which reinforced my impression that his troubles were stemming from stress. R.L. said they were building a special facility for washing the bulls and collecting their semen and that he would see that Hercules was washed often to keep his skin moist. They decided to add oil to his feed in the hope of providing some lubrication for the skin and keep him on green grass, more of what he was used to back in Missouri, where he was raised. R.L. told me that Hercules was ten years old, which is getting on for a bull. They usually only live to be about fourteen or fifteen years of age. As we walked away from his paddock, I felt happy that Hercules' people were doing everything they could to make his sunset year's happy ones.

R.L. asked if the ring in Hercules's nose bothered him. He said he would have it taken out if the bull was suffering from it. I checked with the bull and found that it didn't bother him unless someone pulled on it.

R.L. and Susie took me on a truck tour of their eight-hundred-acre spread before I left that day. I felt as contented as the cows as we drove past the various pastures and paddocks. Here was an exemplary balance of life. The earth, the animals and the people were all a part of each other. It was all working as it should.

When I spoke with the Freeborn's several months later, I was told that Hercules had greatly improved. They moved him to the paddock near the office where all the employees spend time each day petting him and scratching his back. The paddock is also kept moist, similar to his old environment. He now seems to be content, standing quietly and no longer owing at people. Best of all, his hair is growing back.

CHAPTER 24

I'D RATHER BE RUNNING

As soon as I knew my itinerary would include northern Kentucky, I called my friend Dr. Marvin Cain, DVM to ask if he could arrange for me to visit the Claiborne Farm in Paris, Kentucky, just outside of Lexington. For years, I had wanted to see the great breeding farm, home of the most famous racing horses of our time, but circumstances of one kind or another had always conspired against it.

Not this time. The arrangements were made, and shortly thereafter, I was heading down Highway 68. On either side of me, fences of fieldstone or immaculate white rail separated huge pastures filled with Kentucky bluegrass and breathtakingly beautiful thoroughbreds. Recently dropped foals gamboled after their more graceful mothers while yearlings competed with each other in play versions of the races they would some day run in earnest.

I turned and drove through the huge stone-flanked entrance to the farm. The narrow road belied the farm's importance much in the manner of a Boston Brahmin's unobtrusive brownstone. The property was perfectly kept; fences looked as if they'd been freshly painted; and, weed-free flowerbeds lined the drive. No one is ever actually visibly present performing the maintenance, but evidence of it is everywhere like an always filled water glass at a good restaurant.

I parked at the office and walked down to the cemetery behind it; the final resting place of some of Claiborne's most famous stallions. I paused for a moment at the grave of Nasrullah, sire of over a hundred stakes winners, before I moved on the final resting place of his most famous son, Bold Ruler. The legend on his tombstone read: Bold Ruler, Sired by Nasrullah, out of Miss Disco, born April 6, 1954, died July 12, 1971. The first date was a double milestone in thoroughbred history, though no one knew it at the time. Two mares went into labor the same night. One was Miss Disco, bred to Nasrullah to produce Bold Ruler, who many consider to be the greatest thoroughbred of all time. The other mare was Knight's Daughter, bred to Princequillo, another outstanding Claiborne stallion. He was famous for producing Round Table, who won so many races he became the leading money maker in racing history. For many years afterward, the two colts of Miss Disco and Knight's Daughter were housed in facing stalls in stud barn number 3.

Bold Ruler seemed beset by troubles almost from the moment of his birth. He developed a hernia as a foal and suffered throughout his life with chronic arthritis, numerous leg problems, and a wrenched back. His career on the track was spotty at best, but his trainer, the legendary "Sunny Jim Fitzsimmons, considered Bold Ruler to have had the greatest heart of any animal he'd ever worked with. Sometimes it seemed he won on sheer determination, not giving in to his beleaguered body. He was the only thoroughbred to ever successfully win a reprieve from cancer. In spite of his ailments, this horse was the leading American sire eight times, seven of them in a row. Two of his get earned more than two million dollars for their owners. At the end of 1975, when his last colts and fillies were still running as three-year-olds, seventy-eight of them were stakes winners. At the same time, twenty-seven of his sons had also sired stakes winners, an almost incredible record.

Early in July of 1971, it became apparent that the cancer which had struck Bold Ruler's throat two years before had metastasized into his head and upper chest. It was inoperable and nothing more could be done for the gallant stallion except to put him to rest. He was led to a van near the cemetery and injected with a lethal dose of barbiturate.

It is said that a hush fell over Claiborne farm at the instant Bold Ruler drew his last breath. Even workers hundreds of acres away on the giant property knew when it happened. In a pasture not too far away, a sorrel yearling with three white socks and a narrow, slightly crooked blaze on his face, stopped grazing and looked toward the stud barn his father had so recently left for the last time. His name was Secretariat, who would, two years later, inherit Bold Ruler's black and gold trimmed stall, having won all three jewels of the coveted Triple Crown of racing - The Kentucky Derby, the Preakness, and the Belmont stakes.

Mrs. Henry Carnegie Phipps, who owned and bred Bold Ruler, had a unique system of stud fees. No money ever changed hands, she didn't need it. She was far more interested in seeing that her great stallion bred only the finest mares available. So when a mare had passed her rigid tests and was pronounced suitable for mating with Bold Ruler, she was bred to him for two years. At the end of that time, the mare's owner and Mrs. Phipps would toss a coin. The winner had first pick of the two foals. The system did much to enhance the Phipps' racing stables; one couldn't go too far wrong with one of Bold Ruler's foals, especially since the quality of the mares was so high it added enormously to the potential of the offspring.

One such mare was Somethingroyal, owned by veteran breeder Penny Tweedy. In 1970, she and Ogden Phipps, who carried on his mother's tradition, tossed a coin; he got a filly, she wound up with Secretariat.

Secretariat was something of a phenomenon on the track. Most race horses have a particular style of running to which they will always adhere. Some are front runners, made angry by the appearance in their peripheral vision of another horse; some prefer to run second or third for most of the race, then push down the homestretch, and some like to hang well back, maybe even last, and dazzle the crowds with a show of speed and stamina at the three-quarter turn, sweeping to victory amid excited cheers. Secretariat did all of these almost equally well.

During his racing career, this great horse earned 1,316,808 dollars. Mrs. Tweedy syndicated him in early 1973 into thirty-two shares, which sold for a total of 6,080,000 dollars. Had she waited until fall of that year, after he'd won the Triple Crown, she could have done the same thing for 13,000,000 dollars. His first crop of foals was something of a disappointment, but the second crop went on to race and did well, but his offspring never came close to the record of their father. He was a great race horse, but not a great sire.

I walked back to the office where the head groom showed me to the stud barns. For those who haven't visited a thoroughbred farm, the word barn is a deceptive term, usually making you think more of modest, Midwestern, farms of draft horses, haylofts and mice in the grain. In Kentucky, a barn is an elegant affair, a stallion barn particularly. The stalls are sixteen by sixteen feet, carpeted in three feet of straw, which is changed down to the last wisp every morning when the horses are led out to their exercise paddocks. The walls are spotless, painted to perfection. The walkway between the stalls is immaculate. The stalls themselves are lined with two-by-twelve solid oak planks, the bloodlines of their inhabitants listed on the outside just above the halter hooks.

One of the grooms led Secretariat out. He seemed immediately curious about me as he stuck his nose next to mine to say hello. We breathed lightly on each other's noses, he seemed satisfied, so I assumed I passed muster and began to ask him about his life as a celebrity. In my mind's eye, I created the finish to a race I had seen him win and waited for a change in my feelings. It came quickly:

I loved winning best of all. I never gave my running all I had; I could have run faster if I needed to. I'm a champion.

I'm not as happy living here as I was when I traveled from one racetrack to another. I liked being loaded into the van and seeing my saddle there because I knew it meant I would run soon. I loved the excitement at the tracks; everyone talking, laughing and cheering for me. At the end of the race, people brought me flowers. It was great!

Eventually, I was brought here to live. I don't run anymore, except when I'm out in the paddock, and even then that isn't much fun because there's no one there to beat and no crowds to cheer me on. Besides, the flies bother me in the paddock. I don't care for the grass out there either. I'd rather eat hay in the barn.

I also miss my friends. I never get to be with other horses except when I go to the breeding shed in the spring. I know my mother is here somewhere and I'd like to go and see her again, but I can't.

When I was younger, I spent lots of time with other horses. There was one, a black filly, who was my special friend. We'd stand in the pasture and scratch each other's backs, then run and play the rest of the day. One day, when they let me out, she was gone and I haven't seen her since.

I miss the man who took care of me when I was racing, too. He used to talk to me all the time. He was so gentle that when he touched me, I hardly felt his hands. I haven't seen him since I stopped going to the track, but I still think about him. It's nice here. I'm well cared for and couldn't ask for better food or a nicer stall, but I'd rather be running. I felt sorry for this gallant animal obviously one of the greatest we will ever see. Too bad we never got to see what his full potential really was.

One of the other grooms appeared, armed with bucket and sponges. It was time for Secretariat's bath, a ritual he evidently enjoyed, for he greeted the man enthusiastically.

After walking through the barn to visit with the other studs, I thanked my hosts and returned to my car. I drove back down the narrow road to the main highway, stopping for a brief moment to watch a group of two-year-olds at play in one of the pastures. One of them, a dark bay filly with one white sock, caught sight of me and pranced over to the fence. She stood watching me for a minute or two, then turned and flashed away across the grass, a perfect feminine miniature of her handsome grandsire. Death has not won. Bold Ruler is still very much with us.

CHAPTER 25

MARINE WORLD/AFRICA USA

I was in my study sorting through some old publicity material in the hope of clearing out my desk for more current paperwork when I came upon a photograph of me with Nadji, a three-hundred-pound Bengal tiger. The discovery gave me an excuse to interrupt my organizing and not being one for drudgery before fun anyway, I sat back to reminisce for a while.

The photographer had captured us in profile, nose to nose, as Nadji planted a wet kiss on my face. I smiled, recalling with amusement, the feel of his sandpaper tongue. The photo was taken at Marine World/Africa USA, a large animal complex near San Francisco Bay, just north of Redwood City that was later relocated to a more suitable area on the bay, North of Berkeley. I was participating in a non-verbal communication workshop at the time. A reporter who had come out to cover the event accompanied me to my meeting with Peter Gross, the devoted young man who raised Nadji from a cub, and took our picture as Nadji licked my face.

Peter's innate understanding of animals was astounding, which showed in Nadji's happy, gentle response to his methods of "affection training". I asked Nadji what his favorite activity was. He had told me that next to playing with Peter, he loved to ride around the compound in the back of Peter's jeep, watching the people stroll past the various enclosures and feeling the breeze on his face.

I remembered the day in 1975 when the three of us appeared on Jim Dunbar's "A.M. San Francisco" talk show. Nadji stole the limelight from Peter and I by hamming it up the entire time the camera was on him.

I had also met Alberta, the baby hippopotamus that day. She had been unhappy because the park had been temporarily closed to the public. Alberta had a shower in her enclosure which needed someone to pull the activating cord. This was evidently a favorite activity of her younger visitors, bur she complained to me that there were no children around to splash water on her back. I offered to assist her with her daily ritual by pulling the cord myself, which she accepted with delight.

I wondered if Alberta or Nadji were still living at Marine World. I glanced guiltily at my messy desk and caught sight of my appointment book sticking out from under a sheaf of book notes. If I could squeeze in a day at Marine World in my next trip to the Bay Area, I could visit them again.

I located my phone under a cardboard box and called Peter Gross. He greeted me warmly, and assured me my old friends were still in residence and he would be looking forward to seeing me again the following week. Cheered by the prospect, I efficiently finished the job of organizing my desk.

As I headed through the morning fog toward Marine World several days later, I was again thinking about the animals. So often, people ask me if I think it's fair to animals to be confined in a zoo. I have to answer that it depends upon the animal and the zoo. An adult animal taken from the wild is obviously going to have more difficulty adjusting than a baby; and, a dirty, poorly run zoo whose attendants don't care for their charges with affection and respect, will be hard on any animal unfortunate enough to be housed there.

Marine World is one of the finest animal parks I have ever visited. The people who work there show a genuine love and concern for the animals, and everything is done to make the compounds and cages as comfortable as possible for them. I think the animals there are as happy as they could be. Because of their protected environment, many will have longer lives than there counterparts living in the wild, hunting for their food and being hunted by other animals intent on making them their next meal.

The fog had burned off by the time I arrived at the large stone gates flanking the entrance. I parked my car, walked around to the back entrance, and entered through the guard gate, along the path near the elephant barn. Several elephants were eating breakfast while two park attendants cleaned their enclosure. I continued up the path and arrived at a large pool where two dolphins and a whale were moving lazily through the water, pausing occasionally to bask in the warmth of the sun on their backs. I asked the dolphins how they felt about living at Marine World; I experienced a strong feeling of contentment coming from them as they began to respond.

We like being here much better than the place we came from. We were born in a large tank that housed several other dolphins. The tank water didn't bother us because it was all we had ever known, but when we came here, we felt much better. The water here is far cooler and cleaner and has a sweet smell. We can breathe easier too.

We were brought here in a large tank with a net inside it. A man stayed with us, pouring cool water on our backs during the long noisy trip. When we were lifted from the tank we were so scared, we shook. But we both held very still while a man ran his hands all over our bodies and looked into our mouths. Then we were put in here. At first the water seemed too cold for us; it took all our energy to stay warm. Now that we are used to it, we play more than we did at the other place.

After we'd been here a short time, a man surprised us by getting into the pool and swimming up to make friends. He scratched our backs and smelled of fish, so we decided we liked him. He still comes and swims with us. We look forward to his arrival. We can always tell when he's coming, because he slaps the water just before he dives in.

He taught us to do tricks for the people who come here; we can jump into the air, catch fish, and even balance a ball on the ends of our noses. Each time we do what he wants us to, he gives us a piece of fish. He rubs our heads, which feels good. We like swimming with him.

I turned my attention to Coco the whale. I wondered whether he, too, enjoyed being petted.

Not at all! I remember living in the ocean and I want to go back. I miss the slimy plants, the coral and the sea anemones. I want to swim through large reaches of water again.

I had already left my mother and was on my own when the net closed around me. I fought hard to get free, but I couldn't. Now all I have for company are these two dolphins, and I don't like them. Another whale that was caught with me and brought here died soon after we came. I still miss him.

The man who swims with the dolphins has tried to make me do tricks too, but I won't have anything to do with him. I don't want to be touched by people. I want to go back to the ocean and be touched by other whales. I don't know where I would look for my family if they put me back though. I doubt that I could find them.

I walked away from the pool to ask one of the park attendants if the whale was going to stay at Marine World. She told me they realized he would never adjust to living there and were trying to find some way to return him to the ocean.

Feeling cheered by this news, I moved on to the lagoon. Visitors enjoy that area of the park from their boats, while hawks and vultures screech overhead. Most of these birds have been given to Marine World by people who could no longer take care of them. All the animals seemed content with their lives there.

Abasi, an African hawk eagle, seems to enjoy watching the people as much as they enjoy watching him.

When I see the woman who feeds me approaching with a leather band on her arm, I fly to her right away. I know it means she's going to take me outside the aviary so I can swoop down on the people as they walk by the animal pens. People are interesting. I'm bored when the park is empty, but I also love being with the other birds. It makes me feel secure. Sometimes I fly close to the other birds to tease them. I love to do that to the eagle because he gets so angry with me that all he can do is sit on his perch and scream at me.

Igor, the twenty-five-year-old female vulture who had appeared on the "Addams Family" television series, had this to say about show business.

I loved performing. I also liked the other actors in the show. The only thing I didn't like were the long periods of time I had to be by myself in a box. I prefer to have company most of the time.

I love Mary, the woman who takes care of me here. She took me home with her one night and fed me at her table. I got the same food she had and it was delicious! There were lots of things I hadn't tasted before. I especially loved the ice cream; it was cold and sweet in my mouth. I'd like to go home with her every night.

I like people better than birds because people pay more attention to me. Mary taught me to do tricks for the park visitors. I enjoy that very much; it makes me feel important.

I'd like to have some babies to raise, but there isn't a male of my kind here and I sure don't want to mate with those other kinds of birds.

I left the birds and walked along the path, passing the food and souvenir stands mobbed with park visitors. The road forked so I took the left branch to the dolphin petting pool. Crowds of children screamed with delight as the dolphin jumped into the air and sent streams of water over them. Nearby at the whale pool a show was just ending. I went over to ask Yaka, a female whale, if she enjoyed performing.

I love it! I work even when I don't feel well. I want to be admired and praised.

I have a new mate now. After my first mate died, I was terribly lonely; then the people brought Nemo to live with me. He makes me angry sometimes because he tries to push me around. He doesn't work as hard as I do, either; he's lazy. But I'm much happier with him here than I was when I was alone. We're kept separated most of the time, but we call to each other across the tank divider. Sometimes I wish I had more room to swim, but I don't want to live in the ocean where Nemo lived. I wouldn't know what to do there.

I glanced across the lagoon and saw a young park employee playing with an enormous tigress. As I watched, I checked the animal's feelings for her handler.

What do you want, my friend? I was napping and would really rather not be disturbed, but I love you and know you want me to come to you. Do you want to play?

Her question was accompanied by a playful swipe at the man. Since she seemed to think like a dog rather than a wild animal, I wondered about her early life.

I remember a man who played with me a lot when I was very small. It was fun, but I learned that he wouldn't play with me if I played rough. Once I scratched someone here and made him bleed. No one talked to me for a long time after that, which made me sad. Now I'm very careful when I play with people.

I then asked the tigress if she wanted to live in the wild, and I received a blank response of *"what's the wild?"*

Overall, I was impressed with the attitudes of all the big cats at Marine World. They've all been affection - trained resulting in healthy, happy feelings toward people.

I moved on to the Llama compound. When I reached out to touch a nine-year-old Llama named Put Put, he backed away from me.

I don't like being touched by strangers. I love the people who feed me and take care of me, but other people are different; they smell strange to me. I know my friends by the way they smell.

I like to pose for pictures, though. Sometimes when people come to my pen, I see a picture in their minds of me standing proudly, looking at them. Usually I do just that.

One of the women who used to take care of me was my special friend. She had long yellow hair and a sweet odor. I miss her very much. She used to take me for walks around the park so that people could stop and admire me. She was very proud of me, so I always behaved myself when I was with her. One day when she came to my pen, she was very sad. Somehow I knew it was her last visit. I looked for her every day for a long time anyway, but I haven't seen her since.

I won't have anyone riding on my back. My body is my own. I have another Llama in my pen now that I like a lot, except when he teases me. I don't like games as well as I did when I was young.

I went on to visit with Sarge, the water buffalo. I leaned against the fence around his compound and complimented him on his fine appearance. I asked him where he'd come from.

I lived with my mother and a large herd of water buffalo when I was small. Our home was hilly and hot with lots of room to move around. I remember being petted by the woman who brought us our hay each evening. She always spoke to us and handled us gently. I loved the salty taste of her skin.

One day some men herded several of us into a truck. The next thing I knew, I was in a pen with some other baby water buffalo. I was frightened by being away from my mother and called loudly for her, but she didn't come. The others were lonely and crying too, so we stayed close together for comfort.

We were in that pen a long time, gradually getting used to it. The attention of the children who came and petted us helped me forget how much I wanted to be with my mother.

One day I was loaded into another truck, where I rode from sundown until the next morning. When the truck gate was opened, I found myself here.

At first, I didn't like the cool air. I missed my friends too. I was put into a small pen by myself; the other animals were too far away to nuzzle or be close to. I was miserable.

Then one day a young woman came to my pen and put a rope around my neck. She took me out of the pen and led me around the park so I could see all the other animals. I liked being with her so much that I walked slowly to make our outing last longer. When she took me back to my pen, she sprayed water on my back and cleaned my fur. I loved the feeling of the water running over my body and moved closer to her for more. She scratched my neck and rubbed behind my ears, even let me lick her hands. I sure felt a lot better.

She came to my pen often after that. One day when we were out walking, she stopped and put a small child on my back. I've always liked children. I felt very important being allowed to carry this one on my back through the park. I've carried many children since then and some adults too. In some ways, I'd rather carry the adults. They don't pet me as much as the children do, but I can walk faster when they're riding me. I love being admired. I also like to watch the people.

Some mornings, I don't want to be bothered by anyone and the people who feed me, leave me alone - they seem to know how I feel. I'd never hurt anyone on purpose. I'm fond of most people. I do want a mate though. I want to be close to another buffalo.

I left Sarge and walked on to visit with Alberta the hippo; the baby, who had loved her shower, had grown into an adult. Curious to learn if her attitudes had changed with maturity, I asked Alberta if she still liked children.

No, I've grown tired of them. They aren't as nice to me as they were when I was small. Then, all they wanted to do was make the water run onto my back; now, they throw sticks at me and try to make me eat pieces of paper. I don't want to have any young of my own. I still love adults though.

Feeling a bit sad, I moved on to encounter two elephants and their handlers, all out for a stroll around the compound. I asked the elephants if they were having a good time.

As long as we're together, we're happy. We couldn't stand to be without each other. We like people and enjoy giving them rides on our backs. They seem very light to us, and the walk is relaxing. At least we get some exercise which we really enjoy.

We love being washed with the hose when it's hot or before we have to work. We really enjoy going to the island where the giraffes live. It's pleasant there with plenty to eat.

The only thing we don't like is having our barn dirty or smelling badly, but it's usually very clean. All in all, we're happy here.

Next I went to visit Kari the cheetah, who is housed in the cat area. A long, sleek animal, Kari conveyed the impression of viewing everything around him with disdain. I ask him if he felt as superior as he appeared.

I'm different from these others. I was born in a jungle. I caught my own food when I was young and took care of myself. I loved outwitting another creature and eating his still-warm flesh.

I was chasing a gazelle the evening I was trapped. I tried to run, but my way was blocked. I was furious at being caught. I wasn't afraid, just angry that they'd caught me. I knew they didn't mean me any harm.

I was taken a long way from the jungle, to a place where people came and looked at me. For a long time I refused to return their looks. Eventually one or two people started coming into my cage for short periods of time, bringing me fresh meat to eat - fresh, but cold; not like what I used to eat. The people seemed to want to make friends with me. I snarled and swiped at them, but they kept on trying to come closer. They smelled interesting to me. Now people are fun to play with as long as I don't scratch them.

I've been here a long time now. I'm used to people and their ways, but I still think of the jungle. Back home I used to stretch my legs and run for the joy of running. I still miss that, but not as much as before. My legs get stiff sometimes now, so I like having a warm place to sleep at night. I spend a lot of time sleeping, too.

Kari's adaptation to captivity pleased me. I was now feeling relaxed and happy as I moved toward Charlie the Lonesome Cougar. I was quite unprepared for the emotions I experienced from him. Anger and loneliness showed clearly in his flashing eyes and in his defensive posture. I asked him the reason for his unhappiness.

I hate being near all these other cats. I don't like being near many of the people either.

I lived with a young man before I had to come here. I was content then. He used to take me for rides in his car. I loved moving along quickly, watching the trees flash by. I loved him. In the evenings, we often sat together on our couch. I enjoyed our friendship.

He taught me to perform in front of cameras. I didn't like the hot lights overhead or the women I had to pose with, but I did it anyway, just to please him.

There's one man who comes to visit me occasionally here who reminds me a little of my old friend. I have plenty to eat here. I like to watch the elephants lumbering around when I'm in the pen next to theirs. I suppose I could get to like it here if my friend were with me.

I was saddened by Charlie's feelings and resolved to share them with Peter Gross about his preference for men. I knew Peter would arrange for one of the male handlers to spend more time with Charlie.

I visited next with a dolphin in the sea mammal compound. As I approached, I experienced a strong feeling of sadness. I asked him what was wrong.

I've lost two of my friends and I'm unhappy. I miss them terribly. One of them was very old and couldn't seem to breathe well. We tried to hold her near the surface so she could get enough air, but she died anyway.

The new shade over the pool keeps us cool when the sun is high. I like people, because they feed me. Sometimes they come into the pool and swim with us and that's fun. I know the difference between the people who work here and the park visitors, especially the children who poke at me and dig into my hide. My friend over there will come and see you if you feed her. She doesn't like people otherwise.

I wished the dolphins well and moved on to the macaw aviary, where I was greeted noisily by Moria, a twenty-year-old macaw. She offered the following information.

I was raised by a man and a woman in a house when I was small. For awhile, I lived near horses too, first in the stables and then in the race track clubhouse nearby. I liked watching all the people go by and listening to the sound of the races.

One day I was put into a small cage that I couldn't see out of. When the cage was uncovered, I found myself here.

At first, I missed my people and the smell of the horses, but now I feel comfortable. A red-haired woman taught me to do tricks for the people who come to the park. I enjoy performing. I feel important when the people clap their hands for me.

I then walked to the compound where Rosie the timber wolf was housed. I was surprised at how much she resembled a domestic dog in her attitude. I concluded that she must have been several generations into domesticity. She confirmed that she had lived with a human family, in a back yard, with their dogs. Other than not understanding why she had to leave them, she seemed content with her life.

Nadji the tiger lived in the adjacent compound. As I was getting ready to leave, Peter Gross entered the big cat's cage. Nadji ran to greet him, eager to go for his daily walk. The last thing I saw as I headed for the exit that day was Nadji and Peter making their rounds, side by side.

The sight of these two moving companionably along, served to crystallize my impressions of Marine World and its inhabitants, both animal and human, into a definite pattern. Everyone there is a part of everyone else while yet an individual. The animals are kept in such a way that they're able to forge relationships with one another and with their handlers. The people work with, as much as for, their charges. Their mutual respect and affection preclude intruding on another's privacy or enforcing one's will just for the sake of doing so. When Sarge the water buffalo isn't feeling up to seeing people, his handlers recognize that and are considerate of

MARINEWORLD/AFRICA USA

him. They don't assume that he owes them an unchanging disposition any more than they would assume it of another human being. And when the huge tigress who was awakened from her nap greeted her trainer with affection, she put aside her own wishes out of consideration for him.

This is the way we should all behave toward each other, recognizing each individual's rights, yet complying with one another's wishes when it is possible to do so. If it can be done at Marine World, it can be done elsewhere, too.

CHAPTER 26

CRUSTACEAN CONTRAST

On a trip back to the United States after a tour of Canada, I decided to stop and see my brother Milnor, who lived in Jay, Maine. Jay is a tiny place about thirty miles west of Augusta.

Maine is my favorite part of New England. There's something about the Atlantic coast—the feeling of privacy and the cragginess of the seal rookeries, that appeals to me, especially during periods when I've had too much contact with too many people. This was one of those times that I just drank in the scenery greedily as I drove along the ocean.

I was looking forward to this visit for another reason. My nephew Edward was home for a brief time. He was being assigned as pastor to a new church on Prince Edward Island. I hadn't seen him for several years.

Edward is one of those dear, considerate people who have a special knack for remembering the likes and dislikes of others. All my life I have loved to eat lobster. Edward was aware of this so shortly after my arrival, he suggested that we drive to a small bay nearby. He knew some of the fishermen and thought perhaps we could bring back the makings of a lobster dinner. Naturally, I agreed immediately. The thought of real Maine Lobster was more than sufficient to make me forget how tired of driving I was.

We set off together and soon turned onto what looked like someone's driveway. It proved to be a long, winding road which led to a small, secluded harbor. It was the kind of place you had to know about to find.

Dusk was gathering as we pulled the car to a stop. Three boats were moored to a small pier where men were unloading the day's catch. As they saw us approach, one of them quickly stuffed something into a sack. I waited as Ed went to speak with them.

A few minutes later he returned, a big grin on his face. "Come on, Aunt Bea," he said. "They're going to let you see it."

Curious about what "it" was that I was going to see, I hurried over to the fishermen. There, lying in almost majestic isolation from the rest of the catch, was the biggest lobster I have ever seen.

It must have weighed at least twenty pounds. Ed explained that it's illegal to bring in a lobster weighing more than three and a half pounds. The men had been in a hurry to dock while there was still daylight so they hadn't checked their traps carefully before heading their boats toward shore. They would, of course, throw the lobster back. In the meantime, they would also let me see if I could communicate with it.

I knelt and examined the lobster. He appeared calm, in contrast to the other lobsters who were snapping their tails at the men, trying to hurt them with the thorn like pieces of shell that protruded between the joints of their tails.

Just as well he was calm, I thought. One swipe from a tail that size could do considerable damage to one's hand! The long body moved a bit as the lobster turned to look at me. I asked him how he came to be in such a predicament, and then translated his story for the fishermen.

I was moving along slowly, minding my own business, looking for food as usual, when I came upon a large, lush patch of plants. There were other lobsters eating there too, much smaller than I. They moved away when I went near them. I never have to argue with anyone over food; I always get the best there is.

The next thing I knew, I was being hauled out of the water with the others. I know that this is the end for them. They'll be killed by the men who caught us, as so many of us have been. Our beds are becoming thin. There just aren't as many of us as there used to be.

But I'm not worried about dying. I know they'll throw me back because they always do. This isn't the first time I've been caught. They always keep the little ones, but never me.

I'm getting mad, though. This is longer than I've been out of the water in some time. If you're through looking at me, I'd like to go home.

It was almost dark when the lobster finished communicating with me. We watched as the fishermen complied with the lobster's request and returned him to the sea. Ed asked if we could buy some of the smaller ones and some crab for dinner. The purchase was soon completed and we set out for home.

CRUSTACEAN CONTRAST

I wanted to watch the crab and lobster being cooked. Since I have become sensitive to the thoughts and feelings of animals, I have not eaten animals whose lives or deaths are painful. No living thing wants to die, but it has been my experience that most animals are able to accept death as a natural part of life. They know they will survive in spirit and while they may not wish to leave their bodies at the particular time they do, they are not afraid of death as such, only the process if it is painful.

I had decided that if crustacean death was cruel, I would never eat shellfish again. I tuned in to the lobsters as they were waiting to be put into the kettle of boiling water. There was no panic there at all. They knew their lives were going to end soon, but they remained quite calm in contrast to their earlier behavior on the pier. I stayed with them mentally as they were put into the kettle and experienced a feeling of suffocation quickly followed by numbness. Apparently, the steam paralyzed their nervous systems almost immediately, for I received no further communication from them. Feeling somewhat relieved, I turned my attention to the crabs.

I was not prepared at all for what I felt. I have rarely encountered such emotional violence in any animal with whom I have communicated. It took my breath away. I asked Ed if crabs ever fight much once they are away from the ocean. He told me that they seem to "go out fighting." Experienced seafood cooks know better than to leave a number of crabs together in the kitchen for long; they will tear off each other's claws in short order.

I watched as the first one hit the boiling water. I continued to feel the crab's rage until the steam killed him.

I feasted on lobster that night, but I have rarely ever eaten another crab.

CHAPTER 27

GOODBYE

Of the many benefits that have come to me from my ability to communicate non-verbally with animals, perhaps the one I find most precious is being able to "converse" every day with my own animals. This sharing of experiences and feelings with those animals I call my family has enriched my life immeasurably. Of all of them, perhaps, the dearest was my Pomeranian, Blacky. Not that I could ever say which animal I have loved the best. They're like children; you love the sick one most until its well and the unhappy one until it's once more content.

However, Blacky lived with me for fourteen years during which time I went from being a concerned, somewhat inexperienced pet owner, to being a full-time animal consultant, always, until recently, with this little ball of black fur at my side.

I shared my triumphs and tragedies, my divorce and homelessness with my best friend as I knew he could understand me. Afterward, he shared the story of his life with me.

The first person in my life was a woman named Julie, who loved me dearly. She used to call me her special friend. She took me nearly every place she went.

Julie brushed my fur often and gave me frequent baths. One day, after she had cleaned me with special care, we got into her car and went to a place where there were lots of other dogs of all shapes and sizes. There was a ring there where people were walking their dogs. They walked around in circles while a man stood in the center and looked at them.

Soon, Julie put my leash on me and we walked around the circle too. After awhile the man in the center told us to stop walking. He came over to Julie and handed her a blue ribbon. She was so excited she almost cried. She fussed over me and petted me. I was very proud of whatever it was we had done. She got quite a collection of ribbons—blue, red and a few yellow ones because we kept going to more of those rings over the months that followed. She was very proud of me. I got to know many of the other dogs well, because we saw them at each place we went. I enjoyed visiting with them.

One day Julie left me in the car while she went to buy us some food. I was sitting there waiting for her to come back when a man came along and looked at me through the car window. Suddenly he broke the window with a stick and grabbed me.

I screamed for Julie, but she couldn't hear me. I cried and struggled to get away from the man, but he was so much bigger than I was that it was useless. He ran to his car and drove away with me. In the back seat I was still calling to Julie, trying to tell her where I was. In my mind's eye, I could see the horrified look on her face when she came out of the store and found me gone. I knew she was as unhappy as I was. I could see her crying and searching for me. I never saw her again.

The man drove for a long, long time. Darkness came and then it came again. Finally we stopped. He took me into a house where a woman was waiting for him. I learned they were going to sell me.

I was so wretched, I couldn't eat. I looked for a way to get out, but there didn't seem to be any. When I had been there for several days, the man left the back door open just a little. I saw him pull the door shut, but I didn't hear the latch click. I knew I could work the door open if I had a chance. Eventually, the man and woman went into another part of the house and I carefully edged the door open and ran quickly outside.

I tried to figure out where I was. I wanted to go home, but which way was home? Nothing smelled or looked or sounded at all familiar. I was confused and very frightened, but I kept moving. Anything was better than being with that man.

I was walking down the street, looking for something to eat, when a young couple came along. They stopped and looked at me admiringly. I went over to them and offered the man my paw, trying to tell them about me and Julie. I hoped maybe they could help me get back to her, but I couldn't make them understand what I wanted. The woman picked me up. She said they would take me to their home and then try to find my owner.

I was happy to be with someone who cared for me once more. These people were kind; they fed me well and petted me often. I knew they were trying to find Julie, but she was so far away they couldn't locate her. After several days, they decided to take me to his mother's house.

That worried me. The only place I wanted to go was home. The next morning, we got into the man's car and set off. I began to feel a pull toward home and tried to tell the man and woman to turn toward it, but they kept on going straight. Soon the feeling passed. Then I felt worse than ever.

After three days of driving we arrived at his mother's house. She had a lot of dogs living there with her, all very bossy. They told me right away that this was their home and I'd better do as they wanted. I ran and hid under the couch.

Living there was another bad time in my life. This new woman didn't have enough time to take care of me. Though she fed me, she never petted me and her dogs did their best to make my life miserable. I also got a bad case of fleas, something Julie would never have let happen to me.

Then things changed. Bea came to the house one day asking a lot of questions. Said something about taking census? whatever that is. As soon as I saw her, I knew she loved animals. I wanted her to take me with her. I ran from behind the couch and went to her. I wagged my tail furiously and licked her hand to let her know I needed her. She looked at me for a moment and I knew she wanted me! I could hardly believe my good luck. When Bea left, it was with the understanding that she would come back that night and take me home.

I waited for her, hoping she would come back and get me. I wanted to go with her so much I couldn't think of anything else. It started to get dark and she still wasn't here. Then I heard the sound of a car in the driveway and a knock at the door. There she was. I jumped into her arms right away, and then we left for my new home.

When we got there, Bea gave me a bath to get rid of my fleas and tried to comb my fur. Some of it was so matted, she had to cut it off, but I didn't mind, it felt so good to be clean again.

The next morning she put a collar and leash on me and took me for a walk. I wanted to make her proud of me. I strutted along beside her as I had beside Julie in the ring. Bea saw how hard I was trying to please her. Soon I was going everywhere with her and I was happy again.

Not long after that, Bea put all our things into her car. We drove to the airport where she pushed a pill down my throat and put me into a wooden box. I started to feel dizzy and sick to my stomach. After takeoff, the air was suddenly very cold; it was hard to breathe. I began to shiver violently, my head heavy, my tongue thick, my heart pounding. I vomited and gagged. Things around me looked dim and fuzzy. I could hardly even see the sides of my box. The noise was deafening.

Finally the air became a little warmer, it was easier to breathe and the noise stopped. I was moving somewhere. Then I saw Bea.

I was too weak even to wag my tail. She looked at me, horrified at the state I was in. She took me out of my box right away and carried me to a car where her mother and father were waiting for us. All the way to their house, Bea fussed over me and tried to clean my fur. The air was hot and damp and I felt listless.

We stayed for some time at her parents' house. After the first couple of days, I began to feel like my old self again. I soon made friends with her family. I liked her mother, but one morning she came into our room while Bea was still sleeping. I ran out from under the bed and bit her foot as she leaned over to touch Bea. She screamed, and suddenly Bea was wide awake and very angry with me. I couldn't see why. I was only doing my duty, trying to protect her. I was so hurt by the scolding they both gave me that I refused to have anything to do with them the rest of the day.

Soon after that, Bea and I moved into our own house near a lake. I had a friend to play with, a poodle who lived with the people next door.

Things were going along fine until Bea brought another dog home. It was a puppy, but very, very big—much bigger than I— who wanted to play all the time. I would have let her play with me if she hadn't kept pulling my tail and stepping on me. Finally I made her understand that I would only play with her if she was gentle. Bea named her Princess Royal. She and I became close friends.

We eventually took another trip. We moved again to the same warm, sunny place we had lived before, though to a different house. *We had been there a long time when Princess Royal became very ill. I knew her head had been hurting. Both of us had tried to tell Bea about it, but we couldn't make her understand the deep pain.*

One night, Princess Royal began twitching and jumping in the most awful way. I called to her, but she didn't seem to hear me or to even know I was there. Bea came running and took her to the doctor's right away. Princess never came back.

Bea cried for a long time. I tried to let her know I understood her grief. I went to her and licked the salty tears from her face. I had my own grief, too. I had loved Princess and missed her company terribly. I had no one to share my feelings with. Sometimes I felt the loss so deeply that my chest hurt.

Once, when I was sitting with Bea, both of us crying over Princess, I had trouble breathing. My chest hurt as if it had been poked with a sharp stick. Bea took me to the doctor who gave me a pill. I've had to take pills every day since then, but I do feel better.

One day, when Bea came home, I found I could see my thoughts in her mind. I had always been able to see her thoughts, but this was the first time I knew she could see mine. It was wonderful living with her after that. If I wanted something, all I had to do was hold a picture of it in my mind and she'd give it to me.

Bea brought another big puppy home soon after that. She named the puppy Princess II. This Princess and I became friends quickly, but I wasn't too happy when she gave birth to a lot of puppies. I've never liked living with a lot of other dogs. I'd rather be the only one. I learned to put up with the others, however, I had to. There were more puppies after the first bunch and soon the house was filled with dogs.

Bea got a camper and we started taking long trips together. The other dogs all came too, which made it pretty crowded, but I always sat up front next to Bea, where I could see everything we passed.

I'm getting old now. My fur doesn't grow in as it used to. Bea gave me a bright red jacket to wear during the cold weather. It isn't as nice as the thick fur I used to have, but it keeps me warm, I'm grateful for that. I have to take several pills each day now and I hate them. I've lost most of my teeth so I can only eat soft food.

GOODBYE

Sometimes, when I see the puppies gobbling their food, I'm jealous. I used to eat that way and I miss it.

Bea has asked me if I want her to take me to the doctor so he can give me a shot that will make me sleep forever. I don't yet, but I think the day is drawing near when I will. I'd love to stay with her always if I felt well, but the pain in my chest comes more often now. Sometimes it's awfully hard to get out of bed in the mornings because my legs are stiff.

I can't complain, though. I've had a long and full life that I have lived with someone who understands and loves me very much. She says I'm nearly 20 years old now. When I'm ready to go, I know she will respect my wishes.

On January 11, 1979, Blacky indicated he wanted to leave. He awoke late that morning, around eleven o'clock, and after our morning greetings, he went outside for his customary tour of the back yard before breakfast.

He had eaten his morning jar of baby food and was settled under the table where I was working on some correspondence. He let out a sound I can only describe as a scream. I dove under the table and brought him out. He looked up into my eyes and I knew it had been a painful heart spasm—he'd had them for years, ever since his friend Princess Royal had died. I asked him, as I had so often before, if he wanted to sleep without waking. This time he did.

I phoned my veterinarian immediately, but was informed it would be several hours before he could see Blacky. Blacky had never cared much for being held, but this day was different. He stayed in my arms until it was time to go.

At about four o'clock that afternoon, we walked into the office of Dr. Joel Rossen, my vet. I explained to Dr. Rossen, who is aware of my ability to communicate non-verbally with animals, that Blacky had asked to die. He examined Blacky and agreed it was time. There really isn't anything you can do for a 19 - year - old dog to stave off the ills of old age except to relieve him of them altogether when the time comes. Dr. Rossen gave my little friend an injection and after hugging me briefly, left me alone with my dear friend during his final moments of this existence.

I felt Blacky relax in my arms and as I stood there with tears streaming down my cheeks, I saw something so phenomenal I will remember it always. There, above the table, was the image of my Princess Royal, whom Blacky had helped raise and who had been his friend and companion for two years of his life. She was standing there waiting for him to join her. As he did, his body became whole and strong once more. He shook himself as he did after a bath, only this time he wasn't shaking water from his small frame. As he shook, his old body dropped from him in pieces and he emerged as the beautiful, young, full-coated animal I had taken to live with me fourteen years earlier.

It was like watching a butterfly emerge from a cocoon. When he stopped shaking himself, he began to dance around Princess Royal as he had used to do and she in turn, nuzzled him, affectionately. She wanted him to come with her and kept urging him to move. He stood looking at me for a moment, waiting for me to release him spiritually. Somehow I managed to say, "I love you, Blacky. Go with Princess and have a good time. I'll see you later." As he said goodbye to me, I felt his extreme pleasure at being free. Then the image faded.

I looked down at his remains, still cradled in my arms. I took his body home and laid it in front of the other dogs so that they too, would have a chance to say goodbye to him and to know that he was gone from us, but only for a while.

PART III

HOW TO TALK WITH THE ANIMALS

LEARNING THE ANIMALS LANGUAGE AND HOW TO USE IT

PART III

HOW TO TALK WITH THE ANIMALS

The greatest pleasure I have enjoyed in my entire life, second only to my relationship with God, has been the communication I have enjoyed with animals. This has broadened my world beyond anything I could have ever imagined and given me "many true" friends. Getting to know the animals the way I have, has changed the way I treated them before I was able to talk to them. The greatest gift I can give you and the best way to improve the lives of all animals everywhere, is to give you that same ability, for if you can talk to them it will definitely change the way you relate to them and care for them. My hope is that through the sharing of these techniques, you too will begin to experience the wonders of this world that I do. I often hear people say, "When this pet is gone, I'm not getting any more. I just don't want to be tied down and I don't want the responsibility." I have a hard time with that idea, for I can't imagine my world without them. My prayer is that you too will soon feel that way as you learn how to talk to them. Welcome to our world. May you find it as exciting and fulfilling as I have!

In learning to communicate with the animals, you are entering a new dimension of living. This is more than body language, it is actually learning how to "hear" their thoughts and respond on a non-verbal or physical level. The words, "horse whisperer," "dog whisperer" etc., are overused today, for what you are seeing are people who have learned the animals' body language and how to use that to train the animals. The word "whisperer" to me indicates the ability to transmit ideas, thoughts and feelings. That is a two way street, but in the connotation in which it is being so widely used, it is showing people training an animal to mold to their wishes and teach them how to live in our society, not necessarily a two way conversation. I truly wish they were called trainers, and not "whisperers". I want you to experience far more than what they are doing, learn "their" language and have a two way conversation with them. It is a true language that is different from body language, being used between the animals themselves all the time, an exchange of thoughts, feelings and ideas.

The basis to learning to communicate with animals is for you to be able to respect the animal's ideas, attitudes and feelings. If you want to have a true conversation with anyone, human or animal, you must first be willing to "listen" to their ideas and realize that their motives for what they do may be different from yours. What they value and hope for in life may also be far different than yours. This was brought home to me one day when I was out in the cold rain to potty my little Chihuahua. She kept sniffing and sniffing and finally I lost my patience with her and said, "Come on girl, get it over with. It doesn't matter where you go, just do it!" She looked up at me and quietly responded, "It matters to me." I was taken aback by her remark, but it sure taught me a lesson which I never forgot. I try not to "push" my motives on them anymore, but have learned to respect their views as different from mine.

Sometimes it is hard being the voice for the animals because owners don't always want to hear the truth. What they want is for me to say that the animal agrees with their desires, but if I am to be the animal's true voice, I have to speak what the animal wants which may not be what the owner wants to hear. This doesn't make me very popular and sometimes the owners get downright angry and tell me I don't know what I am talking about, but I have to stand my ground or I won't be doing justice to either the animal or it's owner. This is especially hard when an animal is sick or old and requires a great deal of care from their person. My heart goes out to the person who is struggling to lift the big dog, or has to get up many times a night to help their sick pet, etc. I want to tell them the animal is ready to go, but that isn't always the case. The animal will be fighting to live and isn't ready to go yet. It is very hard, in those cases, to tell the hurting, tired owner the truth, but if I am going to be honest, I have to. And sometimes the table is turned where the owner just isn't ready to let go of their beloved friend (are we ever really ready to lose anyone we love, human or animal?) and the animal is begging me to tell them to let them go. They want out of their suffering or embarrassment, such as in the case of animals who have been so clean all their lives and now can't hold their bowels or bladder. These are difficult consultations, sometimes bringing joy and other times sorrow, but in being the true voice of the animal, both must be faced from time to time.

Some people, who learn this language suddenly feel they can call themselves animal psychologists, but learning the language does not qualify you as such, no more than learning a foreign language suddenly qualifies you to be a psychologist to the users of that language. There are many "psychics" out there who obtain a degree of accuracy in "seeing" into someone else's life. It bothers me a great deal when these so called "psychic readers" suddenly tell you what you should and should not be doing with your life. Even a trained psychologist doesn't tell a person what to do, but guides them in making their own decisions. This was brought home to me very strongly when I was in Texas once, teaching at a Sylva Mind control meeting. A lady came up to me after the meeting, obviously quite distraught. As we chatted, she told me how she had been to a psychic reader who told her she was wasting her life being a stay at home wife and mother, but should be out using her gift to teach. This lady expressed to me how much she loved her life and would hate to give it up to go teach. Standing in front of other people is something she hated to do. She was having a real emotional conflict over what the psychic had told her. When I asked her if her husband was a happy man and could she honestly say she was making his life and work possible because he had a good home and wife to come home to? She answered that he definitely was and she felt she had a big part in that. Then I asked her about her children. She said she had one son who is a professional golfer, a good boy who did well in school and was socially developed. I asked her if she felt she did a good job raising him and by being a stay at home mom, did she contribute to making a good man who would improve society instead of harm it? She said a definite yes to that also. Her son had expressed how much he appreciated her being there for him. Then, I told her not to listen to an unqualified psychic and enjoy the role and blessings God had given her. God generously gives us many talents to enjoy and use for our and our fellow mankind's benefit, but we don't have to use them all. Hers may have been in teaching, but she chose to use her talent as a wife, mother and home maker instead and God was blessing her and her family for it.

I see this in the animal world too. Some of the new age people are using the animals to teach their philosophies. One example of this was with a psychic in San Francisco. I had been called by a family in the Bay area to help them with their sick cat with cystitis. I chatted with the cat to be sure it didn't have emotional problems triggering the illness, but the cat was fine, happy etc. What I learned was that the food the owner was feeding it was causing problems with the kidneys. Because I had the knowledge of animal diseases, anatomy and nutrition, I knew what was wrong and what it needed. Except for the food it was ingesting, the cat had a very health body. I advised them what to feed the cat and with the correction in diet, the cat was well within a couple of weeks and stayed that way, with proper feeding, for the next three years. They had enjoyed their session with me so much, they decided to have their local 'pet psychic" come and talk to the cat too. She did so to the cat's harm for the "pet psychic" who was promoting her metaphysical philosophies instead of having the proper knowledge of animal health, told the owners they had no business making the cat get well, but should have let him pass on so he could have been reincarnated into a new body. Rubbish, I say. That cat was young and had already been given a healthy body for him and his owners to enjoy. It was the food that had caused the problem. Unfortunately, within two months after her visit, the cat who had been healthy to the point of her visit, became sick and died at the early age of 8 years old. In my estimation, she did a terrible injustice to the animal and its' grieving owner. To many of us, it is like telling you to let your child die so he can come back in another body! I hear of far too many incidences like this, that is why I am so adamant that one MUST have the proper knowledge before they are qualified to help anyone with their pet. You can talk to the animal, but don't give advice until you know what you are talking about. You need to have a working knowledge of animal behavior, diseases, nutrition and environmental affects before you give advice that will affect their health and future. People are paying their hard earned money for your help so please, be honest and don't give advice carelessly. Some pet psychics charge $300 an hour to tell you your animal is

270

in spirit when you already know the pet is dead. To be the voice of the animals, you must be fair and honest with what you tell the owner it is saying. Remember; be sensitive for you are dealing with people's hearts. It could be you in that situation, so tread carefully.

This non-verbal language is "spoken" mostly in transmission of feelings and pictures. You will see and feel what the animal experiences. Have you ever experienced your animal sitting and staring at you? What he is doing is "looking" at your thoughts the same way you sit and watch television. You see the action and can even determine the emotions from what you see on the faces of the actors. The animals can also do the same with the pictures they "see" in your mind. This is a very fast language for it only takes a few seconds to think a thought and only a few seconds for the animal to "see" that thought and send back a response to it. Within one minute, you can think a thought, they get it and send you back an answer, even if there are several people asking the same animal questions, just like tuning into a radio wave, they can get many thoughts or questions and send back answers within a few minutes. They just have to change stations, (people asking questions) so to speak.

Let's do an exercise here that will help you understand visualization. Close your eyes for a moment and remember what the room looks like around you or if you aren't home, remember what your living room looks like. Think of yourself sitting in one particular favorite chair or couch and think of the colors in the room as you sit there: the pictures on the wall; what you see out the window; smells that are around you; what it feels like to sit on that chair, the feel of the fabric and how you yourself feel as you relax there! Now, open your eyes and realize that you "saw" in your mind your living room or the room you are in! And that you were looking around that room, not looking at yourself. THAT IS VISUALIZATION. It is just remembering what you have seen and experienced.

We think in pictures and have feelings attached to those thoughts whether we are aware of it or not, you cannot hide your thoughts and feelings from the animals. When we say we are going to go to the park, we put a picture of the park in our minds. We don't even have to say it, as long as the thought is there, the picture is there. An example of that was brought home to me when I was training police working dogs. For most of those dogs, they LOVE their work. One gal in our class just thought about going to class or work and her dog would run, find his leash, her keys, and all their other equipment and pile them by the door where he would sit and wait for her to go.

To me, one of the most beautiful things about this language is that it is a universal language. There are no cultural or verbal language barriers. A tree is a tree no matter what it looks like such as an apple tree versus a palm tree and a home is a home whether it is made from blocks of ice or up on stilts in the tropics, it is still a place where people have families and live from day to day the same way. You will literally "see and experience" what the animal "sees and experiences" with no barriers. This will definitely broaden your world.

Culture can sometimes present a problem until you learn to "listen" to what a person is trying to say, not necessarily the words they are using to say it with. This was brought home to me when I first moved from New York, where I grew up, to South Carolina. The first time I bought something in a store and started to leave, the clerk said, "Ya'll come back, ya hear!" Immediately I turned back and asked her "what did I forget?" She looked at me like I was crazy for you see in New York had someone said that, they would have been calling me back because I had forgotten something or done something wrong, but in this new culture Southern Culture, (new to me) the clerk was telling me she enjoyed serving me and would love to have me come back again!. We were using the same words, but with a different meaning or motive behind those words. LEARNING TO LISTEN WITH OUR INNER EAR AND NOT THE OUTER EAR OF WORDS, IS AN IMPORTANT SKILL TO REGAIN. I say regain because as children we had it, but as we learn to speak, we depend more and more on words until we finally go to school where we fully depend on words and shut off the 'INNER EAR". Another example of this "inner hearing" is the mother who wakes up in the middle of the night and says, "Something is wrong with my son (or daughter or spouse). I can feel it!" Soon afterwards they get a phone call saying that person was in an accident or something. Sometimes it works in reverse when the military comes to the parent and says your son is dead or missing in action and presumed dead and the parent says "no, I can feel he is alive" only to have him reappear later on. It is very well documented that twins seem to experience that even more than other siblings or parents. No one knows how, they just do. Another example of that "inner hearing" is when anyone you are close to comes in the door and you just "feel" something is wrong. They don't have to say or do a thing; you can just "feel" it. How many times have you experienced that, asking the person what is wrong and they just mumble, "Nothing". You know better and if you keep probing, they will often blurt out their problem, one that was there all the time that you "knew" about because you were hearing it with that inner "sense". Some people call it a 6th sense, but I call it non-verbal communication.

I know that most of you have experienced this next phenomenon. You can be feeling great, full of energy and happy, so you go out for dinner or to an event. Within minutes of sitting there, you begin to feel irritable, angry, sick or just plain very, very tired. You ask yourself "what is wrong? I felt fine when I came in here?" What you are experiencing is the problems that belong to someone else, someone sitting fairly close. Your mind doesn't have the ability to sort out whose feelings it is getting, but absorbs everything around you as though it belonged to you. Just realize that what you are experiencing is not you, but someone nearby. Ignore the feeling and keep telling yourself "I am fine", act happy and energetic and you will go back to your old self.

One time I had a funny experience about that. I was teaching a class in communication. The students were practicing on each others animals and when we got to the Irish Wolfhound, everyone started feeling nauseated. What they were experiencing was the animal telling them it was sick to the stomach and wanted to throw up. I told everyone to now focus on something else, ignore the feelings they had in their stomach and it would go away. Everyone did so successfully, except for one girl. She kept telling herself, "it is going to go away, I know it will go away, etc." in reality focusing on the problem instead of ignoring it and going on to something else. The more she focused on trying to make it go away the worse it got until she literally had to excuse herself to go out and throw up. You just have to totally ignore it and focus on something else because as long as you focus on trying to get rid of it, the more it becomes yours. She just couldn't separate the two. It was funny when, several years later, she called for something and reminded me of whom she was by telling me, "Remember when I had to leave your class and go throw up from the Irish Wolfhound?" You bet I remembered.

There are two kinds of people you will encounter in this world, Givers and Sappers. By this I am referring mostly to energy. You have those who you sit next to for just a few minutes and suddenly feel full of energy, just as though you had just had several hours of recuperative sleep. Then there are those you sit next to and within minutes you are exhausted and you feel so irritable, you want to snap their head off. What you are experiencing is the energy some people exude to you that refreshes you and those who sap your energy, (these people are usually negative in conversation and actions, nothing is ever right, woe is me, etc.) making you feel exhausted and irritable. The more sensitive you are, the more you will react to both kinds. One of the main reasons people get so refreshed when they get out into nature, is that the earth and nature, gives energy while draining off your negative energy. Some people, who are positive givers, can break off a leaf from a plant, stick it in water and it will grow and yet you take a negative person, a sapper, and watch how plants just die when they are around them a lot. I can't explain to you how this happens, I just know it does.

I am going to give you a little experiment here that will further help you with visualization. Some evening when you are just sitting around, think about going to the refrigerator to get a piece of cheese or something your pet really likes and watch them jump up and head for the kitchen. When you do this, be sure to follow through and go get it for them or you will have them ignore you the next time you try it because they will think you are lying to them. Later on, get up and head for the kitchen while thinking of getting a glass of tea or a cup of coffee and watch the difference in their reaction. Think of giving them a bath and see if you can find them, versus thinking of going for a fun walk and watch them beat you to the door.

Animals learn word association the same as people do. A little child learns to sit up at the table because we tell them to sit at the "table" while moving them to one. They learn that a table is a flat piece of furniture on legs that you sit at to eat, or? We then teach them to spell t-a-b-l-e when looking at one or a picture of one. Animals learn the same way. When we are training a dog to sit, we tell it to sit while we picture them with their butts on the ground and their front end up. If we give them the wrong picture, telling them to sit while thinking of them standing, we will confuse them and they will think that sitting means to be up on all fours. I am not saying that it is easy to do this, it takes practice, but you can eventually discipline yourself to match your mental thoughts and pictures with your verbal instructions. I have had some funny experiences though because the animals do have a mind and will of their own. Mark Anthony, one of my German Shepherds who was trained in police work, pulled a lot of tricks on me. One day we were in an obedience trial. It was the long sit, where they must stay on one side of the ring and the owner goes to the opposite side of the ring, turns and faces them. They are supposed to stay sitting up for one full minute before we are to return to them. As I stood there looking at Mark, I realized he was becoming restless. I didn't want to influence him with the wrong idea, so I quickly closed my eyes and thought of him sitting there quietly. Suddenly I heard a lot of snickering by the spectators who knew me and knew what I was doing. I opened my eyes only to find Mark lying down looking coyly at me. He pulled a lot of stunts on me like that because he found obedience to be very boring after the extensive police training. Another time he was on the long down stay exercise. He looked at me across the ring and said *think I am doing it right?* With that, he rolled over, right out of the ring, shook himself off and walked over to the pond to cool his feet. He fixed me alright for making him do that obedience stuff. We never did get his obedience title so he went back to work, doing what he loved, with a police chief friend of mine.

Another aspect of this is in showing dogs. I remember one time when I was in Virginia at a dog show. A lady there asked me if I would take her Rottweiller into the ring for her. I wasn't doing anything so I said sure. I knew the dog wouldn't win anyway because it was too fat, but since I enjoy showing dogs, it was just for fun. The dog behaved beautifully, no problems. I didn't expect any because I know show dogs are trained and usually behave themselves in the ring, which is what I expected this dog to do. When I came out of the ring, the owner took the lead and said, "Wow that is the first time she hasn't tried to bite the judge!" I am so glad she didn't tell me that before we went into the ring, because that mental picture would have been on my mind whenever the judge approached us. This would have made her back off and act badly or even get excused from the ring, but she is a show dog and I held the right picture in my mind, of her behaving, she did. If someone gives me a dog to show, the last thing I want to deal with is trying to make correct mental pictures when I know I am really dealing with a problem.

This same problem happens a lot with horses that are hunter-jumpers. Maybe one time the horse's timing is off and they stop at a jump. The next time the horse approaches that jump, the rider starts thinking *He stopped at this jump the last time, I hope he doesn't do it again.* This puts the picture of the horse stopping at that jump in the rider's mind. The horse gets that picture and decides that is what the rider wants it to do; it thinks, *oh, she wants me to stop at this jump? Ok, I will.* Now the rider thinks the horse has a problem and every time they approach that jump, what is the rider thinking? You got it, and the horse responds accordingly. Soon it becomes a chronic mental communication problem and the horse is branded as a difficult animal that is afraid of jumping. All of it could be avoided had they been able to "think" correctly in the beginning. I know this is true because I have been called by too many owners to find out what the problem is with their jumping horses. This is what I found.

Most of the time, the animals that love you and bond to you, will do what they are asked to. When your animal, who usually works well for you, has an off day, you need to respect that. You don't get up every day feeling great either and neither do they. Give them the benefit of the doubt and put them up. If it becomes a pattern, that is a different story, but give them a break if it only happens occasionally. If you are feeling irritable or badly, don't try to work them because they will feel your emotions and since they can't distinguish who you are feeling badly towards, they will automatically think it is them and react adversely. You don't want to ruin a good relationship.

Believe me, animals get the picture of what you want, so don't let them get away with pulling tricks on you. Princessa taught me that. Her son, Loverboy, had the bad habit of stealing my shoes, taking them out, chewing them up and burying them. When I caught him doing that, I would picture Princess going after him, taking the shoe away from him, bringing it back to me, and me giving her a treat for her good deed. One day, I caught Loverboy going out with one of my shoes; I called Princessa by name to get her attention, and pictured her going out to get my shoe and bringing it back to me. She promptly lifted her head up to look at the ceiling and said *I'm just a dog, I can't read minds! I don't understand!* I was absolutely floored as she had never done that before. I told her verbally, "you know exactly what I said (never repeated the picture or command) now go do it." She heaved a big sigh, got up, gave me a funny look as she went out the door and returned with my shoe a few minutes later. Of course, got her treat-she was quite a dog. Always follow through with your commands, but be careful not to nag your dog. Princessa and I had a very special bond. She usually loved to please me. When we went to police training class, all I had to do was think the exercise I wanted her to do and she did it. She would look at the other trainers who would say over and over, "sit, sit, sit" and have to force their dogs down. She just did it when I said the word or pictured it. She would look up at me and ask, *what's the matter with them? Why do they act that way? Can't they do it and why do their owners have the wrong thoughts from the words?* She just didn't understand why they were so confusing. When I hear someone repeating a command over and over, it reminds me of the mother you see in the grocery store who tells the kid to put something down. She keeps at it, "put that back, I said to put that back, if you don't put that back I am going to punish you, knock it off and put it back." The kid is thinking, while ignoring his mother, "sure you are going to make me put it back, when hell freezes over." After awhile, you just want to shake her and tell her to stop "nagging" the kid and make him do it. Because animals react much the same way as children, don't keep repeating your commands to them either, but picture the right movement and then follow through with physical training if they don't respond. They are getting it, so follow through with your commands. If you treat them well, with love and respect, most animals will soon respond correctly, but not if you nag.

I loved watching Barbara Woodhouse work with an animal. She would watch the owners bring their dogs into her class and "nag" them. The dog would spin every which way, refuse to sit, etc. You could tell the owner was totally frustrated and the dog was winning and he knew it, resulting in behavior that became worse and worse. Barbara would walk over, take the end of the leash and immediately the dog would settle down and respond to commands. The difference was in the attitude. She knew she was the boss and could handle that dog and the minute she took the leash, the dog knew it too. He could read her mind and boy he cut out the shenanigans immediately because he knew he couldn't get away with it with her.

Tone of voice can also affect the animal in training. One of the best trainers I ever met was Chief Kimball Vickery of Mt. Angel, Oregon. He was so soft spoken and gentle, you wondered how he could get anything to respond, but boy he did. He had a way of saying "No" in a soft but firm way, backing up his commands with an "I know how to make you do it, I am the boss here" that the animals would think *I'm so sorry, I'll never do it again, never.* He had some of the best working dogs I've ever seen and they just adored him. Just remember this, the louder you yell, the higher the pitch of your voice, the more they tune you out, you are losing control and they are gaining it. Attitude on your part, correct mental pictures, and love and respect are the keys to a happy, working animal. Kimball Vickery and Barbara Woodhouse possessed all three and it showed.

One thing you never want to do is baby a "fear or shyness". I hear people saying in a sympathetic tone, "come on, it's all right," while bending down, trying to coax the animal into facing what they are afraid of. Your sympathetic attitude that it gives in to their fear, only makes things worse. Tell them instead, in an authoritative, confident voice, "knock it off, you're fine. You're a big dog and you can handle this." Just move forward like everything is fine and even though they may have a problem for awhile, your positive attitude will help them get over their fear and develop courage. Once they learn you are ok with it, it will help them cope better.

Whatever you do, you must use positive statements with your animals. They don't understand and thus disregard words like, "can't, won't, shouldn't, wouldn't, not, etc. and all they hear or see in your mind is the positive part of the statement. For instance, when you say to a dog, "don't get on the couch,' they throw out the word "don't" and get on the couch. Why? Because you have literally held a picture of them getting on the couch. You can't visualize a negative idea. Young children react the same way because animals and children think alike in this aspect while they are very young. How many times have you seen a child standing and staring at an article on the table you don't want them to touch, so you quickly say, "don't touch that! " only to have them grab it instead. You think the child is being disobedient, but in their understanding and "non verbal language" you just told them to touch it when in reality they may not have even been thinking about the item. You brought it to their attention. You have to tell them what to do instead of what not to do such as "look here and see what I have for you" getting them interested in something safe. For an animal, tell them, "stay on the floor, if you get on the couch I'm going to punish you" Picture them on the floor and being rewarded and then think of them getting on the couch and you putting them out or in a cage. Negative commands are the hardest habit to break, but you can do it with practice.

The word NO is a positive statement. It means, whatever you are doing, stop it, but when you combine it with another positive word such as NO BARK, NO BITE, ETC., you turn it into a negative idea and literally visualize to them doing the barking, biting, etc. There is another phrase that works magic. Said in a soft, firm tone, "LEAVE IT" makes them back off. I was working with a police dog training session one day because the officer couldn't get his dog to let go of the "bad guy" once he got a hold of the sleeve. No matter how hard he pulled or yelled, the dog just wouldn't let go until he quietly and firmly said, LEAVE IT. The dog dropped immediately. It works in almost all circumstances whether it is a working situation or something they want: simply say NO or LEAVE IT.

Your visualization techniques work with most things, but you cannot visualize an animal from reacting to its' natural instincts. You may approach a bear with her cub, or stand between a starving animal and food. Don't try visualizing to them that you are a friend and its ok for you to be there because you cannot override their natural instincts to guard their food or protect their young from strangers and predators. In this instance, to them, you are the stranger or predator, so you better get out of there or you may become their dinner instead of the food you are blocking.

Animals don't have any real concept of time. You may go out for an hour or just go out for a minute to the mail box; you will get the same greeting when you return, just as if you had been gone for days. Animals don't sit and watch the clock to count minutes when giving your attention to them. They don't care that you gave one animal ten minutes and only gave them six minutes. All they care about is that they get individual attention without interference from other animals. Another aspect of time with them is a biological time table associated with eating and routine such as the owner coming home every day at the same time. Their built in clock takes over and they know when it is time to eat.

When communicating with the animals, you need to realize that the pictures you pick up from them will be from their perspective, not yours. A Chihuahua will talk about the tall man while the horse will call that same man, small. When people talk about going in the car, they will see it as a white car because they look at the outside which is white, while the dog may call it a red car because where does he ride,? On the red seat. When they talk about their home, they will tell you what they see when they are there, which may not be their house, but the neighbor's house that they sit and look at all day from their yard. Sometimes a solid wall can either be wood, brick or a wire fence that has so many bushes along it that it looks solid. The Chihuahua may say he has a big yard while the Great Dane will describe it as cramped and small.

Sometimes they will feel like there is a fence when in reality they don't have one, but they feel confined because they have been trained to stay within certain parameters while another animal may feel like they have a huge yard with no fence because they don't feel confined. Learning to "see" things from their standpoint is a lot of fun, but comes with practice.

When you first start, do not try to interpret what you are picking up, just describe it. One time I was talking to a dog that only showed me pictures of piles of bricks everywhere in his yard. My natural instinct said he was a guard dog in a brick yard, but I had learned to describe what I saw, so I told the owner that all I could see were piles of bricks everywhere. The owner laughed and said, "the dog is right. I am building a brick barbeque and patio and the bricks are all over the yard right now."

The mode of transmission of what you will feel from the animals is your subconscious mind. It never sleeps nor does it have the ability to distinguish whether it is your thought or someone else's, it just absorbs what is going on around you like it originated with you. This can present a problem if you are feeling someone else's pain, whether it is a person or animal that is standing near you, because you will experience it like it is your own. Since your subconscious mind lives in your body but isn't really attached to it, when you feel their physical pain, you may think it is your own. Look away and think about something else and it should go away. Sometimes when I am walking down a shed row in a horse barn, I will feel pain from a horse I am talking to. I then look away and concentrate on another animal. The pain usually goes away, but when I look back at the first horse, it comes back again. I know then for sure which animal the pain belongs to. I can remember an incident that happened when I was learning this new language, but still didn't understand this phenomenon or how to shut it off. I was communicating with a dog that had a severe headache. When the dog left, I still felt his headache. Thinking that I too had a headache, I took some aspirin to try to get rid it. Of course it did no good because it wasn't really coming from my own nervous system, but from the dog through my subconscious mind. Now, when I experience something from the animal, I tell myself, "it belongs to them, I am fine," Ignore it and it goes away.

Focus on something else, not the problem, and it will disappear as I have explained earlier in this section about the student and the Irish Wolfhound.

Another way you can tell when the emotion you are feeling belongs to an animal and not you is when you start craving something like a dog cookie that you know is not something you would want That is pretty obvious. The animals will send you their desires, hungers, fears, etc. and at first you can't tell if it is your own problem or that of your animal. An incident happened in Florida once that brought that fact into reality for my student. She woke up one morning, on a hot summer day, 98 degrees with a 90% humidity and felt very thirsty. She drank water, coffee, tea and everything she could, but to no avail. The more she drank, the thirstier she felt. She remembered what I said in class about assuming animal's feelings as your own and thought she had better call the barn to see if the girls had watered her old horse that day. When she did, the stable owner reassured her that they had all been watered and everything was fine. She believed her so she didn't go out to check even though she couldn't shake the violent thirst. Later that evening it suddenly stopped and she was fine. Within an hour she received a call from the stable owner saying that the girls had not watered the horses and her horse had just died of dehydration. She told me that it was a hard lesson, but one she would never forget. When you feel something like hunger or thirst and you eat or drink and it still doesn't subside, check your animal's food dish or water bowel. They may be trying to get your attention because they need help.

Another time, a client of mine in Pennsylvania, who was very good at communicating with animals, had also learned to respond to feelings she got. One evening, she and her husband put the dogs in their crates and went out to dinner. In the middle of dinner, she suddenly had a terrible feeling that something was wrong at home. In just a few minutes, her anxiety grew to where she could hardly stand it so they immediately left the restaurant and headed for home as quickly as they could. What a surprise to find that someone had broken into their home, robbed them and the dogs were going crazy because they couldn't get out to protect the house. Had they ignored the feelings and delayed going home, things could have been much worse. At first you cannot tell if it is your own apprehension or if it is something coming from your animal, so you MUST RESPOND every time in order for it to improve to the point where you can tell the difference.. It is a VERY important skill to learn in order to be a good communicator. Only in time will you be able to tell for sure and even then, not always. It is better to respond and be wrong than to ignore it and have a disaster.

Most people learning the skill of non verbal communication, receive it in pictures, so that is the technique I will describe below. If you don't get pictures, you should get feelings, so respond to what you get and things will develop from there. I am going to describe the steps I have used successfully in teaching hundreds of people this wonderful skill. We learn on the animals, but the techniques are exactly the same when applied to people. Since the subconscious mind does not sleep, even a person in a coma or under anesthesia can hear everything that is going on around them, they just can't respond. It is like they are hearing everything around them from the far end of a tunnel.

When you learn a new language, you start out with simple phrases like, "Hello, my name is, what is your name, where is the house or restaurant, what do you like to eat, it is cold, it is hot, etc. etc. Learning the animal's language is the same way. Start by asking very simple questions. ONE CAUTION HERE, DON'T TRY TO PRACTICE ON YOUR OWN ANIMAL OR ONES YOU KNOW WELL. You will have a tendency to say that what you are picking up is your own imagination since you know the animal. As you talk to new animals you don't know, the owners can confirm what you pick up, and with each confirmation, you will gain confidence. Even to this day, I have one of my students talk to my animals when I have a problem because I am too emotionally involved with them to always get the truth or a clear picture of what they want and not what I want to hear. Also, don't let pet owners tell you about their animals as it will influence your communication and you can't tell if it is something the animal is telling you or if you are being influenced by what the owner said. You will make a lot of mistakes at first, we all did, but don't give up. But just like learning to speak any new language, you have to practice to get it right. Now, let's get started.

Pretend you are that animal. Let's, for the sake of simplicity, pretend you are the dog sitting in front of you. Start by asking a simple question like what is your yard like? Imagine that you are that dog sitting in the yard on a patch of grass. Imagine what you would feel like sitting in that grass, looking around. Don't try to imagine anything else, but mentally ask the question, "What is your yard like"? The first picture, even if it is just a tree or a wall, or anything no matter how minute, the first idea that comes into your head, is the accurate one. Grab that thought and write it down, because your logic starts entering in and it changes your pictures or impressions. Sometimes you will get a blank. If this happens, the dog may be telling you he doesn't have a yard and doesn't go out on the grass, so think of him sitting on cement or in a crate or cage. The picture should change. Another thing that happens is this, best described by an experience I had with a cat in California. I asked the cat what its' yard was like. The pictures he sent were very clear. When I described them to the owners, they kept saying, "No, that is not his yard now, that is his former yard." I just couldn't understand what was going on, so I asked the cat why it wouldn't tell me about this yard. I was quite surprised when he said he couldn't "see" his yard. It was then that the owners confessed that the cat had gone blind just before they moved to the new place. The cat was right, he couldn't "see" his new yard so, of course, he couldn't describe it. You see, there are different things that can happen to effect your communication. When you don't get an answer to one way of asking the question, think of different circumstances that could be going on with the particular animal you are talking to, and try asking the question differently.

Do not concentrate on what you are thinking, but focus on the animal, looking at it and imagining what it is like to be that animal. If you keep trying to "see" the pictures in your mind, you will be concentrating on your own mind and not the animal. It will just happen as you focus on the animal, all of a sudden you will "see" it. It almost reminds me of the way you sort of see something out of the corner of your eye, you are looking ahead, but are aware that something went by.

When you want to ask an animal about a problem in the show ring, just think of them in the ring. Picture them looking at a man judge and a woman judge and see if there is a difference. You may also need to ask them about indoor shows, so picture them inside a building then picture them in an outdoor ring. They may have a problem with one situation and not the other, or with men judges versus women judges or even a judge wearing a hat versus one that doesn't. As you focus on the animal and not on how your feelings change, you will suddenly feel the difference. It comes so subtly you will hardly notice, but suddenly you will feel it. Remember, don't get frustrated when it doesn't happen immediately or every time you try it, just keep trying and it will happen eventually. This exercise reminds me of an incident I had in Minnesota. I was called in to talk to a horse that was viciously attacking his owner, a man who truly loved this horse who had always been kind to him. When I asked the horse why he was attacking the man, he said, *he hits and whips me. I hate him for hurting me and I'm going to get him before he can get me.* His owner was absolutely flabbergasted as he had never raised a hand or a whip to this horse. I thought about it for a minute and remembered how they sometimes see us differently when dressed differently, so I told the man to remove his cowboy hat and put it some place where the horse couldn't see it. Immediately, the horse saw him for who he truly was and approached him in a friendly manner, nuzzling him with affection. In checking the horse's background, the owner later found out that he had been trained by a cowboy who always wore a big cowboy hat and had abused the horse with a whip. Another time on that same visit, I entered a home to chat with a parrot. The minute I entered the room, the parrot started to screech, flew across the room and viciously attacked me. The owner was shocked and very embarrassed to see this behavior because the bird was normally very friendly to everyone. After they were able to peel him off of me, I asked him why he had attacked me. He replied, *I hate you because you tease me every time you come near my cage.* When I explained to the owner that animals do not always "see" us as we are, but that there may be something about me that reminds them of someone else, the bird's owner did say that I looked a lot like their old housekeeper, same color hair, dressed similarly and about the same size. After checking with her, she did admit that she hated the bird and used to tease him when the owner wasn't around. She had been fired because they had been suspicious something wasn't right. It seems that they did the right thing.

To find out what they like to eat, think of them looking at a food bowl, feeling very happy. Suddenly you will see a mound of white stuff that tastes cool and sweet. They could be telling you that they love Ice Cream. Think of them looking at a bowl and being disgusted or unhappy and suddenly you may see a bowl of dry food.

To learn who their friends are, think of them looking at another animal or at a person. Suddenly you will "see" an outline of a person, maybe tall with dark hair, glasses, etc. Just describe the person to the owner, don't try to say that it is a man or a woman. Sometimes they don't see us as a certain sex, but as a personality. The one you think may be a man could be a strong, aggressive woman, so just describe the outline of the person and maybe the personality. When you want to find out who they don't like, think of them looking at a person or animal and project the feeling of anger or dislike and see what you get. Again, do not interpret what you get, just describe it, person or animal. I don't understand why a Siamese cat looks gray in my mind's eye, but it does, so when I see a gray cat, I usually say, "your animal likes or dislikes the gray cat which could be a Siamese, I'm not sure", Sometimes a small fluffy animal they show you could be a fluffy dog, cat or rabbit, so again, just tell the owner the pet's feelings about the small fluffy light or dark animal, don't interpret. Let the owner do that.

It used to be believed that animals couldn't see color, but they can. They describe color to me all the time, but brown, gray and black often look the same and red and orange usually look the same to them, too. Animals express favorite colors to me all the time, especially horses. They definitely have preferences to what colors they want in their blankets.

I have talked to animals that have been dumped by people who think the animal instinctively knows that the rat or bird is food. These animals who start out in homes where food comes from a bag or can, will often starve to death when dumped. They have no idea about predators either. All these things have to be taught to them by their mothers, it isn't just instinct.

Be careful when talking to an animal's owner. As you receive images or feelings or thoughts from the animal, tell them, "This is the impression or picture or feeling I believe I am getting from your animal" then go ahead and describe it. Your tendency is to say, "Is your dog or cat laying on a red blanket, etc." Be careful as that comes across to the owner that you are guessing or that you are trying to get them to tell you about the animal. People love to talk about their pets so they will blab all and you won't get the important feedback you need to gain confidence in what you have picked up from the animals. Just tell them your impressions. You may be wrong and feel like an idiot, but that is part of the learning process. No one will hate you for being wrong, but Aha, you may also be right and boy does that boost your confidence. You will make mistakes, expect it and roll with it, but don't quit. The rewards are life changing and wonderful.

As you learn to master the simple questions, you will be able to go on to more complicated questions later on. Just learn to focus on the animal and mentally ask them the question you want to know. Since they do not have a concept of time such as we do, you cannot ask about incidences that happened on certain dates, such as at a show on the 14th. You will have to ask the owner to give you something specific that happened that day so you can picture them in the specific event where the problem occurred. You have to mentally picture them in the situation, ask what happened to either frighten them or make them happy or whatever the situation was that the owner wanted to know about. This will trigger the event for them and you should get the answer.

One final thing, animals don't "see" situations the same as we do. I have had owners ask me about a "trauma" their pet experienced. The animal will give me a blank feeling and ask what "trauma" only to find out the situation was a trauma to the owner, but the animal took it in stride. Here again, you must realize animals are different from us and often react to situations differently than we do.

If you have purchased the video with this book, you will find a lot of repetition in teaching, but it will just reinforce what you are trying to learn. There are also exercises on the video that will further clarify what you have learned. Now, go out and practice and enjoy your new depth of life.

SUCCESS COMES IN CANS
IF YOU BELIEVE YOU CAN, YOU WILL
IF YOU BELIEVE YOU CAN'T, YOU WON'T.

HOW TO COPE WITH THE DEATH OF A PET

ONLY AN ANIMAL? BUT SUCH LOVE HE GAVE,
I DON'T BELIEVE HAS PERISHED IN THE GRAVE,
SO CONSTANT AND FAITHGUL AND TRUE A HEART,
WILL IN ETERNITY HAVE A PART,
I AM GRATEFUL TO KNOW WHEN I'VE CROSSED LIFE'S SEA,
I'LL FIND HIM WAITING TO WELCOME ME
Author Unknown

After reading my books, "WHAT THE ANIMALS TELL
ME" and "STORIES THE ANIMALS TELL ME," many have written asking
for help in understanding what happens to their pets when they die and how to
eventually cope with their loss. The grief over the death of a pet can be as
devastating as losing a human loved one. I would like to share with you what
God has revealed to me concerning our animal friends. You may not agree with
all that I say, but my prayer is that this will help many of you through a difficult
time.

We get attached to our pets because it gives us another living
being to love and care for that doesn't judge us, and gives us back
such unconditional love. They ask for little and give so much.
When the time comes and they are suffering or are too old and
tired to go on, most of them want me to ask the family to let them
go. All they want is for you to be with them and hold them as they
pass. It is the least we can do for a faithful friend. They know our

grief is really for ourselves and they are comforted by our love for them.

The first feeling you will experience is a sense of GUILT. "If only I had known earlier! If I had just found the right veterinarian!" and on and on it goes. This is NORMAL. Be comforted in the fact that you are not alone, but EVERYONE experiences this whether it is over the loss of an animal or a child. Decide right now that no matter what you did or did not do; this just may have been their "time," no matter what the age. Guilt is a lie from Satan who delights in causing people confusion and grief, so don't let him have a place in your mind. Put this thought where it belongs, as far from your way of thinking as you can get it.

I have been in the presence of many animals as they have left their bodies, and I am happy to tell you THEY NEVER LEAVE ALONE. There is always another animal or person present who had been around them on earth. There seems to be a point right after death, when the animal's spirit stays close to the people or animals it loved. It could be as little as a few seconds or as much as a few days—it all depends upon how long it takes for you to release them. Many of us have been taught that animals are annihilated when they die: that death is the end of their existence. That theory emanates from a misreading of Ecclesiastes 3:21 that says "Who knows the spirit of man, whether it goes upward, and the spirit of the beast, whether it goes downward to the earth?" The book of Ecclesiastes is written to give an idea about how man looks at life without God. Verse 3:21 is not stating a fact, but is posing a question. "Who knows if the spirit of man rises upward, and the spirit of the animals goes down to earth...? The misconception stems from man's own pride that makes him think that humans are the only important part of this universe that God really cares about. I have a great news-flash for these people, "God is the CENTER OF THE UNIVERSE" and man is only a small part of it. His other creations include animals, plants, and the earth itself, not to mention the many galaxies that make up the rest of it much less the many other beings mentioned all through the Bible called principalities and powers that we can't even see. When we try to base a doctrine or belief on ONE VERSE of

Scripture, especially from Ecclesiastes, we are in trouble. This is the ONLY verse I've found that even questions the destiny of animals, while others indicate they are intelligent beings with an eternally living part. Let's look at some of them.

In GENESIS Chapters 1 & 2, we learn that God first created animals, and THEN, He created man 'in His Image' indicating there is a part of man that is not in animals.

Let's first look at how are we alike? Biologically, we are the same as all other mammals that give birth to live offspring. We have the same 'systems', many of the same diseases, and even conceive in the same wonderful, miraculous way as all animals do, by the joining of sperm with an egg.

Secondly, we all possess a soul that is the seat of the emotions. Like us, animals are capable of feeling all the same emotions we feel-love, anger, hatred, frustration, disappointment, fear, excitement, etc., and possess a limited reasoning ability. All you have to do is watch them for a while and you can see it.

What is the IMAGE OF GOD? It is the part of humans that animals do not have. The ability to make intricate plans for the future, an understanding of philosophies and abstract ideas, a concept of value systems, the expression of sexuality that is controllable by us and used for other than reproduction, and moral values resulting in the knowledge of sin and the violation of God's laws. Animals don't experience this and do not sin, they only feel guilty when they have hurt you or disobeyed their owner.

How did Adam relate to animals? After God created Adam, He said in Genesis 2:18, "It is not good that man should be alone; I will make him a helper comparable to him." Although he had the animals, they were different, not quite enough, so God made Eve, another human. While animals are wonderful companions and fill a gap in our lives, they cannot replace human relationships. When we try to make them people, we put a terrible emotional burden on them, creating stress-related problems for them while becoming unbalanced ourselves.

As you read in the beginning of Genesis, it is obvious Adam and Eve had a very compatible relationship with the animals and had some type of ability to communicate with them. Why would

Eve carry on an intelligent conversation with an animal and believe what it said if it weren't a normal thing to do? Again in Numbers 22: 21-31 God opened the mouth of the donkey to verbalize her feelings, showing that animals do have a clear thinking ability and easily see non-physical beings God finally opened Balaam's eyes to 'see' what the donkey already understood and allowed him to speak with her in an intelligent manner! Animals do 'see' non-physical beings and often describe them to me. Another example, I believe, is clear when the animals went onto the ark. Why do you think the animals went into the ark with Noah and lived peacefully for the time they were there?

In Genesis 1;29,30 it says that all men and animals ate grass, herbs and seed bearing fruit. Science teaches us that the animals' teeth changed over time and some of them became carnivores. In Genesis 7, it says that the clean animals went into the ark in pairs, in groups of seven per species, while the unclean animals went in only one pair of each kind. Until the flood, man still had that same kind of relationship with animals that made them truly compatible friends, as originally created, but in Genesis 9, AFTER THE FLOOD, that relationship was broken by God, who gave some of the animals to man for food and placed the fear of man in them.

When God gave us dominion over the animals in Genesis 1, 2, it implies responsibility, a caring for them, not the right to abuse them or do what we want with them. Genesis 9:4,5 indicates that man will have to give account to God for causing suffering to animals especially if we eat their flesh while the lifeblood is still in them. This is done in some primitive tribes where they cut off pieces of meat for eating and let it grow back again to be eaten later. This is just one of the examples of the cruelty I believe God was referring to in Genesis 9 that man will be accountable for: the cruelty to animals as its LIFE'S BLOOD, suffering while alive, not just the blood being drained from it after death. Other examples are dog and cock fighting, starving and beating them, etc.

I eat meat- God delivered animals to us for food, so I know He will take care of their souls. I have talked to many animals being killed for food and they do not resent it, they only fear the method used, or being hunted, or dying for no reason. I am comforted by

Job 12:10 that says, "In His hand is the soul of every living creature and of man."

God doesn't waste anything, for even the leaf that falls from the tree becomes food for the tree and plants below. I believe that that same God will not annihilate something as wonderful as the pet I have known and loved so deeply and then create new ones to populate heaven. I'm afraid heaven wouldn't be heaven to me without my beloved pets.

I have 'seen' some of my pets after they have left and they have ALL told me they were not allowed to stay with me, but were allowed to come back and tell me they were alright. Don't get me wrong. I do not seek communication with the dead – it is forbidden in the Bible, but in my own grief, during the loss of an especially dear pet, while in prayer, a vision of my dog was given to me. She was 'allowed' to come and comfort me, to let me know she was alive and well in a place that fit all the descriptions I've since heard given by Christians who have died and come back to life, describing what they saw. It was a very similar place. It was not a vision I sought, nor did I expect it, as I had also believed animals were annihilated. I was in deep, deep sorrow over what I thought was a permanent parting.

All through Scriptures, God uses the animals as symbols. They took a clean animal, without blemish, laid hands on it, and sacrificed it for that person's sins. This was a symbol that some day Jesus, the perfect Lamb of God, would take the sin of man on Himself and He would be slain as the ultimate sacrifice to pay for our sins. When Jesus died, all animal sacrifices stopped as there was no more need for them.

I believe God talks sparingly about the destination of animals in the Bible because He knows He has taken care of them: they don't have to make a choice like man must. It is you to whom He gives the choice. Romans 3:23 says, "All have sinned and come short of the Glory of God." You see, only man has the image of God in him, so when sin entered the world, it did so through man, the only one of God's creatures that could disobey, or sin, unto spiritual death. The serpent was punished because it allowed Satan to use it, but its punishment was to crawl on its belly in the dirt and be despised by man. When man sinned, it was unto spiritual death, not just a physical punishment. The Image of God became marred, and distorted in man. He developed a reprobate (misused and off track) mind. Romans 6:23 says "the wages of sin is death, but the gift of God is eternal life through Jesus Christ our Lord." John 3:16 says, "For God so loved the World that He gave His only begotten Son, that whosoever believe in Him, should not perish, but have everlasting life." It's a free gift, given for the asking only to those who repent of their sins and invite Jesus into their hearts. Ephesians 2:8,9. "For by grace are you saved through faith and that not of yourselves, it is a gift of God, not of works, lest any man should boast."

Some people believe their pet will be reincarnated. I have asked hundreds of animals if they were ever here before, but have never found any support for that belief. The one instance I thought that might substantiate the reincarnation claim was really a dog trying to 'copy' what he 'saw' in the owner's memory of the deceased pet. He knew the owner really didn't want him, but wanted his former pet back and because he wanted the man to accept and love him as he had the dead dog, he did all he could to mimic the deceased animal. When the man released the former pet, the new dog's personality changed to who he really was. Many things that people say their new animal does that reminds them of their old pet are really actions that are characteristics and behaviors particular to that breed and because they want their old pet back so badly, they misinterpret that action to be the dead animal reincarnated in the new one. When you understand the limitless abilities of the human mind and how the spirit world influences man, those principalities and powers on high spoken of throughout the Bible, such as in Ephesians 6, 11, 12, most of the 'proofs' of reincarnation are easily explained. Besides, reincarnation doesn't even apply to animals as the whole premise of that philosophy is to keep coming back to this world to pay for past mistakes (sins) until you get good enough to accept Christ or until you reach the state of Nirvana (a Sea of Nothingness), whichever idea you embrace. Animals don't sin, so they don't need to come back, but it's us who want them to come back because we can't let go of those we love. Just because we want them to come back, doesn't make reincarnation a fact.

I can't imagine why anyone would want to go to Nirvana or embrace the Eastern religions that teach this, religions that have kept their countries in cast systems where a man can never rise above the state in which he is born or kept women in such subservient positions, holding animals in higher regard than women, instead of holding to the Scriptures, the loving Word of God. Take I Corinthians 2:9, "Eye has not seen nor ear has heard, no mind has conceived what God has prepared for those who love Him," and John 10:10, "I am come that you might have LIFE and that more abundantly." The Bible is full of statements like that. Since I love my animals so much and they are such a part of me, these statements give me joy and hope that they will be with me throughout all of eternity.

If we could come back and 'pay' for past sins, then Ephesians 2:8,9 are false and Jesus died in vain. God says in Isaiah 64:6, "All our righteousness is as filthy rags," that all the BEST we can do is unacceptable to God because He will not accept anything that tries to bypass His provision of the sacrifice of His Son on the cross. Reincarnation appeals to man's pride and is man's way of leaving Jesus out of his destiny. Just because man believes it, doesn't make it true. Man believed the earth was flat at one time too, so there have been a lot of sincere people in history who have been 'sincerely wrong'. If reincarnation is wrong (and I believe it is), isn't that an awful chance to take with your soul when facing eternity? It also says in Hebrews 9:27, "And as it is appointed for men to die once, but after this the judgment." This and other scriptures indicate there is no second time around.

Besides, if God can make a universe as grand as this one, don't you think He has enough room to accommodate everyone and everything He's ever made here, on our one planet that is only a dot of light in ONE Galaxy? Remember, God is the Center of ALL THE UNIVERSE, OF ALL THE GALAXIES, not man, not this Earth. When you look at the expanse of all His creation, it is breathtaking to me that He loved us enough to shed His glory, come to this tiny dot in the universe and incredibly lay down His life for me, for us, so that we might live eternally!

Remember when Jesus was praying in the Garden before His death? He prayed that the cup, the pain and suffering of Hell that He would endure for us, would pass from Him, nevertheless not His will, but God's be done. Do you think for one minute that God the Father, would have put Jesus through that and Jesus, a part of the Godhead, would have allowed man to do that to Him, if there was any other way? By virtue of the fact that He laid down His own life and allowed man to nail Him to the Cross, (He could have stopped it at any moment, for remember, He is God) tells me there is NO OTHER WAY that man can have his sins forgiven and come to God. In John 14:6, Jesus said, "I am the Way, The Truth and the Life. No one comes to the Father except through me."

What has God prepared for those who accept Him as their Lord and Savior? I don't know all of it, but I do believe there is going to be a great reunion with all my wonderful pets. I believe your animals will be there. Will you? The decision and choice is yours. Won't you accept Christ and join us by praying this Prayer of Salvation?

Heavenly Father; I come to You in the Name of Jesus. Your Word says, "Whosoever shall call on the name of the Lord shall be saved." (Acts 2:21). I am calling on You. I pray and ask Jesus to come into my hear and be Lord over my life according to Romans 10: 9-10. "If thou shalt confess with they mouth the Lord Jesus, and shalt believe in thine heart that God hath raised him from the dead, thou shalt be saved. For with the heart man believeth unto righteousness; and with the mouth confession is made unto salvation." I do that now. I confess that Jesus is Lord, and I believe in my heart that God raised Him from the dead. I confess my sins and ask you for forgiveness for those I know and those I can't remember. I thank you that I John 1:9 says, "If we confess our sins, He is faithful and just to forgive us our sins and to cleanse us from ALL unrighteousness."

I am now reborn! I am a Christian—a child of the Almighty God! I am forgiven, saved! I John 5:11, 12 "And this is the record that God hath given to us eternal life and this life is in His Son. He that hath the Son (Jesus) hath life and He that hath not the Son of God, hath not life. This is referring to eternal life in heaven with Him, our loved ones and our precious animals

For further help or for more questions, please feel free to contact us at 1-800-258-8589 or

15443 So. Latourette Rd. Oregon City, Or. 97045

Email: Bealydecker@ccwebster.net

Website: www.bealydecker.com

Beatrice has appeared on many television and radio shows over the past years. These appearances include "The Oprah Winfrey Show," "The Tonight Show starring Johnny Carson," The Dinah Shore Show," "Joan Rivers," "The Tomorrow Show," "Late Night with David Letterman, "PM Magazine," "Two On The Town," "In Search Of," "To Tell The Truth" and too many more to mention.

Her foreign appearances in Canada include: "The Don Harron Show," "Canada After Dark," "Take Thirty" and "Cross Country." In Holland she was a guest on "The Tineka Show," and in England: "Barbara Woodhouse In Hollywood," "The Dave Hill Show," "Saturday Childrens' Shows," and "The Last Resort."

Articles have been written about her work by the press in many major newspapers and magazines around the world. In the United States she has been featured in such periodicals as *The Wall Street Journal, Los Angeles Times, The Enquirer, Star Magazine* and *People Magazine* among many others.